In the Land of the Magic Pudding

Barbara Santich has an international reputation as a food writer and historian. Currently lecturer in gastronomy at the University of Adelaide, South Australia, she has written five books and numerous popular and academic articles. *In the Land of the Magic Pudding* is the product of her love of literature and her abiding interest in the history and culture of food and eating.

By the same author

The Original Mediterranean Cuisine
What the Doctors Ordered
Apples to Zampone
Looking for Flavour
McLaren Vale: Sea and Vines
Bold Palates
Dining Alone (ed.)
Enjoyed for Generations
Wild Asparagus, Wild Strawberries

In the Land of the Magic Pudding

A gastronomic miscellany

Edited by Barbara Santich

Wakefield
Press

Wakefield Press
16 Rose Street
Mile End
South Australia 5031
wakefieldpress.com.au

First published 2000
Reprinted 2018

Cover painting *The Snake is Dead* by Annette Bezor
Designed by Liz Nicholson, design BITE
Typeset by Clinton Ellicott, Wakefield Press

National Library of Australia Cataloguing-in-publication entry

In the land of the magic pudding : a gastronomic miscellany.
Bibliography.
ISBN 978 1 86254 530 4.
1. Food habits – Australia. 2. Food – Anecdotes.
3. Food habits in literature. 4. Food in literature.
5. Gastronomy – Anecdotes. I. Santich, Barbara.
641.300994

CORIOLE
McLAREN VALE

Wakefield Press thanks
Coriole Vineyards for
continued support

For Jean Smith, who honours tradition as cheerfully as she discards it.

'I have everything I require, except food, except food;
but without food everything is rather less than nothing.'

Bunyip Bluegum, from *The Magic Pudding* by Norman Lindsay

Contents

Preface

For as long as stories have been told, food and eating have entered into the narrative. From Homer to Chaucer to Patrick White, novelists – and dramatists and film makers, storytellers equally – have taken a wholly natural and mundane occurrence and woven it into the fabric of their stories. They have used food to convey character and emotional state; they have contrived meals as a means of bringing people together and facilitating dialogue; they have inserted eating episodes as a pretext for surprise encounters or impromptu confessions; and they have created scenes of food and eating which have furthered the plot or suspended it, which have brought characters face to face or even lips to lips, which have heightened the tension or moderated its development. All these from something as simple as food and an event as ordinary as eating!

But how effective they are! I remember one brief scene in Balzac's *Eugenie Grandet*, when cousin Charles takes breakfast, that manages to highlight M. Grandet's miserliness, Eugénie's eager desire to please, Charles' profligacy – and, at the same time, demonstrates the contrast between Paris and the provinces. Equally, the sharp observations of Marjorie Barnard, describing the Bowker family at lunch in her short story 'The Dressmaker' (page 145), point up the pretentiousness and self-centredness of her characters.

The images retained from this story, together with scenes recalled from reading the novels of Australian writers such as David Malouf, Marion Halligan and Norman Lindsay, meandered about my mind for years before they gradually coalesced to form the germ of an idea: a collection of popular writings by top authors focusing on food and eating in Australia. And the longer I reflected, the more I remembered from countless hours in countless libraries, enjoyably engrossed in novels and newspapers as I researched the history of tomatoes or the origins of carpetbag steak.

Initially, my intention was to select only fictional writing and, with a few exceptions, all the pieces from the 1950s onwards are from novels or short stories. Fictional accounts from the nineteenth century proved far more elusive. On the other hand, I discovered that the most entertaining writing on food and eating in this period was contained in a diversity of non-fiction forms. *In the Land of the Magic Pudding* therefore mines diverse literary lodes, with extracts from novels and short stories, memoirs and reminiscences, biography and auto-biography, travellers' tales, journalism, letters and diaries, books of etiquette, menus, cookbooks and books of household management. Fictional works predominate at the end of the twentieth century, non-fiction in the early nineteenth. Both are equally valid; fiction can be just as reliable – or unreliable – a source of information on the subject of food and eating as first-person accounts in letters and diaries, just as credible as the reports of an 'impartial' observer.

There's another reason for widening the compass of this book to include both fiction and non-fiction. With few exceptions, it is only recently that novels and short stories have incorporated details of what was eaten and drunk, how they were prepared and served, what they smelled like, looked like, tasted like. This trend towards greater emphasis on the materiality of the event has even reached a point where the recipes themselves are often incorporated into the text. Medieval verses and tales, on the other hand, dwelled on the lav-ishness of the feast and generosity of the host, often making lengthy enumerations of the various species of fish, poultry, meat and game that arrived in the kitchens without mention of the dishes created by the cooks and presented at the table.

At a recent symposium at the University of Adelaide on Food in Literature – how writers bring in references to food and eating and for what purpose, whether for vicarious pleasure or as an essential function – there was resounding agreement from speakers that food fulfils an essential function. It can underlie (and underline) a principal theme, sustain a plot, enhance characterisations and be absolutely vital to the development of dramatic tension and narrative force. In short, if references to food and eating were omitted the story and the writing would be all the weaker.

The diverse texts gathered together in *In the Land of the Magic Pudding* have several features in common. First, they all relate to Australia. Second, the authors are all writing of the period in which they lived, of which they had direct, personal experience, even if as adults they are writing about days of their childhood. *Labourers in the Vineyard* by Colin Thiele – born in 1920 – is set in the Barossa Valley of the late 1930s (pages 127 and 158); Miles Franklin, writing in the 1950s, describes in *Childhood at Brindabella* an orchard at the end of the nineteenth century (page 35).

Third, and most significant, the extracts all focus on food and eating in Australia in the nineteenth and twentieth centuries (with one exception: Joseph Banks was writing at the end of the eighteenth century). They talk about buying food, or finding it, growing it, killing it, cooking it, standing in line in factories packaging it. They describe what people eat or used to eat, and how and when and where – a family Sunday lunch or a party supper, at school or in a shearers' mess, roughing it in the bush or dining at an exclusive restaurant. They demonstrate the development of Christmas customs and of concepts of an Australian cuisine. Together they form a mosaic which, viewed as a whole, illustrates the development of Australian food traditions.

How little we know of our food traditions! Too often we don't see them for looking; they can be under our noses and still we fail to recognise them. There are some who would, without hesitation, state that Australia has no food traditions. Assuming that Australians inherited and unthinkingly applied British traditions they allow no credit for originality, ingenuity and independent thinking. We may have perpetuated the baked (or roast) dinner, but we added pumpkin and sweet potato to the vegies around the joint of meat. We continued to bake scones, but we also deep-fried them to make puftaloons, and served them with golden syrup. We took a standard lemon curd recipe and substituted passionfruit, to produce passionfruit curd. While we might have inherited, we also adapted.

Take the pie floater, a meat pie served in a sea of pea soup with a slash of tomato sauce, a dish which is probably unique to Australia (not only Adelaide; Brisbane, too, has or has had its floaters). Its exact origins are blurred in a swirl of faded memories and vague hearsay, but it seems to have been the result of a fortuitous proximity. The 'fast foods' of the nineteenth century, often sold in the streets, included pies – pie stalls had been around since at least the 1870s – and mashed peas. In Britain 'mushy peas' made with split yellow peas are sold as a takeaway in pie shops and fish-and-chip shops. Louis Stone's novel *Jonah* describes 'a basin full of green peas, boiled to a squashy mass' which were eaten sprinkled with pepper and vinegar (vinegar was an alternative to tomato sauce in the early days of the pie floater, too). Yet another street food, saveloys, were also eaten with mashed peas.

As for the name, an English slang compendium of the late nineteenth century records 'floater' as a suet dumpling in soup. In Suffolk something similar is known as a 'Suffolk swimmer'. Logically, then, a pie on a puree of peas, or in thick pea soup, should be called a pie floater. It's an adaptation and progression of an English custom, but it is authentically Australian.

And how easy it is to dismiss the past as unpalatable and indigestible, to sneer at the customs of our parents and grandparents, to turn up our noses at vegetables cooked in mutton fat rather than today's trendy olive oil, to disdain dishes such as chops in parsley sauce, scalloped sheep's head, suet pudding, marrow bones on toast, prunes and junket, and toast water for those feeling poorly. Tastes change. These dishes might not suit today's tastes, but they are not, in themselves, abominable (at least, not if they're cooked properly, with care and good ingredients). They might not be part of the modern repertoire but they are still deserving of respect.

At a conference on Australian food habits some years ago, British sociologist Anne Murcott accused nutritionists and food scientists of 'hodiecentrism', by which she meant interpreting the past in terms of the values of the present (and therefore finding it lacking). In her view, it represented an attitude analogous to ethnocentrism, judging other cultures according to the (superior) standards of one's own culture. The word is too good to ignore, despite its absence from dictionaries, and totally relevant. Too many Australians – food writers included – could similarly be described as hodiocentric, in that they have eyes (and words) only for the here and now – unless, announcing the most recently discovered, most fashionable food/ingredient/cuisine, they are anticipating the future.

Hodiecentrism translates as a prejudice against the past, and in gastronomic terms this means disparaging the foods and dishes of earlier generations while imagining fine dining, and the appreciation of good food and wine, to belong to one's own generation – to have begun, perhaps, in the post-war fifties, or to have blossomed in the wake of the nouvelle cuisine revolution of the seventies, or even to have its roots in the multicultural east–west fusion of the 1980s and 1990s. Yet the magazine *The Home* shows that even in the 1920s society hostesses in Sydney, Melbourne, Adelaide and Brisbane could imagine (we don't know if they actually served them!) menus such as these, replete with oysters and caviar, lobster and foie gras, quail and pigeon.

And in the 1930s the Adelaide market offered, in addition to the usual lamb and beef and pork, 'thousands of pairs of poultry and game, from chaste little squabs and quail, their knees tucked in and neatly

MENU
Crayfish Cocktail.
Turtle.
Scalloped Whitebait.
Vol au Vent of Sweetbread,
with Mushrooms.
Saddle of Mutton.
Snipe, with Orange.
Asparagus.
Rhum Omelette.
Roe on Toast.

From Lady Frank Moulden, Adelaide.

MENU
Cantaloupe.
Creamed Lobster
Américaine.
Chicken with Mushroom.
Filet Mignon.
Quail and Orange Salad.
Ice Bomb Maraschimo.
Paw Paw Salade
with Port Wine.

**Mrs Norman Armytage, 'Alta Vista',
Melbourne, favours this dinner.**

MENU
Caviare on Toast.
Purée of Tomato Soup.
Lobster Patties.
Roast Turkey with Chestnuts.
Asparagus Salad.
Chip Potatoes.
Banana Cream Ice.
Hot Chocolate Sauce.
Cheese Soufflé.
Dessert. Coffee.

**Dinner Selected by Mrs Sep. Levy,
'Hillside', Woollahra, Sydney.**

MENU
Slices of Rock Melon.
Ground Ginger and Sugar.
Lobster au Gratin (hot).
Pigeons in Casserole with
Mushrooms and Sultanas,
Nuts and Bacon.
Peas and New Potatoes.
Mousse au Chocolat.
Stuffed Prunes (with Chutney)
on Croutons.
Dessert. Coffee.

**From Mrs Hector Clayton, 'Woodlands',
Edgecliff Road, Woollahra, Sydney.**

MENU
Caviare.

Pochés à la Peru.

Smoked Russian Salad.

Black Duck.

Fresh Asparagus.

Rhum Omlette.

Mushrooms on Toast.

**'Inspiration' from Mrs James Burns,
6 Macleay Street, Pott's Point, Sydney.**

MENU
Lobster Cocktail.
Oyster and Asparagus Omelette.
Poussin with Mushrooms,
Salade Japonaise.
Filet de Boeuf with Small
New Potatoes and Petit Pois.
Rock Melon Ice.
Caviare.
Strawberries on Maraschino.

**Mrs Arthur Whittingham, 'Mayfield',
Brisbane, chooses the above menu.**

sewn with cotton, to old-man turkey gobblers and Toulouse geese that weigh 13 pounds without the feathers', together with freshwater and saltwater fish and 'the festive scarlet crayfish that belongs to Saturday night' (*Advertiser*, 9 June 1934). The vegetable supply included mignonette lettuce and curly kale, bouquets of parsley and thyme; on other stalls were 'pots of jam and jars of pickles, horse radish for the roast beef and capers for the mutton'. In 1935 Sydney society ladies enjoyed a Danish-style charity breakfast, with open sandwiches and pastries and coffee. The following year Madame Leo Cherniavsky, wife of the celebrated Russian violinist, gave a cooking demonstration at the Adelaide Town Hall featuring recipes from her book, *Continental Recipes*, for dishes such as blanquette de veau, boeuf à la bourguignonne, risotto a la Milanese, Hungarian chicken and zabaglione.

The excuse, if one is offered, is that Australia is too young to have developed gastronomic traditions, too young to have a history of food and eating. Or, alternatively, that if Australia is to claim a genuine cuisine and food traditions, we have to look to the Indigenous Australians. Weak arguments, both. It's not necessary that traditions – the beliefs, stories and customs handed down from generation to generation, especially by word of mouth or by practice – rest on a solid base of five or more centuries in order to justify their existence. In the gastronomic world some dishes are genuinely archaic – the Italian broad bean purée, for example, which could just as easily have been eaten by the ancient Greeks, or the Burgundian preserve of pears in concentrated grape must, which would have been equally at home in Caesar's Rome. But pasta with tomato sauce, which we see as so ubiquitous as to be timeless, probably only dates from the late eighteenth century, about the time that Europeans arrived in Australia.

As for the argument that the only Australian cuisine belongs to the Aboriginal peoples, this ignores the fact that the population of Australia is multicultural. No one refutes the authenticity of indigenous food traditions but in a democratic society these can co-exist with other beliefs and practices.

The important thing is to acknowledge the traditions we have – for they are still traditions even if no longer practised. Burgundy has, or had, a particular tradition of treading the grapes – the Musée du Vin in Beaune displays a photo of a handsome young trio in a large wooden tub, arms around each other's shoulders, discreetly thigh-deep in the dark mass of juice and berries, and not a stitch of clothing in evidence anywhere. Today you could probably travel through all the villages at vintage-time without ever encountering such a scene, no matter how hard you looked – but the custom is no less a part of Burgundian tradition.

There is a great danger that any traditions we can identify in Australia – the roast lamb with all the vegetables, the toast-and-Vegemite for breakfast – will be overtaken and swept aside by the waves of fashion which surge and break with ever-increasing frequency. We might not wish to be constrained by the past, but nor should we ignore our traditions; and while a book such as this will not necessarily revive them and keep them alive, at least it might invite their spirits to dance.

As a collection of writings about food and eating in Australia, this book is also about (dare it be said) Australian cuisine.

Australian cuisine? If there is such a thing as Australian cuisine, what is it? What is so characteristically Australian about our food and the way we eat? Why do we need to identify and define an Australian cuisine?

Asking the question is itself a peculiarly Australian habit – or perhaps was; we seem less obsessed today than we were a decade or so ago. As food writer Paul Levy observed on a visit here in 1987, Australians have a concern with Australian food, with being Australian, which is generally not shared by other nationalities. As early as 1967, television chef Graham Kerr reflected on the idea of an Australian cuisine in the pages of the *Australian Women's Weekly*, suggesting even then that perhaps we should be concentrating on regional cuisines instead of a single national one.

As I understand it, cuisine is the product of foods and people. It is a cultural product; it is what people do to and with foods that results in cuisine. In Australia our cuisine – however it might be described or defined – has changed as new foods and new products have become available and as people of different national or ethnic backgrounds have made their home here. Our larder holds a vast diversity of ingredients, from the rediscovered indigenous 'bush foods' to the lamb and olive oil we have naturalised and now call our own. In the same way, Italy naturalised the tomato, Hungary paprika peppers, Hawaii the macadamia nut and south-east Asia chillies. We have borrowed and incorporated culinary techniques (stir-frying) and genres (Thai-style green curries) in the same way as France has adopted the north African méchoui (whole barbecued lamb) and couscous.

Challenged to define Australian cuisine, the response is often to equivocate, to dodge the issue and apologise. But does something have to be defined before it can be recognised? In the reasoning of philosopher Raimond Gaita, 'Generally it is not true, however, that a deepened understanding of what is fundamental in our lives . . . depends on our finding definitions. We seldom come up with any that are worth much. Often, we must be patiently open to aspects of experiences that invite – sometimes compel – us to reach for a particular concept' (*Australian's Review of Books*, June 2000). While he was not specifically discussing cuisine, the argument is still valid.

It might not even be possible to define Australian cuisine by reference to a corpus of dishes or recipes, but we know that what is cooked and served in moderately expensive Australian restaurants is different to what is offered in similar restaurants in Paris, for example, or in Rome or Bangkok. Even at the level of the cheaper café with its daily specials, Australia differentiates itself from countries such as England, Japan and Spain. Without specifically pinpointing the identifying characteristics, we recognise Australian-ness through eating it. And we refer to a contemporary Australian style, the product of inventiveness and a certain insouciance applied to a strong foundation combining familiarity with, and respect for, other culinary traditions.

In the Land of the Magic Pudding is not intended to supply answers to any of the questions but will, I hope, provide evidence to sustain hypotheses. The writings in this miscellany are a sample of my discoveries over many years, kept because I enjoy and value them. Growing older has its benefits; you gain immeasurably in understanding. As you learn more about the object of your passion – for me, the history and culture of food and eating – you appreciate the knowledge so much more. These extracts are evidence not only of gastronomic traditions but also of a robust literary tradition – though serious consideration of what Australian literature might be predates by at least half a century the same kind of attention to Australian cuisine.

Each of the pieces included stands on its own merits. The sequence is roughly chronological. Rather than incorporating them into a narrative of my design I prefer that readers create their own stories. At the same time, however, I should admit it is not a random collection; the various extracts represent my selections, arbitrary or deliberate, chosen as much for the quality of their style as for their content. If they arouse controversy through favouring a certain viewpoint, a particular understanding of the development of food traditions in Australia, so much the better.

Author David Malouf said recently that Australians had, until quite recently, been inhibited by 'the idea that we had an empty past', having been told so often that we had no history, or that our (white) history was too short. In his view, writers now feel a compulsion to explore the past (*Australian*, 3 July, 2000). He was talking about history in general, but the same goes for culinary or food history – and this book offers an invitation to explore it.

Cut-an'-Come-Again Puddin'

Norman Lindsay

Norman Lindsay's *The Magic Pudding* is probably Australia's best-loved children's story, continuously in print since its first publication in 1918. Along with May Gibbs's gumnut children and wicked banksia men, Lindsay's magic cut-an'-come-again Puddin' has entered the Australian vernacular and mythology.

Though chronologically out of place, an extract from *The Magic Pudding* seemed an appropriate start to this collection – partly because of the title reference and partly because its irreverent larrikin humour typifies a particularly Australian approach to life.

The Magic Pudding, 1918

Bill was a small man with a large hat, a beard half as large as his hat, and feet half as large as his beard. Sam Sawnoff's feet were sitting down and his body was standing up, because his feet were so short and his body so long that he had to do both together. They had a pudding in a basin, and the smell that arose from it was so delightful that Bunyip Bluegum was quite unable to pass on.

'Pardon me,' he said, raising his hat, 'but am I right in supposing that this is a steak-and-kidney pudding?'

'At present it is,' said Bill Barnacle.

'It smells delightful,' said Bunyip Bluegum.

'It is delightful,' said Bill, eating a large mouthful.

Bunyip Bluegum was too much of a gentleman to invite himself to lunch, but he said carelessly, 'Am I right in supposing that there are onions in the pudding?'

Before Bill could reply, a thick, angry voice came out of the pudding, saying –

> 'Onions, bunions, corns and crabs,
> Whiskers, wheels and hansom cabs,
> Beef and bottles, beer and bones,
> Give him a feed and end his groans.'

'Albert, Albert,' said Bill to the Puddin', 'where's your manners?'

'Where's yours?' said the Puddin' rudely, 'guzzling away there, and never so much as offering this stranger a slice.'

'There you are,' said Bill. 'There's nothing this Puddin' enjoys more than offering slices of himself to strangers.'

'How very polite of him,' said Bunyip, but the Puddin' replied loudly –

'Politeness be sugared, politeness be hanged,
Politeness be jumbled and tumbled and banged.
It's simply a matter of putting on pace,
Politeness has nothing to do with the case.'

'Always anxious to be eaten,' said Bill, 'that's this Puddin's mania. Well, to oblige him, I ask you to join us at lunch.'

'Delighted, I'm sure,' said Bunyip, seating himself. 'There's nothing I enjoy more than a good go in at steak-and-kidney pudding in the open air.'

'Well said,' remarked Sam Sawnoff, patting him on the back. 'Hearty eaters are always welcome.'

'You'll enjoy this Puddin',' said Bill, handing him a large slice. 'This is a very rare Puddin'.'

'It's a cut-an'-come-again Puddin',' said Sam.

'It's a Christmas, steak, and apple-dumpling Puddin',' said Bill.

'It's a – . Shall I tell him?' he asked, looking at Bill. Bill nodded, and the Penguin leaned across to Bunyip Bluegum and said in a low voice, 'It's a Magic Puddin'.'

First Tastings

Joseph Banks

Joseph Banks (1743–1820) was an enthusiastic amateur botanist who accompanied Captain James Cook on his voyage of discovery to the eastern coast of Australia, by way of Brazil, Tahiti and New Zealand. Fascinated with the plant world from an early age, Banks was elected to the Royal Society at the age of 23, and through the Royal Society

requested to be received on Cook's ship. The expedition landed at Botany Bay in April 1770 and spent a little over three months exploring the coast northwards from Botany Bay; the plants mentioned in this extract from his journal all grow along this coast. Banks' main interest may have been botany, but he was curious enough to conduct palate tests. His bleak prognosis for Australia: hardly a gastronomic paradise, but endurable.

The Endeavour Journal of Joseph Banks 1768–1771

A Soil so barren and at the same time intirely void of the helps derivd from cultivation could not be suppos'd to yeild much towards the support of man. We had been so long at sea with but a scanty supply of fresh provisions that we had long usd to eat every thing we could lay our hands upon, fish, flesh, or vegetable which only was not poisonous; yet we could but now and then procure a dish of bad greens for our own table and never but in the place where the ship was careend met with a sufficient quantity to supply the ship. There indeed Palm cabbage and what is calld in the West Indies Indian Kale were in tolerable plenty, as was also a sort of Purslane. The other plants we eat were a kind of Beans, very bad, a kind of Parsley and a plant something resembling spinage, which two last grew only to the Southward. I shall give them their botanical names as I beleive some of them were never eat by Europeans before: first Indian Kale (*Arum Esculentum*), Red flowerd purslane (*Sesuvium Portulacastrum*), Beans (*Glycine speciosa*), Parsley (*Apium*   ), Spinage (*Tetragonia cornuta*). Fruits we had still fewer; to the South was one resembling a heart cherry only the stone was soft (*Eugenia*   ) which had nothing but a light acid to recommend it; to the Northward again a kind of Figs growing from the stalk of a tree, very indifferent (*Ficus caudiciflora*), a fruit we calld Plumbs like them in Colour but flat like a little cheese (   ), and another much like a damson both in appearance and taste; both these last however were so full of a large stone that eating them was but an unprofitable business. Wild Plantanes we had also but so full of seeds that they had little or no pulp.

Palms here were of three different sorts. The first which grew plentifully to the Southward had leaves pleated like a fan; the Cabbage of these was small but exquisitely sweet and the nuts which it bore in great abundance a very good food for hogs. The second was very much like the real cabbage tree of the West Indies, bearing large pinnated leaves like those of a Cocoa nut; these too yeilded cabbage if not so sweet as the other sort yet the quantity made ample amends. The third which as well as the second was found only in the Northern parts was low, seldom ten feet in hight, with small pennated leaves resembling those of some kinds of fern; Cabbage it had none but generaly bore a plentifull Crop of nutts about the size of a large chestnut and rounder. By the hulls of these which we found plentifully near the Indian fires we were assurd that these people eat them, and some of our gentlemen tried to do the same, but were deterrd from a second experiment by a hearty fit of vomiting and purging which was the consequence of the first. The hogs however who were still shorter of provision than we were eat them heartily and we concluded their constitutions stronger than ours, till after about a week they were all taken extreemly ill of indigestions; two died and the rest were savd with dificulty.

The sea however made some amends for the Barreness of the Land. Fish tho not so plentyfull as they generaly are in the higher latitudes were far from scarce; where we had an opportunity of haling the Seine we generaly caught from 50 to 200 lb of fish in a tide. There sorts were various, none I think but Mullets known in Europe; in general however they were sufficiently palatable and some very delicate food; the Sting rays indeed which were caught on the Southern part of the coast were very coarse, but there little else was caught so we were obligd to comfort ourselves with the comforts of Plenty and enjoy more pleasure in Satiety than in eating. To the Northward again when we came to be entangled within the great Reef (within which we saild to our knowledge o Leages and we knew not how many more, perplexd every moment with shoals) was a plenty of Turtle hardly to be credited, every shoal swarmd with them. The weather indeed was generaly so boisterous that our boats could not row after them so fast as they could swim, so that we got but few, but they were excellent and so large that a single Turtle always servd the ship. Had we been there either at the time of Laying or the more moderate season we doubtless might have taken any quantity. Besides this all the shoals that were dry at half Ebb afforded plenty of fish that were left dry in small hollows of the rocks, and a profusion of Large shell fish (*Chama Gigas*) such as Dampier describes Vol III, p. 191. The large ones of this kind had 10 or

15 lb of meat in them; it was indeed rather strong but I beleive a very wholesome food and well relishd by the people in general. On different parts of the Coast were also found oysters which were said to be very well tasted; the shells also of well sizd Lobsters and crabs were seen but these it was never our fortune to catch.

Upon the whole New Holland, tho in every respect the most barren countrey I have ever seen, is not so bad but that between the productions of sea and Land a company of People who should have the misfortune of being shipwreckd upon it might support themselves, even by the resources that we have seen. Undoubtedly a longer stay and visiting different parts would discover many more.

Feasting on Kangaroo

Robert Dawson

Early white settlers are often portrayed as hostile, unjust, harsh and dispossessive in their treatment of Indigenous Australians. Among European colonists, however, were many who tried to understand the ways of the Aborigines and to learn their languages, who respected them as equals and who pointed out the superiority of their intelligence in so far as the natural environment was concerned. One such was Robert Dawson, whose attitude was far more enlightened than that of most of his contemporaries. Dawson explored the Port Stephens area of New South Wales in 1826 in order to identify suitable sheep grazing country for the Australian Agricultural Company and subsequently helped open up the area for settlement.

The Present State of Australia, 1830

On our arrival at the camp we found every thing in readiness for dinner. The place looked like a flesh-market, with such a quantity of kangaroo hanging in quarters upon the trees. The blacks were all in high good-humour at the idea of so much 'patter'. They had got a blazing fire, and had reserved a luncheon (part of a kangaroo's head) for Wool Bill; but the superior tit bit (the entrails) had been previously disposed of. In an instant my companion was seen gnawing, like a dog, a half-roasted kangaroo's head; thus at one moment displaying an intelligence worthy of civilisation, and in the next indulging in habits but little above those of the animals of prey in the forest.

But let us be just towards them. I know the poor and unprotected natives of Australia have been traduced by many, who have ascribed to them, exclusively, customs and practices which are common to *all* human beings in uncivilised life; and I have seen observations made upon them in print by well-meaning people, who write without the necessary information, attributing to them habits which have no existence amongst them, and which would place them *quite* upon a level with brutes.

It has been said that they will eat even dogs in a state of putridity, and that they will drink polluted ditch-water. I can only say, that I never saw an instance of their attempting to eat flesh of any kind uncooked: on the contrary, they have a great aversion to it, although, as I have before stated, they are not in the habit of roasting it according to our notions and tastes. As to their eating putrid animals, I have many times seen them take up dead and putrid kangaroos in the forest, and throw them down again with looks and gestures expressive of abhorrence; and the same with fish, which are sometimes found dead and putrid on the seashore. Both from observation and conversation with them on this subject, I can say that they are remarkably particular in this respect; nor did I ever hear, out of England, that dog's-flesh formed any part of their food. I am satisfied it does not; but supposing it to have been the case, they have the example of some of the eastern nations to keep them in countenance, and especially the Chinese, who expose for sale in their shambles both dogs and cats for the table.

In their choice of water they are particular above all things. It sometimes happens, in dry seasons that water is very scarce, particularly near the shores. In such cases, whenever they find a spring, they scratch a hole with their fingers (the ground being always sandy near the sea), and suck the water out of the pool through tufts or whisps of grass, in order to avoid dirt or insects. Often have I witnessed and joined in this, and as often felt indebted to them for their example.

They would walk miles rather than drink bad water. Indeed, they were such excellent judges of water, that I always depended upon their selection when we encamped at a distance from a river, and was never disappointed. I speak only from my own experience. It is possible that other practices may prevail in other districts, but as I was in almost every part of the colony during my residence in New South Wales, and was never an uninterested or inattentive observer of the habits of the natives, I think, if such practices as I have denied the existence of had prevailed, I must have heard of, though I did not witness them.

The most revolting custom that I ever saw amongst them, was their manner of eating the entrails of birds and beasts, which, though they always emptied, they never would wash. They cooked them, however, much longer than any other food, and as they were always taken out of a hot fire much shrivelled and rather burnt, the substances left on the inner coat were probably consumed in a great measure, if not entirely, by the fire; but I do not pretend to *know* this, never having gone so far as to join in a repast of the kind. I think, however, that even this practice, in *a savage*, is as easily to be justified as many which we know of in civilised life, when the comparative advantages of men in their respective states are fairly estimated. The Russians, it is said, are fond of train oil; and I have also heard it said, that in one of the most considerable cities in England, a dish of stewed snails was considered a delicate supper; and I have often seen the very blood of animals, which the Australian savage abhors, collected as it flows from the dying victims, to be afterwards served up in the shape of puddings at the tables of those who consider themselves the most civilised and refined!

It is curious to observe the progress in refinement of taste in uncivilised as well as civilised men. I have seen the Australian natives eat, with much relish, the damaged and musty flour scraped from the side of the casks. By degrees, as they became acquainted with that which, to *our* tastes, was of a better description, they refused that which before they so much enjoyed, and which appeared to have agreed perfectly with them. I apprehend that a refinement in animal tastes usually accompanies intellectual improvement to a certain extent, if not, the Australian savage has in this respect the advantage of us. His fare is simple, his cookery equally so, his tastes are not vitiated, and the means therefore of his subsistence are every where within his reach. He has no occasion to dig or saw, or to build houses and plant vineyards. He can eat either the kangaroo or the lizard, the oyster or the grub, all of which exist in the greatest abundance around him. We can join him in the kangaroo and oyster, while we recoil at the lizard and the grub. Where is the difference? the latter are as tender and as wholesome as the former. The black eats the grub without cooking; do not we the same with the oyster? He laughs at us for our distinctions, and cannot understand them; and I suspect it is habit only, and not reason, that enables us always ourselves to understand them.

I would therefore recommend those who would place the Australian natives on the level of brutes, to reflect well on the nature of man in his untutored state in comparison with his more civilised brother, indulging in endless whims and inconsistencies, before they venture to pass a sentence which a little calm consideration may convince them to be unjust. But I must leave my moralising, to join my friends round the fire in the forest in their feast of kangaroo.

A Choice Cutlet of Turtle

Samuel Mossman and Thomas Banister

Those who settled or travelled in Australia during the first half of the nineteenth century often suffered from an inordinate urge to publish accounts of their experiences, frequently under pseudonyms such as 'An Old Hand', or 'One Who Lived There'. Samuel Mossman himself, as 'An Australian Colonist', wrote *A Voice from Australia, giving practical advice and true information* (2nd edition, 1852). Demand for such narratives was strong, and they found a ready market in England. In *Australia Visited and Revisited* Mossman and his co-author, barrister Thomas Banister, gave an account of their travels through Victoria to Sydney and as far north as Moreton Bay (Brisbane), visiting many of the new gold diggings. Their observations are unusual in their thoughtful objectivity.

Australia Visited and Revisited, 1853

The Aborigines of the northern districts are also a more robust people than those inhabiting the south; most probably from the country yielding them a greater abundance of natural food, and the temperature of the climate being more congenial to their attenuated bodies. Moreton Bay, in these respects, is essentially the paradise of the Australian Aboriginal inhabitants; there they may revel in the freedom and nakedness of mother nature throughout all seasons, without the encumbrance of opossum-skin rugs and blankets, which are necessary to protect them from the cold south winds in the higher latitudes; and the waters of the bay furnish them with an abundance of nourishing animal food, which the bays on the southern coast do not possess. What will our aldermanic readers think of the condition of these poor natives, when we state the fact, that they dine frequently off roasted turtles? In our sojournings amongst the many interesting localities of this extensive bay, we have often partaken of a choice cutlet of turtle with our sable brethren, from a five-hundred-weight animal, cooked in its own shell; and we can aver that it was far more savoury than the spiced dishes John Bull has served up from *calipash* and *calipee*, in the shape of turtle-steaks and turtle-soup. The fact is, the *chef de cuisine* at the Mansion House might add a recipe or two worth knowing to his cookery-book from these natural gourmands. We confess ourselves a little bit of an epicure in the mode of cooking fish; and their simple method seems to us the best we have ever seen for preserving the natural juices of a delicate fish. They first collect the hot ashes from a large fire made of the mangrove-tree, which are white and free from burning embers; then the fish is taken 'all alive', without being gutted or scaled, and buried in these hot ashes for a quarter of an hour or twenty minutes. When it is sufficiently baked the gut comes out in one mass, and the skin peals off whole, leaving the flakes of meat firm, white, and savoury, with the natural fat and gravy of the fish, which in civilised cookery are lost; the former being thrown away with the gut, and the latter escaping through the scraped skin.

Fishing and Foraging

Jane Isabella Watts

Jane Isabella Watts (1824–1894) was one of the daughters of William Giles, who came to South Australia in 1837 to take charge of the whaling station at Kangaroo Island. The family later moved to Adelaide, William Giles ('Mr A.' in his daughter's memoirs) serving as manager of the South Australian Company from 1841 to 1861. Her writings show Jane to have been a girl of lively intelligence and curiosity with a mischievous sense of humour. Despite the primitive conditions in the rough-and-ready settlement on Kangaroo Island and the trials and tribulations of baking bread in a camp oven, she clearly found pleasure in her new environment and described with light-hearted amusement the eccentricities of its inhabitants.

Memories of Early Days in South Australia, 1882

That night, while seated around the old-fashioned supper-table, they learned that Mr A. had received official intimation of the Governor's intention to land the next morning, to inspect the township and hold a levée. It was at once settled that he must be invited to dinner, together with his suite, and the captain of the Queen's ship, the *Pelorus*, as they were to sail again immediately, the gentlemen on the island being asked to meet them. Now this, it must be owned, was rather startling intelligence. For when it is taken into consideration that the family had only just moved into the house, which was in the greatest state of confusion, with not a room in order; and moreover that they were living in a place where frequently provisions of even the plainest description could not be procured for love or money, it must be admitted that their position was a perplexing one. To provide, at only twenty-four hours' notice, a suitable dinner to set before twenty-four persons, was no easy task.

Fortunately, Mrs A. proved herself equal to the emergency, notwithstanding the ludicrous difficulties to be encountered. Her great ally on the occasion was a young man – one of the steerage passengers of the ship they came out in, who happened to be over from Adelaide at the time, on a visit to their maid servant to whom he was engaged to be married. He was a fine, hearty, good-natured young fellow, a sort of 'Mark Tapley' in his way, delighting in difficulties for the pleasure of overcoming them, and he agreed to start at daylight for the Farm on a foraging expedition. Another messenger was then told off to go to the township before breakfast, with orders to bring back anything in the way of provender he could honestly come by. This one speedily returned with the overwhelming intelligence that not one pound of meat was to be got upon the island, save a solitary loin of mutton, kindly sent by a friend, which, with four eggs, was all that could be had.

Matters now began to wear a very serious aspect. The morning was passing away. Mary, the cook, had finished her pastry, and was in a state bordering on distraction, for how she could be expected to have a dinner ready by six o'clock that night, and no material in the house to cook it with, seemed to her unsophisticated mind a problem impossible to solve. At length the happy thought occurred to Mrs A. of sending off to one of the ships, to see if the good natured captain L–, of the *Goshawk*, would prove a friend indeed in this dire time of sorest need, and to the credit of humanity be it said, he 'was all their fancy painted him', bountiful and generous as a prince – placing at their disposal, in the kindest manner possible, a boat load of good things. There was a splendid ham, an English cheese, tins of soup, roast veal, preserved fruits, and hosts of other dainties, with some excellent light dinner wines – sauterne, hock and claret – all of which, with a sailor's generosity, he begged their acceptance of – refusing to take a shilling in payment.

Mark Tapley, too, returned in high glee, on the only 'Rosinante' the island possessed, with a turkey dangling on one side of the saddle, a goose on the other, and, strapped before him a 'wallaby' fat enough to make the old geologist's eyes twinkle with delight. Now their fears vanished in a trice! Cook, they knew, was admirable in her line of business, Patty neat-handed as a waiter, and Mark Tapley a host in himself, a veritable tower of strength, skinning that wallaby and plucking that poultry as if he had not done anything else since his birth, and then turning to and washing the vegetables with a skill and deftness worthy of the 'old girl' in Dickens' *Bleak House*.

After all their gloomy forebodings, when the dinner-hour came, and the guests arrived, everything was in readiness for their entertainment. The carpet had been laid down in the dining-room, curtains and pole affixed to the windows, pictures hung upon the walls, and with good napery, and a sufficiency of glass, silver, and wax lights upon the tables, as excellent a repast was provided as anyone not absolutely an epicure could possibly desire, the wallaby soup in particular being much enjoyed from its rarity. The drawing-room, though furnished, still wore a dismal look, from its new plastered walls and generally unfinished state; but 'Rome was not built in a day', and no small amount of energy and pluck must have been exerted by those pioneers of civilisation in surrounding themselves with the comforts here recorded, so early in the colony's history as June, 1838.

Staff of Life

Robert Dundas Murray

The monotony of mutton, tea and damper, the staples of bush living in the nineteenth century, was often deprecated; but for every writer who reviled the inoffensive damper another rose to praise it. Robert Dundas Murray kept a relatively balanced opinion, though Louisa Meredith was later to write that damper was 'the worst way of spoiling flour'.

A Summer at Port Phillip, 1843

Our accommodations within are, for the bush, on a superb scale: a real table and real chairs – not the few planks nailed together, nor the wooden stools which you find as substitutes in other huts; and, moreover, an old deal packing-box figures as a book-case, and contains a dozen well-thumbed volumes; and there are doors to the inner apartments, and curtains to the four panes of glass that admit the light, while everything is scrupulously clean – thanks to my entertainer's housekeeper, who is regarded as the paragon of her profession all over the country side.

At the early hour of six we have tea served up. This is the beverage of the bush; master or man, you will find no other liquid but this to moisten your clay; and if you wish to indulge, you must be satisfied with the kettle and its temperate contents. At dinner, the cups are ranged beside the plates as at breakfast, and the servant pours out as many libations as you please. The same thing is done at supper; and between meals, whenever you feel thirsty, the cry is for some more tea, which speedily makes its appearance. The oceans that are thus disposed of amount to something quite incredible; and confirmed topers never emptied so many hogsheads as a regular bushman does boxes of tea. Certain it is that the former never feels half so happy over his bottle, as the other when his cup or tin pannikin of sugarless and creamless tea is in his hand – the only refreshment he seeks after his long and wearisome journeys. All other liquids of a stronger description are almost universally banished; not so much, it must be confessed, from choice as from the utter impossibility of obtaining them in the interior. Before a keg of rum reaches its destination, unnumbered are the dangers through which must run the gauntlet. Drays *will* upset on bad roads, and their cargo be wrecked beyond the hopes of salvage; faithless drivers *will* broach the cask, and make merry with what was to gladden their masters' hearts; and, worst of all, should it safely arrive, on the news being spread, the whole country side will flock to judge of its quality, and *will* remain until the last drop is drained, and the possessor nearly driven to the brink of despair. No wonder, then, that the prudent settlers prefer loading their dray with something more enduring than the ill-fated fire-water.

As a substitute for bread, we have damper – the staff of life in the backwoods of Australia. Take a mass of dough, shaped like a thin cheese, cover it over with hot embers, let it remain till the crust is hard, and then scrape away the ashes, and you have damper before you. With your knife cut off a wedge and hand the loaf to your next neighbour. Be not particular if the aforesaid knife has just been employed about your mutton chop, as spare ones are a luxury you must not expect in the bush; and if, as a last resource, you think of wiping yours on the table-cloth, ten to one such an article is unknown within the compass of twenty miles. To well-baked damper you speedily become reconciled, despite of its inferiority to the leavened loaf, in comparison with whose spungy lightness the close grain of the other tastes to great disadvantage. The very best, however, is rather apt to awaken visions of dyspepsia among those who are strangers to the free air of the forest.

I am sure our entertainer's dinner equipage must be a source of grief to his fellow-settlers. You may search far and wide in the bush before you find anything half so magnificent. No tin or pewter ornaments the board, as among the envious; but we are regaled with plates of delft, and dishes of the same; and not more than the half of them are cracked. This is an extraordinary pitch of refinement; and, to crown all, the contents of the dishes, besides the everlasting mutton that figures at every meal, display some unusual dainties, in the form of potatoes and other vegetables; and what hut can equal that? Truth to say, at most stations, the bill of fare is reduced to two dishes and no more. You have mutton and damper to-day – mutton and damper will appear tomorrow; and, from that day till the end of the year, your dinner is mutton, boiled, roasted, or stewed, or otherwise dressed as seemeth good to the hut-keeper. Dinner is no sooner despatched, and the last bowl of tea swallowed, than each guest draws forth his tobacco-pouch, and smoke begins to ascend in clouds. Give a thorough bushman his tea and pipe, and his enjoyment is complete.

Sydney Markets, 1840s

Louisa Ann Meredith

English-born Louisa Ann Meredith (1812–1895) was a respected author and illustrator whose first book about colonial Australia was *Notes and Sketches in New South Wales*. Her clear-headed observations provoked an angry response, colonists objecting to her frank and outspoken criticism of 'this new and generally too prosaic Colony, where the cabalistic lettres £.s.d. and RUM appear too frequently the alphabet of existence'. She also reproached Sydney women for taking more interest in fashion and the length of a sleeve than in literature, art or politics.

Notes and Sketches in New South Wales, **1844**

The market in Sydney is well supplied, and is held in a large commodious building, superior to most provincial market-houses at home. The display of fruit in the grape season is very beautiful. Peaches also are most abundant, and very cheap; apples very dear, being chiefly imported from Van Diemen's Land, and frequently selling at sixpence each. The smaller English fruits, such as strawberries, &c., only succeed in a few situations in the colony, and are far from plentiful. Cucumbers and all descriptions of melon abound. The large green watermelon, rose-coloured within, is a very favourite fruit, but I thought it insipid. One approved method of eating it is, after cutting a sufficiently large hole, to pour in a bottle of Madeira or sherry, and mix it with the cold watery pulp. These melons grow to an enormous size (an ordinary one is from twelve to eighteen inches in diameter), and may be seen piled up like huge cannon-balls at all the fruit-shop doors, being universally admired in this hot, thirsty climate.

There are some excellent fish to be procured here, but I know them only by the common Colonial names, which are frequently misnomers. The snapper, or schnapper, is the largest with which I am acquainted, and is very nice, though not esteemed a proper dish for a dinner party – why, I am at a loss to guess; but I never saw any native fish at a Sydney dinner-table – the preserved or cured cod and salmon from England being served instead, at a considerable expense, and, to my taste, it is not comparable with the cheap fresh fish, but being expensive, it has become 'fashionable', and that circumstance reconciles all things. The guard-fish is long and narrow, about the size of a herring, with a very singular head, the month opening at the top, as it were, and the lower jaw, or nose, projecting two-thirds of an inch beyond it. I imagine it must live chiefly at the bottom, and this formation enables it more readily to seize the food above it. They are most delicate little fish. The bream, a handsome fish, not unlike a perch in shape (but much larger, often weighing four or five pounds), and the mullet, but especially the latter, are excellent. The whiting, much larger than its English namesake, is perhaps the best of all; but I pretend to no great judgment as a gastronome. I thought the rock-oysters particularly nice, and they are plentiful and cheap; so are the crayfish, which are very similar to lobsters when small, but the large ones are rather coarse. I must not end my list of fish that we eat without mentioning one that is always ready to return the compliment when an opportunity offers, namely, the shark, many of whom are habitants of the bright tempting waters of Port Jackson. Provisions vary much in price from many circumstances. Everything was very dear when we landed in New South Wales, and at the present time prices are much too low to pay the producers.

Belgravia in the Antipodes

G.C. Mundy

Lieutenant Colonel Godfrey Charles Mundy (1804–1860) arrived in Sydney in June 1846 for a five-year term as Deputy Adjutant General of the military forces in Australia. During this time he travelled extensively in New South Wales, visiting also Victoria and Van Diemen's Land. His book was published in three volumes in 1852, after his return to England, but was so successful that it was subsequently re-issued as a single volume. Mundy was a perceptive and witty commentator, combining chatty diarising with

thoughtful and critical observation ('The construction of the buildings is blameably ill-suited to a semi-tropical climate – barefaced, smug-looking tenements, without verandahs or even broad eaves') together with factual information such as details of current food prices and the servants' wages.

Our Antipodes, 1852

June 29th

The well-known hospitable spirit of the Sydney society developed itself in my favour this morning, in the shape of a mound of visiting cards, interlarded with numerous invitations to dinners and evening parties.

I dined this day with my respected chief, Lieutenant-General Sir Maurice O'Connell, at his beautiful villa of Tarmons; and I mention the circumstance merely to have an opportunity of remarking that there were brisk coal fires burning in both dining and drawing-room, and that the general appliances of the household, the dress of the guests and the servants, were as entirely English as they could have been in London. The family likeness between an Australian and an Old Country dinner-party became, however, less striking when I found myself sipping doubtfully, but soon swallowing with relish, a plate of wallabi-tail soup, followed by a slice of boiled schnapper with oyster sauce. A haunch of kangaroo venison helped to convince me that I was not in Belgravia. A delicate wing of the wonga-wonga pigeon and bread sauce, with a dessert of plantains and loquots, guavas and mandarine oranges, pomegranates and cherimoyas, landed my imagination at length fairly at the Antipodes.

Sticker-Up

Louisa Ann Meredith

Louisa Ann Meredith's vivid descriptions of colonial life and wildlife betray a keen spirit of adventure and sensitivity to nature. She illustrated many of her books, and her delicate wildflower drawings were awarded prizes at the Melbourne Exhibition of 1866. Contemporaries praised her writing as among the most reliable and practical. She arrived in New South Wales in 1839 and soon after accompanied her husband to Van Diemen's Land, where they established a farm – no easy task, but Louisa clearly enjoyed the new experiences the bush offered.

My Home in Tasmania, 1852

In the afternoon we reached a solitary public-house, where we purposed resting for an hour, but finding a large party of rather riotous guests already in possession of its wretched little rooms, we hastened on for a short distance, and paused on the next hill, where the horses were tethered to graze, and we soon made a fire to grill our cold meat and warm baby's food; and so, under the shade of some sombre gum trees, had a pleasant pic-nic sort of repast, far more to my taste than a sojourn in the unpromising dingy little hostel we had left.

Here I was first initiated into the bush art of 'sticker-up' cookery, and for the benefit of all who 'go a-gipsying' I will expound the mystery. The orthodox material here is of course kangaroo, a piece of which is divided nicely into cutlets two or three inches broad and a third of an inch thick. The next requisite is a straight clean stick, about four feet long, sharpened at both ends. On the narrow part of this, for the space of a foot or more, the cutlets are spitted at intervals, and on the end is placed a piece of delicately rosy fat bacon. The strong end of the stick-spit is now stuck fast and erect in the ground, close by the fire, to leeward; care being taken that it does not burn. Then the bacon on the summit of the spit, speedily softening in the genial blaze, drops a lubricating shower of rich and savoury tears on the leaner kangaroo cutlets below, which forthwith frizzle and steam and sputter with as much ado as if they were illustrious Christmas beef grilling in some London chop-house under the gratified nose of the expectant consumer. 'And gentlemen,' as dear old Hardcastle would have said if he had dined with us in the bush, 'to men that are hungry, stuck-up kangaroo and bacon are very good eating.' Kangaroo is, in fact, very like hare.

On this occasion, however, as our basket was town-packed, our 'sticker-up' consisted only of ham.

Tea, Damper and a Fry

William Howitt

William Howitt (1792–1879) arrived at Port Phillip, Victoria, in September 1852 with his two sons, Charlton and Alfred. Four weeks later the trio, plus William's nephew Edward, set off for the diggings, and the next eighteen months were spent on the Victorian goldfields. Here William not only found time enough to write the 'Letters from Victoria' which eventually became this book, but also to pen a promised letter to Eliza Acton, then the doyenne of English cookery writers – not on the Australian bush, as she might have anticipated, but about food and cooking on the diggings.

Letters from Victoria, 1852–1855

We place the cart so as to be convenient to get what we want out of it; then pitch our tent opposite to the fire, but so that the smoke shall blow from us. Charlton takes the horses, gives them water, and tethers them out where there is the best grass. Meantime Alfred and I make the beds up in the tent, and the two Edwards make a fire, get out flour, and prepare a damper or a leather-jacket for tea. The damper, the universal bread of the bush, is a mere unleavened cake of a foot diameter, and from an inch to an inch and a half thick, baked in the ashes. The leather-jacket is a cake of mere flour and water, raised with tartaric acid and carbonate of soda instead of yeast, and baked in the frying-pan; and is equal to any muffin you can buy in the London shops. A fat-cake is the same thing as a leather-jacket, only fried in fat, and is not only much sooner done, but is really excellent. After tea they bake in the camp-oven, in the embers of the fire, a loaf, raised also with acid and soda, and which is equal to any home-baked bread in England. A suet pudding, called a dough-boy, or a dish of rice or potatoes, if we have them, are put into the fat, and when ready, beef steaks or mutton chops are fried; and our tea-dinner, you will admit, is not to be sneezed at, especially with the Spartan sauce of a day's travel. It is amazing what a quantity of tea is drunk in the bush. It comes upon the table everywhere in the bush or on the road. Two or three pannikins, that is, from a quart to three pints, are thought no extraordinary quantity for one person after the copious perspiration of a day's travel in this warm, dry country.

After tea Alfred gets his cigar; we talk over our affairs, and retire early to bed. We are up at peep of day, that is, from four to five o'clock, breakfast again on tea, damper and a fry; pack, and move on till noon, when we stop near some stream, get a luncheon pretty much like a dinner, lie down for a couple of hours, and then on again till four o'clock. That is our routine, except getting a bathe, or good cool wash from head to foot, where bathing is impracticable, after we have camped.

Melbourne and the Diggings

William Kelly

An unlikely assortment of individuals was attracted to Australia by the goldrushes: the shady, the downright criminal, the profiteers and the educated English gentry such as William Howitt and William Kelly, both of whom seem to have been sufficiently aware of history as to recognise the value of their journals to a 'home' audience. While generally open-minded, Kelly seemed to retain an English xenophobia when faced with unfamiliar food.

Life in Victoria in 1853, and 1858

1853

It was now getting duskish, and the day's work gave us a good appetite, which we went to appease in an eating-house in Great Collins-street East, a little below the level of the street. I thought I heard my friend – who was a member of the Wyndham – heave a gentle sigh as, surveying the rough-and-ready dinner apartment, he endeavoured to sidle into a seat opposite me, where we were obliged to dovetail as in an omnibus, the table betwixt us being barely broad enough to sustain the pair of half-wiped plates. We ordered steak and potatoes as the safest dish, and, while waiting for it – as we were not allowed any bread to pick at – we endeavoured to derive edification from the general conversation. One good-natured, communicative man in a jumper, who saw that our attention was directed to his box – moreover perhaps moved by the destitute appearance of our table, which was simply decorated with a single salt and an egg-cup of mustard – jumped up with a bottle and glass, and insisted on our joining him in nobblers. As there might have been danger in declining the intuitive hospitality, we made a virtue of necessity, and swallowed the potions in so clean, off-hand a manner, as to charm the heart of our unknown entertainer, who smiled affectionately, shook our hands vehemently, exclaiming, in guttural ecstasy, 'X-cuse me, gemmen – you're town folk – I don't make me money like as you do; I makes mine by fair bloody diggin'.' Saying which, he gave the bottle a flourish over his head that sent a shower of brandy about the room.

Our dinner arriving at this juncture, he retired, with a propriety of demeanour scarcely to be expected. But how shall I attempt to describe the meal I have designated a dinner? Each plate contained a calcined lump of meat, which might have been flat in its raw state, but was now shrivelled up into a black ball about the size of the cold potato beside it. Gravy there was none; and so far from there being any succulence about the unsightly cinder, the fork went into it as if it was entering a rusk, causing a shedding of sooty scales about. There was no butter, and there was no use in complaint; we, however, got a bit of gritty bread, and a glass of saccharine ale, as extras; the whole repast costing the small sum of 8s 6d.

1858

I had anything but an agreeable time of it in my boarding house. The meals were well enough in their rough-and-ready way, for the boarders, who paid liberally, would not tolerate any palpable inferiority of fare. They entertained, in their own phraseology, 'a dead down' on all made dishes of the hash, haricot, or Irish-stew school. The refinements of the French cuisine had not as yet penetrated into the Bush, and therefore all disguises were forbidden. Whole quarters of mutton and sirloins of beef, with entrées of steaks and chops, were the prevailing regimen, but food in any unrecognisable shape was treated by a process of summary ejection. Hot mutton-pies were an innovation which progressed by slow degrees, and sausages for a long time were regarded as an abomination too strong for civilised stomachs. And this suspicious fastidiousness was all the more strange from the cheapness of meat, and the difficulty of finding a substitute; for dogs were too highly prized to be used indiscriminately, and the 'feline seasoners' were then unknown in Victoria, cats being positive curiosities. I believe myself that the explanation was to be found in the fact that nine-tenths of the people who sat down to meat meals three times a day in the colony, used it so unfrequently in their early days, they had the same fears of being imposed on that a rural swell entertains lest gooseberry should be imposed on him for champagne by London landlords. As I said before, the food was well enough, and I could even wink at the greasy enamel of the wiped tin plates, or the deltas of unctuous deposit which settled between the prongs of the fork or round the hafts of the knives, if I were allowed any moderate period for undisturbed repose on my corded boxes; but rest in the refreshment tent was even more impossible than on the boiler of a steam-engine with the rivetters at work. The senses, after a lapse, may become reconciled to a repetition of torturing sounds, provided they all come of the same family, but where they are capriciously afflicted with an infernal medley of oaths, thumps, screams, drunken songs, and a *delirium tremens* of bottles and glasses, nothing short of death, or at least that partial phase of it which follows an excess of whisky, could even feign composure.

Oysters and Pleasure

G.C. Mundy

Godfrey Charles Mundy was one of the most informative and ostensibly trustworthy documentarists of social life in the colonies in the mid-nineteenth century, enjoying all the opportunities that passed his way to participate in the rituals of colonial society. While he thought little of fishing excursions in Sydney Harbour (groups would return 'with a good basket of schnappers and flatheads – perhaps a rockcod or two, and with every bit of skin burnt off their noses and chins') he enjoyed shark-hunting: 'the best sport to be had in New South Wales; and [it] affords a wholesome stimulation to the torpid action of life in Sydney.'

Our Antipodes, 1852

Considering the unrivalled suitability of Port Jackson for aquatic pursuits, the citizens of Sydney appreciate pastimes on the water little more than they do the rides, and drives, and gardens. There is, however, connected with the shores, and islets, and coves of the harbour, one pursuit peculiarly congenial to the tastes of the people – a pastime half jaunting, half sedentary; a little sea air, a very little personal exertion, and a large amount of gastronomic recreation; I mean, oyster-eating. Every inch of rock from Sydney to the Heads is thickly colonised by these delicate shellfish; that is, every inch would be so peopled, but for the active extermination incessantly going on.

On any fine day select parties of pleasure-and-oyster seekers may be seen proceeding by water, or land, furnished with the necessary muniments for an attack, or actively engaged in it. A hammer and a chisel, an oyster-knife, a bottle of vinegar, and the pepper-pot, with a vigorous appetite, sharpened by the almost impregnable character of the foe – such are the forces brought into the field, and the inducements to distinction. It is needless to add, that the garrison are quickly shelled out of their natural stronghold.

I enrolled myself more than once in an expedition of this kind, and only regretted that 'my great revenge had stomach' for only one-half of the luscious victims demolished by my companions. The small rock-oyster of New South Wales is excellent in its way, although inferior to the Carlingford. The great mud-oyster of the rivers is too unctuous for delicate appetites, although it is swallowed *ore rotundo* at the street-corners and stalls by those who prefer quantity to quality. Not much can be said in favour of the other fish of the colony. The guard-fish, which resembles a little sword-fish, and is somewhat smaller than the European herring, is delicate; and the schnapper, when on the table, looms like the cod, but is a decided impostor as far as flavour goes. There is an inland, tramontane, fresh-water cod, strange to say, worth all the sea-fish of the Australian coasts. I am afraid to state the weight that this species sometimes attains, but in naming 60 lbs I am surely within the mark.

There did exist, during part of my sojourn in Australia, and long previously perhaps, an association of the aristocracy and bureaucracy of Sydney, whose members once or twice a month indulged in piscatory excursions down the harbour. It was generally believed that they went out with the intention and purpose of 'roughing it' on the fruits of their skill. Furnished with an immense seine, or hauling-net, they put into any of the numerous sandy coves of Port Jackson favourable for the purpose of the expedition; and having launched their net, and lighted a fire of drift-wood under some sheltering bank tufted with gum or fig-trees, nothing could have appeared to the eyes of a stranger more miraculous than the repast which resulted from the experiment. The gentlemen did not over-fatigue themselves by personal exertion, for half-a-dozen boatmen, who looked wonderfully like convicts, hauled the seine, while one or two others, assisted perhaps by an amateur, busied themselves among pots and pans round the fire. Presto! appear spread on the sward a boiled schnapper or broiled flathead, with oyster sauce. That was natural enough. It looked like practising Ichthyophagy in its purest sense – as it is practised, in short, at Blackwall or Greenwich in the whitebait season. But pigeon pies, turkey and tongues, ham and chicken, champagne and bottled ale – where did they come from? It was quite plain that all was fish that came to the net of these famous fishermen.

Christmas Dinner, 1858

Blanche Mitchell

Blanche Mitchell (1843–1869) was the youngest of the eleven children of Sir Thomas Mitchell, Surveyor-General of New South Wales from 1828, explorer and early advocate of olives for Australia. She spent a comfortable childhood and early adolescence in the grand family home at Darling Point, Sydney, but after Sir Thomas's untimely death in 1855 she and her mother and siblings were obliged to move to a much smaller house in what is now King's Cross. Her diary from January 1858 to February 1861 is a record of family life and the social events which shaped the life of a teenage girl.

Blanche: An Australian Diary, 1980

First course was a pair of fowls – a very large ham – roast beef and horse radish, potatoes, beans, vegetable marrow, cabbage etc. When all were satisfied, and the dishes removed, visible anxiety was painted on each countenance for the safety of the pudding, which was rather long in coming. But soon it made its arrival, and Roddy shouted with joy at seeing its good natured face, speckled with plums and currants and a goodly branch of Christmas waving from its crown, inviting all to partake and taste of its merits. And taste all did, for who would not eat of a plum pudding on Xmas day, and plates were replenished and filled again, and it was pronounced excellent by all around. Even though a rhubarb tart graced the upper end of the table, it was left untouched, and all at last being satisfied, and praises echoed from all around, the signal was given, and the silvery tones of the tinkling bell warned the servant to take away.

The wine being freely spread, some joviality began to creep in amongst the family party. Mr Uhr reasoned, and entered into an interminable argument, about some unknown subject. Jessie entered into quick repartee, and cut him short at every word. Campbell and Alice laughed, quarrelled, and made up again. Roddy and I fought half in jest, and half in earnest, and kept up a silent merriment between ourselves, whilst poor Livy sat in his solitary bedroom eating his solitary dinner, and mourning the loss of his health, which prevented him sharing in the fun.

The dessert consisted of apricots, plums, oranges, cakes and biscuits. At last the great affair being over, we adjourned to the drawing room.

Christmas in Melbourne

Anonymous

Blanche Mitchell may have enjoyed her hot roast with all the trimmings, but as early as the mid-nineteenth century an alternative Christmas tradition flourished in Australia: the outdoors and the picnic. For all those who bemoaned the inappropriateness of a hot dinner in the middle of summer – and Marcus Clarke was one of them, as he shows in the piece after this one – there were as many who appreciated the informality of a cold meal outdoors.

Illustrated Melbourne Post, December 1864

Nature holds high festival at Christmas-tide as well as man. Our orchards are ruddy with fruit, our gardens bright with flowers, and our fields golden with the yellowing harvest, at the very time we observe the great holiday of the year. It comes to us in the full flush of mid-summer, and it is celebrated – like many of the religious festivals of ancient Greece – in the open air. It is a prolonged merry-making, for there is a suspension of all business from Christmas Eve until the morrow of New Year's Day. The old year passes away, and its successor is ushered in with general rejoicing.

A Christmas dinner in Australia necessarily takes the shape of an *al fresco* meal. It is eaten under green boughs like the 'feast of taber-nacles' among the ancient Israelites. [At the beach at Brighton] an impromptu encampment springs up among the tea-tree scrub which flourishes upon the sand hummocks. Fires are lit, hampers of pro-visions unpacked, table cloths are spread upon the sand, temporary awnings rigged overhead, and innumerable gypsy parties, in close proximity to each other, apply themselves with British vigour to diminish the stock of comestibles and drinkables they have brought with them. The clatter of plates, the popping of corks, the jingling of glasses, and the rattle of knives and forks, mingle with peals of merry laughter, with the buzz of conversation, and with the splash of waves upon the beach.

Marcus Clarke's Christmas in Australia

Marcus Clarke

Marcus Clarke (1846–1881) arrived in Melbourne in 1863 at the age of 17 and, after brief and unfulfilling experiences working in a bank and as a jackeroo, settled for a life of writing. He wrote essays, short stories, pieces for the theatre and a novel, *For the Term of His Natural Life* (1874), which has become a classic, but he was most prolific in the field of journalism.

Australasian, 26 December 1868

A merry Christmas! Very merry with the bailiffs drinking beer in the kitchen, and James George Augustus Robinson (*aetat*, 1 hour 37 min) reposing stertorously upon the flock-bed in the dismantled room upstairs! A very merry Christmas, with the roast beef in a violent perspiration, and the thermometer 110 deg. in the shade!

A remarkably merry Christmas, with the hot wind raging, and one's plate of Christmas cheer two fork-handles-deep in gravel! An excessively merry Christmas for John Shepherd, as he sits in the shade of his cabbage-tree hat on the burnt-up grass of the Tartarus Plains, and munches his bread and mutton wearily, while the sheep lie in panting groups, strung out under the haze, away down to the solitary box-tree that stands where the dusty gaping fissure tells where the creek ought to be! The merriest of merry Christmases for young Cuttemoute, travelling on the roads with store-cattle, and unable to make the public house and smithy, which constitute the township, until a week after New Year's Day!

It may be rank heresy, but I deliberately affirm that Christmas in Australia is a gigantic mistake. The keeping of Christmas is a simple waste of time and money. 'Will the Coming Man Drink Wine?' asks a writer in the *Atlantic Monthly*. I may also ask, 'Will the Coming Man Keep Christmas?' and answer it in the negative. I myself take no interest in the Coming Man – (having 'come', for my own part, as far as I can) – but if the gentleman in question is sensible, and possesses digestive organs, it is quite probable that he will refuse to load his stomach with the portable nightmare popularly known as plum pudding, and that he will decline to consider the eating of hot roast beef until his eyelids will no longer wag as a pleasant and Christian duty.

Half a Bullock and a Case of Pickled Salmon

Rolf Boldrewood

Rolf Boldrewood, the pseudonym of Thomas Alexander Browne (1826–1915), is best known for his novel *Robbery under Arms* (1882–1883), one of the classics of colonial Australian fiction. Born in London, he came to Australia in 1831 and spent his early working life running sheep stations in Victoria and on the Murrumbidgee River in New South Wales. This story describes typical conditions before the shearers' strikes of the 1890s.

'Shearing begins to-morrow!' These apparently simple words were spoken by Hugh Gordon, the manager of Anabanco Station, in the district of Riverina, in the colony of New South Wales, one Monday morning in the month of August. The utterance had its significance, to every member of a rather extensive *corps dramatique* awaiting the industrial drama about to be performed.

Tuesday was the day fixed for the actual commencement of the momentous, almost solemn transaction – the pastoral Hegira, so to speak, as the time of most station events is calculated with reference to it, as happening before or after shearing. But before the first shot is fired which tells of battle begun, what raids and skirmishes, what reconnoitring and vedette duty must take place!

First arrives the cook-in-chief to the shearers, with two assistants, to lay in a few provisions for the week's consumption of seventy able-bodied men. Now the cook of a large shearing shed is a highly paid and responsible official. He is chosen and provided by the shearers themselves. Payment is generally arranged on the scale of half-a-crown a head weekly from each shearer. For this sum he contracts to provide punctual and effective cooking, paying out of his own pocket as many *marmiton*s as may be needful for that end, and must satisfy the taste of his exacting and fastidious employers.

In the present case he confers with the storekeeper, Mr de Vere, a young gentleman of aristocratic connections, who is thus gaining an excellent practical knowledge of the working of a large station; and to this end has the storekeeping department entrusted to him during shearing.

He is not, perhaps, quite fit for a croquet party as he stands now, with a flour-scoop in one hand and a pound of tobacco in the other. But he looks like a man at work, also like a gentleman, as he is. 'Jack the Cook' thus addresses him:

'Now, Mr de Vere, I hope there's not going to be any humbugging about my rations and things. The men are all up in their quarters, and as hungry as free settlers. They've been a-payin' for their rations for ever so long, and of course, now shearin's on, they're good for a little extra.'

'All right, Jack,' returns de Vere good-humouredly; 'your order was weighed out and sent away before breakfast. You must have missed the cart. Here's the list. I'll read it out to you – three bags flour, half a bullock, two bags sugar, a chest of tea, four dozen of pickles, four dozen of jam, two gallons of vinegar, five lbs pepper, a bag of salt, plates, knives, forks, ovens, frying-pans, saucepans, iron pots, and about a hundred other things. You're to return all the cooking things safe, or *pay for them*, mind that! You don't want anything more, do you? Got enough for a regiment of cavalry, I should think.'

'Well, I don't know, sir. There won't be much left in a week if the weather holds good,' makes answer the chef, as one who thought nothing too stupendous to be accomplished by shearers; 'but I knew I'd forgot something. As I'm here, I'll take a few dozen boxes of sardines, and a case of pickled salmon. The boys likes 'em, and, murder alive! haven't we forgot the plums and currants; a hundredweight of each, Mr de Vere. They'll be crying out for plum-duff and currant-buns for the afternoon, and bullying the life out of me if I haven't a few trifles like. It's a hard life, surely, a shearers' cook. Well, good-day, sir, you have 'em all down in the book.'

Lest the reader should imagine that the rule of Mr Gordon at Anabanco was a reign of luxury and that waste which tendeth to penury, let him be aware that shearers in Riverina are paid at a certain rate, usually that of one pound per hundred sheep shorn. They agree, on the other hand, to pay for all supplies consumed by them, at certain prices fixed before the shearing agreement is signed. Hence it is entirely their own affair whether their mess bills are extravagant or economical. They can have everything within the rather wide range of the station store – *pâtés de foie gras*, ortolans, roast ostrich, novels, top-boots, double-barrelled guns, *if they like to pay for them*, with one exception – no wine, no spirits! Neither are they permitted to bring these stimulants 'on to the ground' for their private use. Grog at shearing? Matches in a powder-mill! It's very sad and bad; but our Anglo-Saxon industrial champion cannot be trusted with the fire-water. Navvies, men-of-war's men, soldiers, *and* shearers – fine fellows all. But though the younger men might only drink in moderation, the majority of the elders are utterly without self-control, once in the front of temptation. And wars, 'wounds without cause', hot heads, shaking hands, delay and bad shearing would be the inevitable result of spirits, *à la discrétion*. So much is this a matter of certainty from experience that a clause is inserted and cheerfully signed in most shearing agreements, 'that any man getting drunk or bringing spirits on to the station during shearing, loses *the whole of the money* earned by him'. The men know that the restriction is for their benefit, as well as for the interest of the master, and join in the prohibition heartily.

Shooting, Fishing and Other Diversions

James Inglis

James Inglis (1845–1908) settled in New South Wales in 1877 after many years in India. Several years later he founded the business of James Inglis & Co., importers and general merchants, and led a highly respectable life as a member of parliament and Minister of Public Instruction from 1887 to 1889. He contributed articles to the local press under the pen-name 'Maori' and wrote several books, including *The Humour of the Scot*. This extract reveals an extrovert and outdoorsy character, and his inventory of the gargantuan rations required for 'roughing it' during an Easter camp suggests a willingness to enjoy life to the full. As he explains in a footnote, 'camp' is the invariable colonial phrase used to describe an excursion of any sort – to go a-fishing, or a-shooting, is 'to camp out'.

Our Australian Cousins, 1880

Some days before the holidays a trusty friend hinted to me that I should be welcome if I would consent to join himself and a party of friends. I asked him where they were going.

'Oh!' said he, 'we're going to have a regular camp; we've got a steam launch and a boat, and intend going to Port Hacking to have some shooting, fishing, and general diversion.'

Now, I had camped out a good deal in my time. I knew what it involved; and, remembering my corpulent frame and rheumatic joints, I was rather averse to the idea of roughing it, as I knew many enthusiastic young Australians were in the habit of doing, when they went out on an expedition of the nature proposed by my friend. I am just as fond of sport as most men, and, perhaps, have had as large an experience as the majority of my Australian acquaintance. Grouse shooting, partridge shooting, black-cock shooting, I have had. Salmon fishing in the bonny Scottish rivers, in the lovely voes of Shetland, and in the deep blue waters of the Western Islands, I have enjoyed with a delicious zest; but I never found warm dry clothing, comfortable quarters and good cookery detract from, but rather intensify the sport, whatever it may have been. In New Zealand I have been out shooting wild cattle on the back ranges, spearing eels with the Maories, and potting Paradise ducks, and other winged and web-footed birds on the flax-fringed tarns of Canterbury. But I never found a nice tent and warm blue blankets to be at all a bad accessory to one's sport. After a weary day's waiting in the thick *sal* jungle of India, when each rustle made my heart beat high with excitement, as I looked for the expected leopard or lordly stag; or at the end of a long beat through tangled bamboo or elephant grass, as the stately line of elephants bore majestically down on the slouching tiger, the savage rhinoceros, or the ponderous buffalo; a refresher in the shape of an iced hock and seltzer, a sparkling draught of champagne or claret cup, or a long pull at refreshing brandy and soda, has never detracted from the enjoyment of the sport pure and simple, and, therefore, I asked my friend what sort of a camp they were going to have.

Now he was the sort of man who cares not a button so long as there's plenty of wallaby to be shot or schnapper to be hooked, and even when he said that everything was to be quite on a scale of oriental magnificence in fact, I still felt rather dubious, and I said, 'Well, we can go and see G.!' 'All right,' said A., and off we went. My first impressions of G. were decidedly flattering to that excellent fellow, and when we had visited his well-stocked cellar, discussed a flagon of delicious Australian wine, and G. had told me he was to take a tent and I might have a share of it, I began to think it might not be a bad thing after all to have an outing at Easter.

In addition to the steam-launch there were to be two or three tents, two Aborigines to assist the *chef de cuisine*, and the party was to be limited to twenty. For their sustenance and delectation a quarter of an ox, a live sheep, a colossal ham, three barrels of beer, flour, potatoes, tomatoes, cabbages, carrots, cheese, bread, condiments, mushrooms, butter, and all the 'materials' for punch, not forgetting even the lemons, and last, but not least, an enormous plum-pudding were to be provided. Ere he had half finished his tempting category my last remaining scruple had vanished, and even for a time, I must confess with a blush,

I forgot all about the wallaby and the fishing. However, we discussed another flagon, and then arranged for a muster, and talked over every requisite detail. Our luggage was to be sent down from G.'s, and it was finally decided that the party should meet at Botany, at the Sir Joseph Bank's Hotel, on the Thursday night.

Rabbit-in-a-Pumpkin

Agnes Stokes

Originally published as *The Autobiography of a Cook*, the memoirs of Agnes Stokes (b. 1867) were rediscovered by Helen Vellacott who republished them under the title of *A Girl at Government House*. Agnes was clearly an adventurous girl; having seen an advertisement – 'Free Emigration to Australia' – she immediately decided to take up the offer. She arrived in Brisbane in 1887 and spent the next twelve months there, and subsequently worked in Sydney and in Melbourne before returning to England.

The Autobiography of a Cook, 1932

I'd been set against church by my elders, but I'll never forget the camp meetings on Darling Downs. They put the civilised nations to shame. At home it is considered enough to join the nearest congregation, and take your seat easy or kneel on cushions. Out in Australia they'd flock for thirty or forty miles, without thinking about the weather. In they came on horseback, sometimes one behind the other on the same nag. Once there were three weddings and a number of children christened, and the people sang Moody and Sankey hymns at the tops of their voices, and enjoyed themselves so end. Sometimes there were several speakers, all good, and after the meeting I had my first bush dinner. They cut a large Turk's head, a vegetable something like a pumpkin. The top was sliced off, all the pips scooped out; some rabbits were shot, skinned, cleaned, cut up and put inside with onions.

A hole was dug and a pile of wood shoved in. When it was well alight a lot of stones were thrown in, then more wood, next the Turk's head which was covered and left till cooked. Some rabbits they roasted and they made some dampers – bushmen's bread – just flour and water cooked in ashes, and jolly nice they were, eaten as soon as cooked. Altogether, it was great fun, and made me feel as if I'd really travelled far from the little round at home.

Kangarooing

Anonymous

Less than one hundred years after the first English settlement in Port Jackson, Australia had its own comprehensive guide to proper behaviour, *Australian Etiquette*. The chapter on the venerable English sport of 'Hunting' showed how easy it was to transfer to the colonies the defining qualities of a traditional English hunt.

Australian Etiquette, 1885

A hunting sport, which is essentially Australian, is called 'Kangarooing', and is often indulged in by both ladies and gentlemen. In the country districts of the colonies, wherever kangaroos are to be found, they offer most excellent sport to lovers of the chase. The kangaroo, as is well-known to the people of Australia, is a very peculiar creature. It does not, like other quadrupeds, run upon four feet, but jumps along with great velocity, being furnished with powerful and long hind legs, which enable it, aided by its enormous tail, to jump an extraordinary distance for a creature of its size. It is capable of clearing, at every bound, quite as much space as is usually covered by a horse when in full stride at a gallop. Kangaroo dogs are often killed by an 'old man', as a seven-foot male kangaroo is called. Sometimes he will drown them, when, like the deer in England, he has taken to the water in an effort to escape from pursuers. Sometimes an 'old man' will place his back against a tree and keep a pack of kangaroo-hounds at bay, wounding and killing them by blows from his hind feet, the long nails or claws ripping into and disembowelling the dogs. When, in the course of a chase, a kangaroo either 'trees' by placing his back against a tree as just described, or betakes itself to a water hole and keeps the dogs at bay, the struggle seldom ends until the huntsmen gallop up, and the gentleman who is first 'in at the death' dismounts and kills the kangaroo with his hunting-whip, which is furnished with a loaded handle, and is usually carried for the express purpose of giving the object of pursuit the *coup-de-grace*. Should a lady be present when the 'old man' of the Australian bush receives his death blow, she claims and obtains the kangaroo's tail, which most ladies well-know how to convert into 'kangaroo-tail soup' – a dish greatly esteemed by epicures. It is impossible to devote space to a full description of the excitement and pleasurable features of kangaroo-hunting, or of that other native sport, wallaby-hunting, which latter is pursued in a similar way to kangarooing, though the subject is a tempting one.

Harvest Festival

Catherine Martin

Born in Scotland, Catherine Martin (1848–1937) came with her family to South Australia with her family in 1855, and took the colony as the scene for *An Australian Girl,* her first novel. In this extract the heroine, Stella Courtland, describes in a letter the Easter Sunday harvest festival (or 'Dankfest', as she calls it) at St Stephan's Lutheran church at the 'old-world charming little German-looking township' of 'Blumenthal' – a fictional town whose name was probably derived from Blumberg (now Birdwood) and Lobethal, two predominantly German settlements in the Adelaide hills.

An Australian Girl, 1890

Blumenthal, Easter Sunday

I must write to you while I am at Pastor Fielder's. I came on Saturday, so as to be at the Dankfest to-day . . .

My old friends, the Schulzes, Grossvater and Grossmutter, greeted me with all their old cordiality. Their seat was crammed with sturdy young Schulzes of the third generation. I should be afraid to say how many of the sept there were in all. It was good I was in the church before the service began, for I could not have kept my eyes from wandering. Such lavish heaps of flowers, fruit and vegetables! No wonder the good Germans of Blumenthal hold a harvest festival. There are ten windows in St Stephan's, with wide, deep sills to them. On each side of these an overflowing horn of plenty had been emptied.

It was a triumphant exhibition of what Nature can do in our land when her lap is shaken out. The apples alone were a feast to the eyes – so large and smooth and beautifully tinted. As for the pears, they were so ripely yellow one dared not look at them too fixedly lest they should melt at a glance. There were mounds of great purple figs gaping with mellowness. Citrons large as pumpkins, quinces not much smaller, plums of all kinds, from the little piquant damson to the generous Orleans; blood-red mulberries, fragrant peaches with their crimsoned cheeks, nectarines, and oranges of a lordly size, though still, of course, unripe. On the altar – a plain table with a white cloth and crucifix – were grapes, heaped up in splendid profusion. The robust Black Prince, the small berries of the Cabernet Sauvignon – no, I must not put you out of patience by naming all; besides, if I did, half would still be forgotten, if you will pardon the bull. I noticed one bunch of Doradillas which must have weighed five pounds. You are in deadly terror of hearing about the spies and Eshcol – but I spare you. I also let you off in the matter of vegetables. They were all there, from the asparagus to the virtuous potato. The ends of the seats were wreathed with hop and vine leaves, and round the chandeliers were hung sheaves of fine wheat, of oats, of barley, and maize. The pastor preached a divine little sermon – sincere, simple, and to the point. It was the discourse of a man who knows that there are two sorts of ignorance, and two sorts of lying, in the world. The ignorance that knows and cares for little beyond the daily round; the ignorance that cares for so much, yet apprehends that so little can be really known. The lying – that of statements known to be untrue; the other, which takes the form of treating as certainties matters than can never be subjectively proved true. And yet, because he knew all this, it seemed to me that he was all the better fitted to speak with authority on what we do know to be true. We know that if we put aside the baser temptations of life we can bear our share of fruit to nourish man's spiritual nature, even as the fields around us, year in, year out, bear harvests that sustain material life.

Grandma's Orchard

Miles Franklin

Miles Franklin's full name was Stella Maria Miles Lampe Franklin; 'Miles' was the family name of her grandmother's grandfather who arrived in Australia with the First Fleet. Her family were pioneer graziers in the Monaro tablelands of New South Wales and in her mind their property, 'Brindabella', was always her true home. The publication of her first novel, *My Brilliant Career* (1901) brought Miles Franklin (1879–1954) fame plus a certain notoriety and from 1905 to 1933 she lived overseas, writing under the name 'Brent of Bin Bin'. The autobiographical *Childhood at Brindabella* was written in 1952–1953 but not published until 1963.

Childhood at Brindabella, 1963

The diminishing weeks were frantically savoured. I ran hither and yon as intensely as a dog left in charge, trying to garner concretely the intangible. The beauty of the orchard in bloom had excited me as an ethereal wonderland. Those heralds, the peach-trees, had been every-where, almost unregarded, patches of rose amid the native foliage along the race or creeks where their pits had been dropped to make fruit for the possums. The pear, the plum and the cherry-trees were ladies-in-waiting. The quince with her quieter blooms was a hand-maiden. The great apple tree stood like the queen of them all in her pastel rosiness with her promise of substantial gifts to last through the bare months. Her bridal radiance was overwhelming under the fresh warm spring skies. The butterflies paid her court in flickering beauty spots of added adornment.

The cherries ripened first and disappeared quickly. The leather-heads chanting *cholicky-cholicky* sensed their arrival from afar: only sharp-shooting saved for us some of the black and white-heart beauties grown on trees grafted by Great-Uncle William himself. He was a skilled orchardist and agriculturist, one of the ablest pupils of Calloway. Fruit-trees were respected and loved. There was no hacking them to let the riflers or sprayers have easy access. Each tree was a personality like members of the family themselves. When pruned the superfluous limbs were carefully selected, sawn with a surgeon's amputating precision and then plastered with mud lest the powerful Australian sun should prove fatal. Each tree was allowed to develop grandly to its full height and to live to its full age. They responded by bearing nobly for generations.

Another early treat were the apricots on a tall tree that guarded the back gate and threw shade where Grandma had made the splendid swipe at me with the broom. I held an idea that five pips were the correct number for an apple. Mother told us of her grandmother on a visit bringing a beautiful apple, one of several that had come all the way from Prospect by bullock dray. Each one had enjoyed a taste of it and its five pips were saved for increase. Two trees resulted. These were, I believe, the queen already mentioned, and another that stood not far away among the oldest trees near the house. The queen's fruit was large and green. They turned yellow only when ripe. The flesh, juicy when newly ripe, delicious for eating raw or cooking, would mellow to dry flour that could be scooped out with a spoon. When ripe their broad flatness allowed them to be split in halves by hand. The second tree was not so tall and had less massive limbs. The fruit was small. We called the apples 'russets' because they had a tough brown skin. The flesh was yellow with a nutty flavour. Both these apples would remain in the straw in the loft where they were carefully placed till the second season's early fruits would be well advanced. The straw seemed to suck the flavour from the big apples, but the hardy russets retained theirs and were much prized when there was no cold storage, no exchange of fruits from afar. There was also the earliest apple, the Irish peach or the Dunlop, small apples with dark speckled skins. At the head Bobilla homestead too and other haunts of my childhood were numerous unnamed seedling apples equally remarkable. There was no disease, no codlin moth, fruit flies, nor the most insidious of all, the brown rot which was to be seen destroying even King George V's peaches exhibited at the Chelsea Flower Show.

Gathering the apples for winter was a pleasant and satisfying task. The fruit was allowed to ripen to the right degree to retain its full flavour. It was not plucked so green that it never ripened or ripened so unnaturally that the flavour was spoiled. Uncles would ascend the great trees to choose the best apples for eating raw. These were tossed to my aunts to be placed tenderly in the big laundry baskets. My youngest aunt could catch like a cricket fielder. Any apple with a bruise or blemish was rejected. Then came the fuller harvest in various grades, not quite so specially handled but nevertheless sorted and laid on shelves. There were hundredweights in addition that could be eaten all day. The residue fell on the ground and was a tasty dessert for the pigs.

In a corner outside the flower garden was the domain of the gooseberries, the red and white currants and the raspberries. A tall magnolia looked over the flower-garden fence to watch my foraging and feasting.

Thickets of Kentish cherries yielded appetising fruit especially delicious for preserves. The pigs crushed their stones with gusto which, seeing how their teeth are placed, always seemed clever marksmanship to me. Peaches were plentiful. Luscious pears that would melt in the mouth, and others so hardy that they lasted till spring and so weighty that a couple could serve a family, were a treat, baked in the brick oven with cloves stuck in them. The quinces, never to be outgrown in affection, would hang like yellow lanterns on the trees after the leaves had fallen, the most lasting of the orchard's bounty and none more appetising stewed or baked or in pies with clotted cream or preserved in jellies and jams.

Among such riches none was more plentiful, more varied, more luscious than the plums. Strange fruit, among the sweetest raw, among the sourest cooked. I don't know their species but in the gardens of my childhood I can clearly recall eighteen different kinds. Sometimes in the night when sleep will not come I summon them to mind. A small sweet one called the American came first. Also early and one of the choicest was the greengage. There followed the purple and the red, oval or round, large and small, including the big Victoria, and one of the handsomest called the Japanese, which was untameably sour, raw or cooked. It was delightful to shake a tree or to hit it with a prop-stick for the ripest fruit to fall. Plums were with us for the full season right through to autumn with the white and purple prunes, the big whitish floury egg plums, then the small roundish damson plum and the oval damson herself. The damson is the beloved of those reared in the cold country. When truly ripe, stewed with its royally coloured juice, served with plenty of thick scalded cream it is a dish for epicures. And a damson-tree laden with ripening fruit thrills with its dark beauty. The rarest, most tribal plum of all was the gizzard plum. It lasted longest of any and shared with the prunes the honour of best for drying. It was smallish, the size of the damson plum, with the halves plainly indented. Unless quite ripe it was astringent and puckered the lips. Properly ripe it vies with the damson in memory. Dried it turned dark and leathery like the cooked gizzard of a hen, but in pies, with thick cream again, it and the damson had the winter to themselves.

I never saw a gizzard plum anywhere but in Grandma's orchard, and two immense old trees farther up the river in some spot which had been the home plot of a settler long gone. We thought that 'gizzard' was our private name for it, and Grandma did not consider it quite genteel to call it that to topside guests.

One day long after on Tottenham Court Road not far from Oxford Street I was turning over the wares on the pavement outside Shearn's, the well-known fruiterer. A shop assistant brought me to heel with, 'Can I help you to find something, Madam?'

'I was looking for gizzard plums,' I mumbled.

'Ask at the counter inside, Madam; fourpence per pound.'

A pound of fruit in a bag was quickly in my hand. I stuck in my thumb and pulled out a plum, and thoroughly dumbfounded was I. It was ripe and sweet, of rare flavour, unmistakably a *Gizzard Plum*!

I sallied out dazed, never more integrally of the British Empire.

My Queensland friend, she who caressed the carpetsnake, and had inherited a prejudice against the English, laughed merrily, 'Yes! There's no doubt they are the most remarkable people on the globe. I wouldn't believe it with their stick-in-mud tinpot ways and all that broken glass on top of their old walls to keep people out, but one day at Kew I found in a hothouse a pot full of our old sourgrass weed that grows round the stables at home!'

Banana Field

Rosa Praed

Rosa Praed (1851–1935) has been described as the first Australian writer to make an international reputation, though for all her writing life she lived in England and Europe. Of her output of around 40 novels, approximately half featured Australian settings. The autobiographical *My Australian Girlhood* describes with deep affection her early life in the Queensland bush and in Brisbane.

One could write a whole essay about the delights of a banana field – the succulent stems, running with innocent sap, which nevertheless stains hands and pinafores vicious and ineffaceable brown, rousing wrath in the breasts of the governing hierarchy – elders, nurses and laundresses. Then the lovely sheaths of royal purple, unfolding and revealing the creamy blossoms and baby fruit: and lastly, the long-drawn joy of watching the green fingers swell and take a tinge of yellow – and maybe a surreptitious filching, wrongfully charged to flying foxes, before the bunch is gathered and hung under the verandah eaves, when the lawful authorities take jurisdiction thereof.

Ripening plums on a south wall, early pears in an orchard, and the gooseberry border in the kitchen garden, are not in it with the secret excitements of a banana plantation.

Biscuits and Wine

Dame Mary Gilmore

Dame Mary Gilmore (1865–1962) was a poet, teacher, writer, journalist and outspoken advocate of the rights of workers and the welfare of the working class. From 1908 to 1931 she edited the women's page of the *Worker*, using this forum to awaken women to various social reforms but also to pass on household hints and economical recipes, which eventually became *The Worker Cookbook* (1915). These recollections of her childhood probably reflect the period she spent with her grandparents on their property, 'Brooklyn', located near Wagga Wagga.

Old Days, Old Ways, 1934

Besides the removal of the bonnet, and the special seating of the visitor when she came, there was the glass of wine and a biscuit if your wealth ran so far, or cake if you could not afford 'stores'. These I might say were not shop's; they were your own personal or family provision against the period known as 'between the teams'. People had not the water-supplies, artesian and sub-artesian, that they have today, and the teams could only set out when the seasonal rains provided water. We read of the breaking of the ice in Canada and of the melting of the snows on the Rockies as the periods of activities there and in the United States of America. But we had just the same eager stir and the same field for romance in Australia when the creeks ran, the billabongs and soaks filled, and in the towns the gathered army of the teams could start. Then the whips cracked and the voice of the teamster went out into the wilderness; then 'the stores' came out back, and there were wine and biscuits for the visitor.

There were no bridge afternoons then; instead, the visitor would ask for a piece of sewing or some mending, or 'receipts' would be talked, and an orgy of cooking would be indulged in. No visitor was so discourteous as not 'to offer' to do something. An equal courtesy required the acceptance of the offer. 'She did not offer,' condemned any woman. *Her* things went on the bed once, but never again!

A woman once lived near the Narrandera Berry Jerry when Mr Leitch owned it. She was a lover of biscuits. This was regarded as an unnatural appetite, bread being natural and not biscuits. So everyone said she would have something wrong with her if she continued to eat biscuits instead of bread. It was not a proper thing, they said, to eat biscuits instead of bread. Bread was in the Bible, biscuits were not. I recollect, then being about seven, that I remarked that 'cake' was in the Bible, and that biscuits were like cake. I was sternly told that it was 'cakes' in the Bible, *not* 'cake'; that the word only referred to the form and not to the material in the thing baked, and that that was unleavened bread baked on the coals or on hot bricks like a damper in an oven. So damper was legitimate, biscuits were not, and cake did not exist in the Bible. Whether the biscuit-eater died, or 'perished at the waist', as she was expected to do, I know not. Later, my doubts of things accepted were strengthened, but my bewilderment was not lessened, by finding that another neighbour ate biscuits, and she remained plump! The funny thing about it all was that it was customary to eat biscuits with wine. My own people had cracknels with port, arrowroot biscuits with sherry, and a 'plain' biscuit with sweet Madeira and Malaga. So that's that!

Melbourne Restaurants

Marcus Clarke

After the success of his 'Peripatetic Philosopher' series in the *Australasian*, Marcus Clarke became a journalist-about-town, living life to the full – or to the extent that his purse permitted. He seems to have known and frequented virtually every hotel, restaurant and café in the city. Despite his distaste for 'foreign foods', he gives a remarkably comprehensive account of eating out in Melbourne in the late 1860s and 1870s.

Age, July 1879

Melbourne should be a very Paris for cafés. The tastes of the people and the warmth of the climate all tend towards the out-door life. It is remarkable that until very recently there has been no decent dining hall in the city. Between the destruction of the old Café de Paris was a dark age, a feudal period of heavy pastry and colonial beer. Now we seem likely to be embarrassed with riches, for, in addition to the Academy, and Clement's, Mr Gunsler has opened a gorgeous palace, which bids fair to rival the establishment of Spiers and Pond. There are cafés and cafés, clubs and clubs.

The glory, however, of Melbourne was the Café de Paris. It was built, in connection with the Theatre Royal, by Black, in 1857 or thereabouts. At first the place was cut up into bedrooms; but very soon Spiers and Pond, who made their *début* as caterers at the cellars beneath the Elcelsior Hotel in Bourke-street, took it into their hands, and, by their skilful management laid the foundations of their fortune, and, inaugurated at the other end of the world a system of intelligent provision for the wants of the hungry man which has laid the Great City itself under a boon to antipodean enterprise. For the behoof of those who remember it not, and for the pleasure of those who do, let me recall the *grille* where two enlightened cooks broiled – (not fried, oh Bridget-beridden householder!) – the selected steak. Partitions divided the sides of the room into snug boxes which were calculated to hold six persons. Down the centre of the room ran three tables set in line, at which a large party could be accommodated with convenience. The joints were under cover, on moveable stands, which deft cooks wheeled noisily to your side. An adjacent kitchen supplied the soups, entrées, and finer meats, while, from a bright and glittering bar, the proprietors themselves did not disdain to superintend the dispensation of the wines. A billiardroom was on one side, on the other a smokingroom opened into the theatre . . .

The fire of 1870, which burned the Theatre Royal, purged the old place of whatever of geniality and folly then clung to it. It is now a billiardroom, and I cannot but wish that some enterprising fellow would in his fiery turn purge it of white balls and red, and restore the good old days.

When Spiers and Pond retired, the *grille* received Mallam and King as masters. After them came Morton (of the Criterion); after him, Wright (of the London Tavern); and after him, Tipper, formerly of the theatre bars. During all these troubles Foxall, formerly of St Kilda, and now of the Globe, in Swanston-street, held managerial sway. What dinners were given in those spacious times! Sir Henry Barkly was there entertained at a farewell banquet. Barry Sullivan and Walter Montgomery were feasted there by the best literary and artistic talent the town afforded. A series of dinner to consuls, given by Mr Ploos Van Amstel in King's time, was amongst the most notable of records in the *Almanach des Gourmands d'Australie*. The wondrous feast of the Acclimatisation Society took place there. Nothing was eaten on that gorgeous evening that was not of native growth; nothing drunken but what was of Australian birth. The wines of Yering, Ivanhoe and Yarraberg were set out in sparkling order. Iguana steak, roasted wallaby, boiled bandicoot, and emu 'with the hair on', are reported to have been eaten freely by unsuspecting country cousins. I know that there was a dish of sharks' fins, for I partook of it. Rumour suggested gum-tree grubs and flying fox *à la maitre d'hôtel*, but I know not if rumour was correct in such suggestion.

In the wake of the big Spiers-and-Pond argosy many smaller barks followed. There was Nissen's Café, a pleasant place for confectionery, coffee, fruit, dominoes or tobacco. This house was open on Sundays, and as the larger establishment closed its doors on that day, was frequented by many outcasts who, like myself, cared not for 'piano, baths and gas, with all the comforts of a home'. But the real business of Nissen's was done in the daytime. Lunch – an elegant equivalent for dinner with many honest fellows – supplied the sinews of war to most *restaurateurs* who were compelled to keep open until unprofitable hours. The City Buffet and Cleal's Hotel were exceptions to this rule. Each of these places did a roaring trade both night and morning. From ten am until eight pm each place was the haunt of respectable folk – clerks, shopmen, shopwomen and the wives of comfortable tradesmen. But when night fell another class of customers appeared. There is no law, I believe, which insists that champagne and devilled kidneys are not to be served to ladies and gentlemen who fail to produce certificates of moral health.

The Count de la Chapelle – I see that since his return from exile he has written a work on his intimate association with the late Emperor Napoleon the Third – endeavoured to give Melbourne a *Café des Variétés*. He commenced at the Polytechnic Hall, where the adventurous L.L. Smith used to lecture on the Venus – of Milo and others, and ended by an elaborate music hall on the site of the present Opera House. The Varieties, while it lasted, was a great institution. It reminded me of the London Alhambra viewed in the small end of an opera-glass. There were ballets, and boxes 'wired in', where fair occupants awaited the visits of admiring friends prodigal of champagne and chicken bones grilled. The *cancan* was danced there, until poor G.P. Smith, then Attorney-General, discovered that it was exciting, and forbade it. The officers of the Galatea, then in harbour, did not disdain to 'look in', and there was brewed a bowl of Edinburgh punch, round which historic memories linger.

The Varieties could scarcely be called a restaurant proper, though its supper room attracted many people. Hosie and Duncan did the legitimate trade in luncheons and dinners for the people. Their successful efforts have been largely imitated. Every pastry cook attempted restaurant keeping. Some failed, some paid their way, some profited. Among the last is Mr Gunsler, whose café in Collins-street is elegantly furnished, and most expensively decorated. During the day time the Café Gunsler is crammed with people. There are luxurious rooms for ladies, and an excellent bill of fare. The outlay must have been great, and I hope that the speculation will be successful. A man who adds to our small fund of social enjoyments deserves to be supported; and bearing in mind that Collins-street is for all business purposes empty after dusk, it behoves all friends of the Café Gunsler to support it during the working day. Clement's Café in Swanston-street is another excellent house of entertainment, and suited to all purses. The dinner served *à la carte* in the room behind the bar is as good as can be obtained anywhere. Upstairs is a private room for ladies, and a general diningroom, where glass, napkins and little luxuries, appreciated by the fastidious, are cheaply obtained at a little extra charge.

Of chop-houses I know nothing. They do not exist. There is only one place in Melbourne where I ever had a chop properly served for the last six years, and that place is a cellar underneath the Hall of Commerce. When I knew it first it was a billiardroom; then M. Ludovic Marie took it and made it a wine hall. Lots of fine fellows patronised M. Marie, but they were men of ideas so lofty that they disdained sordid notions of finance, and M. Marie had to throw up his venture. An enterprising lad took the unpromising cellar, and so in a short time the verandah were there *en masse*. Why not, indeed? A well-grilled steak, a cool tankard of porter and a smile which begins in the merry black eyes before it reaches the pleasant but very business-like mouth for one shilling. No wonder that Mrs Burton has been able to buy that station in Queensland (all good Victorians go to Queensland when they die) and I only hope that she will not get into the hands of the banks, but, like Dan Chaucer's Wife of Bath, be long both merry and wise.

Of the few houses which offer 'dinner' to the stranger, I choose, for my own taste, the Academy of Music. The café at the Academy of Music cost £7000 to fit up after it was built. The kitchen is on the top of the house, the dishes being sent down by a 'lift'. There is a billiard-room in connection with the café, from which, as in the old Spiers and Pond style, ingress is had to the theatre. The profit of such an under-taking is probably to be found in shrewd attention to minor details. For instance, two farms, owned by the proprietor, supply the vegetables and fruit – even the flowers for decorating the tables. Return carts take back the broken meats, waste milk, &c., to piggeries established at these places, so that while no broken victual is wasted, wholesome dairy-fed pork can be always obtained. The advantage at the Academy Café, to my thinking at least, is the employment of waiters. I detest my dinner service to be rendered by women at any time; and as the girls who wait at the various cafés are generally recruited from a class superior to that in which one obtains domestic servants, the middle-aged visitor can never indulge in the luxury of expressing discontent should the soup be cold, and the sherry warm, while the younger ones are sometimes tempted to neglect, for the pleasure of talking to a pretty woman, the more serious business of alimentation. At the

Academy is a snug well-carpeted room in which your wife or your sister can get her luncheon in peace should she feel inclined to dismiss her carriage, or should you have failed to supply her with the superfluous silver needful for the hire of a cab. In another room the bachelor can obtain an excellent dinner from the carte – say, clear soup, 1s; fried flounder, 1s 6d; slice of haunch of mutton, 1s; sweet omelette, 1s; stilton cheese, 6d; glass of punch *à la romaine*, 6d; glass of sherry, 6d; small bottle of champagne, 6s; coffee and *chasse*, 1s; total, 13s 6d; or if you are prudent, roast sirloin of beef, 1s; rice pudding, 6d; total 1s 6d.

But there are other houses which, if not so elegant in appearance, are perhaps more interesting to visit – the restaurants which rely upon the less wealthy classes for patronage. Let us examine into some of these.

Bourke-street is the legitimate home of the cheap restaurants of Melbourne. Always awake, Bourke-street is the only highway in the city which fairly never goes to bed. There is a succession of eaters and drinkers from daylight till dark, and from dark till daylight. Humanity, whether it breakfasts at the cheap houses near Kirk's Bazaar, lunches at the Albion, takes caviar and white wine at Buschmann's, sleeps in one of Parer's hundred bedrooms, or sups at a coffee stall and dozes in a friendly doorway, must in some sort and shape be fed.

The small houses by Kirk's Bazaar are by no means ill-kept. The food is good, though roughly served, and sixpence is surely a price small enough for a steak and onions, or a bowl of Irish stew sufficient for Gargantua. The company is not select, certainly; but hunger makes men acquainted with strange table companions, and a craving stomach has no conscience. At the Criterion in Bourke-street sixpence secures a plate of soup, the choice of roast joint, cabbage, potatoes, and pudding. There are houses indeed in which tea or coffee is added for the money. The meat and vegetables, it must be said, are perfectly wholesome and well-cooked. Coming to the corner by Dunn and Collins's, the book-sellers, how large a part do the illustrations of the shop-windows play in the education of a people. I turn for a moment to contemplate the hoarding which once was Williams's Hotel and Dining Rooms . . .

The Albion Hotel keeps a capital table, and is well patronised by coach passengers. On the night of the Cup I have seen nearly 200 people at dinner in the long room, which looks like the cuddy of a passenger ship. The first time I heard of the Albion Hotel was when I was on board a steamer on Loch Katrine. A small boy selling papers to the tourists offered me a copy of the *Cornhill Magazine*, then some eight issues old, and I read Henry Kingsley's account of the coach drive to Ballarat. I recognised the big window at once when I – a helpless new arrival – was enquiring my way to the Post Office. If I were suddenly enriched, I think I should gratify a secret ambition I have long cherished, and break that window somewhere about the middle. I don't do it just now because John Cleeland, though an uncommon generous fellow, and as 'straight' a man on the turf as there is anywhere, might not feel inclined to regard the business as the joke I should think it is. The Parrot lives at the Albion now, and if you have not seen him you had better do so at once. Spooner, of the Port Phillip, owned him when I first knew him, but Captain Cook saw him when he landed, and there is mention made of him by Lieutenant Tuckey. The Parrot is a very old bird, and he swears audibly in five languages. He also whistles the music of Pinafore, and sings Pop Goes the Weasel. He sews, dances, stands on his head, tells fortunes, and is darkly supposed (by the opponents of Sir John O'Shanassy's bill) to be a Jesuit in disguise. I am informed that he intends to contest the West Bourke election; if so, let Mr Deakin look out.

The best of the cheap eating houses is undoubtedly the Spanish Restaurant, or the Duke de la Victoria, opposite the Academy of Music. This house may be said to be an Academy Café on a cheaper scale. There are thirty-two persons employed in the house, and nine cooks are constantly at work in the kitchen, while over 100 beds are made up nightly. The story of the owners is a remarkable one. In the year 1858 five Spaniards, brothers, named Parer, started an eating house a few doors above the present hotel. By the year 1861 they had made sufficient money to take larger premises, and now rent, in Bourke-street, three houses which they have turned into a large hotel. In the dining room are nineteen tables, and an average of 600 people dine there daily. On the Cup day and other great holidays 2000 people have been served. Five hundred pounds of fish, 600 dozen eggs, and 3000 lb of meat are consumed weekly. The weekly expense for wages, rent and gas is £95, and the restaurant was fitted at a cost of £5000. There is a fine billiardroom, and the snuggest 'boxes' for supper I have seen out of London. The bill of fare is most liberal. A breakfast (the choice of ham and eggs, steak, cutlet or sausages, together with tea or coffee) for a shilling; the average charge for 'plates' at the dinner is 3d. A visitor can thus order the following menu:– Pea soup, 3d; roast beef, 6d; plum pudding or fruit pie, 3d; cheese, 3d; English ale, 3d; total, 1s 6d. For hot supper a shilling is the uniform charge, and a clean and comfortable bedroom can be had for a shilling. There is a system adopted by the proprietors of issuing tickets for shilling meals at ten shillings a dozen; and this notion is largely favoured by the economical. The clerk told me that he always has 100 tickets out. Bed and board can be had for 20s a week, all boarders being allowed three meals a day. There are larger bedrooms to be had for 2s a night, and I find on inquiry that a stranger, say a man from Sydney come to see our exhibition, could have a large front bedroom looking on to Bourke-street, and three meals a day, from the bill of fare, for 30s a week. As with the Academy Café, a farm owned by the proprietors supplies the bulk of the fruit and vegetables. There are 3000 fruit trees on this farm, and the enterprise of the brother who superintends it may be guessed from the fact that sixty dozen bottles of tomato and other sauce which he showed me in his still-room were, he assured me, the produce of his garden, which gives 400 dozen quart bottles of such material every year. A feature in this house is its Spanish wine, exported by members of the family in Spain to the brothers in Melbourne. The red wine is better than any colonial wine I have tasted; and the white better than many high-priced sherries. It is said that the Parer Brothers (who have married five sisters) have made their fortunes. If intelligence and industry merit success, the fortunes are well deserved, and I hope the ten of them and 'their families may live long and prosper'.

I have no experience of the *Pension Suisse*, or Mr Hartog's boarding-house, or of several other places which claim attention from the foreigner. There is an atmosphere of garlic and strong cheese in these places that terrifies me. I have eaten my food on foot under a hedge, on horseback in the saddle, and on the broad of my back in a boat, but I have never yet been courageous enough to tackle the genuine 'foreigner', as he is to be met with in his most caeparian and caseous moments. My good friend Antonio, whom I remember somewhere between the Houses of Parliament and Sandridge pier selling coffee and hot buttered rolls since the days of the Barmecides, has become a hotelkeeper, and I trust will prosper. But Antonio's cookery, though primitive, was not greasy, and I have heard *bon vivants* praise his coffee. For sixpence one can eat at a coffee stall the weight of a cup-winner's jockey. Hot baked potatoes, hot muffins, hot saveloys, hot rolls and butter! Hot coffee – boiling hot coffee! hot pies – scalding hot pies! tempt with their savour and perfume the home-returning journalist, or the weary outward bound wayfarer. On a heavy 'night' I have seen more than half the respectability, and certainly more than half the talent, of the Melbourne Fourth Estate eating supper at a coffee-stall with the air of young boars roaring for their prey. On an early Saturday morning I have watched the market gardeners regaling their honest stomachs – *dura messorum dia* – with comforting coffee and luxurious toast, and blessed Mr Fitzgibbon and the Corporation for the boon which the Antonio and his brethren confer upon the public.

But there is one foreign house which gives me always hospitable shelter. Marie was good enough for dinner in the early days of the empire, but Buschmann is still provident of sausage. I confess that a very little of the Buschmannian *bratwurst* goes a very long English mile with me. I cannot acclimatise my unhappy English-born bowels to the sufferance of rotten cabbage and pigs'-flesh minced with garlic, and salad made of herrings, chopped in vinegar. Yet I see Germans – aye, and Englishmen, too, for that matter – eat things with relish at Buschmann's, the very thought of which sets my gorge rising. There is caviar in a wood-tub – Lord Bacon never did more than taste it, I am open to assert, though he did insinuate that it was a luxury in his ridiculous play of Hamlet – and there is cheese hermetically sealed in tins like those which hold the powder for the Corporation's cannon. Epicures come and eat these horrors, discoursing glibly the while and drinking red wine by bottlefuls. What glorious stomachs the German race must have! Even Goethe, the magnificent, selfish, immortal old rascal, sent sausages to Frau von Stein, and enjoyed – God of Love and God of Reason, say! – enjoyed his *Limburg* cheese. I meet pleasant artist brain and honest German heart at Buschmann's, and go there accordingly, but when I have eaten a *fricatelle*, some potato salad, some beetroot and *schwarzbrod*, or some grated ham with wine, I am *hors de combat*. But the others – ye powers that smile on virtuous love! – hot ham, cold veal, horseradish, caviar, herring salad, smoked fish, Swiss cheese, *sauerkraut*, bread in basketfuls and butter in knife loads. I have pleaded my liver as an excuse fifty times for not entering the house, but one always wants French mustard, or pressed horse-radish, or pickled anchovies, or chiles, or real olives, or something which Buschmann only supplies, so I go again and again, and am again undone. If the monster had but Bavarian beer my ruin would be complete, but thank heaven he only holds a wine licence. Let me interject here that the man who introduces successfully lager beer into Melbourne will make his fortune.

But, I have to dine at a Chinese cook-shop tonight, and must hurry to my appointment.

Chinatown

Marcus Clarke

By the 1860s Melbourne had a sizeable Chinese community, most of whom had come from southern China in search of gold. As Marcus Clarke's account makes clear, they were disparaged and misrepresented, victims of nineteenth-century xenophobia. The eating house described here was said to be in the 'aristocratic' part of the city, where the houses were 'palaces compared with the loathsome dens' where the poor Chinese lived.

Argus, 8 March 1868

The next place we visited was a chemist's shop. The odour in this place was intolerable. The proprietor and two friends, however, were drinking tea in the back parlour, and seemed rather to enjoy the perfume. The shop was filled with packets of drugs carefully labelled with Chinese characters, and various drawers contained the 'made-up' medicines. A 'jess' stood in the corner with lights burning before it, and a miserable creature, the very model of the 'poor apothecary', stood behind the counter compounding a cough mixture from a prescription a yard long before him. He kindly offered us a portion of the mess to taste, but we declined. It looked not unlike liquid liquorice, and we were informed that the chief ingredients were orange peel, gentian, and laudanum. It was to be taken as a hot decoction and doubtless would not be very unpalatable. On the other side of the road was an eating-house, and the horrible stenches that rolled out of it gave no great promise of good entertainment. Our guide, however, seemed to enjoy the odour, and endeavouring to forget the existence of such things as noses, we followed him in.

The chief curiosities of the place were the loaves, baked with sugar, and made into various shapes. Little tables were ranged along the walls, and the bill of fare in Chinese lay on each. Sucking-pig, roasted whole, was on the *carte*, and a curious mess, called by a name that sounded like 'foo-a-chow', and was compounded of sheep's trotters, sugar, cabbage, flour, and fish, smoked on the copper. The kitchen was appalling. Several boilers were simmering with all kinds of nastiness, and three or four cooks were stirring up the *potage* with iron rods. The usual price charged was about 1s 6d, but an excellent dinner (!) could be got for 3s. We drank a teacupful of 'samshoo', a kind of *vin ordinaire*, with the sleek proprietor, and were thankful to depart. It is only just, however, to state that in the higher class of eating-house, the cookery is cleanly, and the meals well served and cheap.

Mechanics' Hotel and Restaurant, Melbourne

Advertisement, 1882

Soups of all kinds – Scotch Broth and rich brown gravy,
Ox tail and pea soup à la navy,
Roast beef – n'er by Englishmen is scorned,
Also the same joint beautifully corned,
Mutton and lamb, steak puddings, haricot,
Ox heart and Irish stew, a goodly show,
Plum pudding, maccaroni, jam and rice,
Fruit pie – in fact all pastry, pure and nice.
[NB – Bread and vegetables, pickles and sauces are all included in the various courses. – 6d.]

Successful Dinners

Anonymous

Australian Etiquette, or the Rules and Usages of the Best Society in the Australasian Colonies (1885) sets forth the ritualistic formality of a nineteenth-century dinner – presumably for the benefit of those who were

not to the manor born. Additionally, it serves to demonstrate the widespread acceptance of service à la russe, gradually introduced in the first half of the nineteenth century but, as late even as the 1860s, still misconstrued in England.

Australian Etiquette, 1885

The success of a dinner

A host and hostess generally judge of the success of a dinner by the manner in which conversation has been sustained. If it has flagged often, it is considered proof that the guests have not been congenial; but if a steady stream of talk has been kept up, it shows that they have smoothly amalgamated, as a whole. No one should monopolise conversation, unless he wishes to win for himself the appellation of a bore, and be avoided as such.

Dinner a la Russe

The latest and most satisfactory plan for serving dinners is the dinner a la Russe (Russian style) – all the food being placed upon a side table, and servants do the carving and waiting. The style gives an opportunity for more profuse ornamentation of the table, which, as the meal progresses, does not become encumbered with partially empty dishes and platters.

General rules regarding dinner

When the plate of each course is set before you, with the knife and fork upon it, remove the knife and fork at once. This matter should be carefully attended to, as the serving of an entire course is delayed by neglecting to remove them.

Greediness should not be indulged in. Indecision must be avoided. Do not take up one piece and lay it down in favour of another, or hesitate.

Never allow the servant, or the one who pours, to fill your glass with wine which you do not wish to drink. You can check him by touching the rim of your glass.

If you have occasion to speak to a servant, wait until you can catch his eye, and then ask in a low tone for what you want.

The mouth should always be kept closed in eating, and both eating and drinking should be noiseless.

Bread is broken at dinner. Vegetables are eaten with a fork.

Asparagus may be taken up with the fingers, if preferred. Olives and artichokes are so eaten.

Fruit is eaten with silver knives and forks.

You are at liberty to refuse a dish that you do not wish to eat. If any course is set down before you that you do not wish, do not touch it. Never play with food, nor mince your bread, nor handle the glass and silver near you unnecessarily.

Never reprove a waiter for negligence or improper conduct; that is the business of the host.

When a dish is offered you, accept or refuse at once, and allow the waiter to pass on. A gentleman will see that the lady whom he has escorted to the table is helped to all she wishes, but it is officiousness to offer to help other ladies who have escorts.

If the guests pass the dishes to one another, instead of being helped by a servant, you should always help yourself from the dish, if you desire it at all, before passing it on to the next.

A knife should never, on any account, be put into the mouth. Many people, even well-bred in other respects, seem to regard this as an unnecessary regulation; but when we consider that it is a rule of etiquette, and that its violation causes surprise and disgust to many people, it is wisest to observe it.

Be careful to remove the bones from fish before eating. If a bone inadvertantly should get into the mouth, the lips must be covered with the napkin in removing it. Cherry stones and grape skins should be removed from the mouth as unobtrusively as possible, and deposited on the side of the plate.

Never use a napkin in place of a handkerchief for wiping the forehead, face or nose.

Pastry should be eaten with a fork. Everything that can be cut without a knife should be eaten with the fork alone. Pudding may be eaten with a fork or spoon.

Never lay your hand, or play with your fingers, upon the table. Do not toy with your knife, fork, or spoon, make crumbs of your bread, or draw imaginary lines upon the tablecloth.

Never bite fruit. An apple, peach or pear should be peeled with a knife, and all fruit should be broken or cut.

Praising dishes

A hostess should not express pride regarding what is on her table, nor make apologies if everything she offers you is not to her satisfaction. It is much better that she should observe silence in this respect, and allow her guest to eulogise her dinner or not, as they deem proper. Neither is it good taste to urge guests to eat, nor to load their plates against their inclination.

Erkmann's Grillrooms and Ladies' Café, Melbourne

Advertisement, *Table Talk*, 25 June 1886

(next door to Theatre Royal.)
Come and see the novelty yourself. Pick out your
own Chop or Steak.
The Brass Grill is going from 8 am until 11.30 pm
Best pastry, lollies and cigars. Prompt and
civil attention a specialty.
Well appointed Ladies Lavatory.
Another Novelty – You only pay for what you consume.

Leon Erkmann, Proprietor

Through French Eyes

Oscar Comettant

Oscar Comettant (1819–1898) visited Australia in 1888 as one of the French judges at the Centennial International Exhibition in Melbourne. The event, which featured exhibits from each of the Australian colonies plus Great Britain, Germany, France, Belgium, Austria and the United States, was designed to commemorate the founding of the first Australian colony in 1788. On his return to Paris, Comettant published his observations on life in Australia, and on Melbourne in particular, as *Au Pays des Kangourous et des Mines d'Or*, later translated as *In the Land of Kangaroos and Goldmines* (1980). While he had little to say about the exhibition, he concluded that 'it did great honour to Melbourne, city of action, initiative and progress, the city of the future par excellence.'

In the Land of Kangaroos and Gold Mines, 1890

If the reader is curious to know the exact prices of the material necessities of life in Melbourne, I can give him exact information. The English-style bread (that is bread that is nearly all crumb – French-type bread is also made) costs 20 to 25 *centimes* a pound. Beef averages about 60 to 80 *centimes* per pound, mutton 40 to 80, and pork 90 *centimes* to one franc per pound. The price of butter varies according to the season; at a minimum, it is one franc per pound. Much imported butter is old, often mixed with margarine. The cheese made in Australia is only mediocre, and costs from 90 centimes to one franc per pound. Roquefort cheese is imported in little boxes, but it does not keep well, and turns into hair-pomade. Gruyère, Chester, and Dutch cheeses are those most commonly seen at table. Eggs are never cheap in Melbourne, being one franc 50 a dozen, or more. Poultry is not cheap either. It is about the same price as in Paris. Potatoes are eaten with everything, as in England, and are not dear. Rice is 40 *centimes* a pound, soap from 60 to 70.

Now that we know what is eaten in Melbourne, and how much it costs, let us see how it is eaten. Let us go from the markets to the restaurants.

There are two or three good restaurants in Melbourne; the rest are, to French palates, more or less bad. No more than in England do they know how to make stock in Australia. What they call soup is a kind of very thick, highly seasoned sauce, bearing no relationship to what we in France eat under the names of *potage*. The appetising hors-d'oeuvre served after the soup are significant by their absence at restaurant tables. There is no logical order about the serving of courses, which are in any case lacking in variety, and in the true art of cooking. With this *cuisine* the appetite dies quickly. Here I am talking of restaurants in general; I have eaten some good grilled meat and roasts, some quite passable stews, and some good fish at the *Maison Dorée*, the *Crystal Café* and in a little French restaurant called *La Mascotte*. In the big hotels the cuisine is of course better than in most of the restaurants. But, heavens above! What dreadful food you get in the cheap boarding-houses and temperance hotels and restaurants! How can one describe the fixed-price meals at sixpence or a shilling! Although it is also true that in Paris, for the same price, you get literally poisonous food.

The shilling meals consist of one of those soups that are neither soup nor sauce, a plate of tasteless meat accompanied by some even more tasteless vegetables boiled in saltless water, and a pudding that you swallow while reminding yourself that you must eat to live, not live to eat. That lot is washed down with plain water, more or less clear, or cooked water, more or less brown, called tea.

Brillat-Savarin has said that animals gorge, humans feed, and only the man of discernment eats. At this rate there must be many men of discernment in Melbourne and Sydney, for if one only feeds in so many Australian restaurants, it is hardly possible to eat better than one does in the private houses of these great and beautiful cities.

In the luncheon rooms one may eat a modest, but pleasant and well-served meal for two or three shillings. Nevertheless, you do not have to have too many extras to spend ten or more francs if you are not a tee-totaller (that is, a water-drinker) and require a little reasonable wine.

Spongers – who are everywhere, mainly through their own fault – can get a free lunch in certain bar-rooms in Australia. On a table are laid out for all comers slices of beef, sausages, bread, cheese, and biscuits: you pay 30 *centimes* for your glass of beer, and eat for nothing. I believe you can even eat without drinking in these hospitable bars, which is cheap living in the extreme. You find the same benefits in many bar-rooms in New York, where, as in Australia, second-grade meat is very cheap.

Bohemian Eating

Marcus Clarke

'Bohemian Eating' was one of a series of columns in the *Australasian* depicting the dismal underside of life in prosperous Melbourne – the cheap cafés with their solitary diners, late-night bars and dishonourable drunkenness, tawdry streetwalkers and pawn shops.

The true and absolute Bohemian detests fixtures of all kinds, and prefers to take his meals standing, or walking, or lying, or in any posture but sitting. For this purpose the various street stalls sprung into existence. It was found that not only did honest toil going to its work at dawn require a cup of coffee to cheer its honest heart, but that vagabondism and theft, sneaking to their unholy errands, were prepared to pay for a gentle stimulant also. Upon this arose coffee-stalls, apple-stalls, pie-stalls, and trotter-baskets, and peripatetic Bohemia was fed.

The coffee-stall is a disjointed sort of affair, made so that it can be shut up easily. It consists of a barrow upon which is placed a large board, sometimes covered with oil cloth, and protected with an awning. On this board are set forth the luxuries of the stall. *Imprimis*; a huge can of polished tin, with brass nozzle and spout. This tin holds about four or five gallons of coffee, which is kept hot by means of a pan of charcoal placed underneath it. By the side of the tin are ranged cups – very thick and heavy, sandwiches, greasy cakes, and a sort of plum-duff of very satisfying character. The coffee is sold at 1d a cup, and is really very good at the price; the sandwiches are 1d or 2d each, and the cake according to quality. Here is the receipt for it – 1/4 lb currants, 1/2 lb sugar, 7 oz dripping, and a quartern of flour. The coffee is made dark and strong by means of burnt sugar, and is chicoried to a very large extent. Ten oz of coffee make five gallons of coffee-liquid. The average profit on a stall is about 150 per cent – perhaps more. The cost of starting in the business is about £6, according to the 'taste and fancy of the starter'.

The apple-stalls cannot be properly called Bohemian, and the tarts and confectionery are usually the same as those sold in the pie-shops. There are some home-made tarts which are stronger in flavour, owing to the use of rancid butter. The pies are eatable, but peppery. Pepper takes off the 'flavour of the meat'. They are made in batches, and are composed of the 'pieces' of meat from the butchers', baked, and washed over with a seasoning of salt and water and egg. When the pie is baked the pieman pokes his finger through the top crust, and pours in the 'gravy', made of salt and water, by means of a can with a long spout. The meat is always mutton or beef. 'Mutton's cheaper than cat!' said a man to me one day with his mouth full, 'go ahead, it's all right!'

Baked potatoes are pleasant and healthy. Those with a rough skin are selected by Bohemian epicures, because they are the mealiest. Three baked potatoes will be quite enough for any reasonably hungry person. But the trade is not a good one here, except in the winter time. Who could eat hot-baked potatoes with a hot wind blowing! Another miserable sort of trade is that of trotter-selling. Our Bohemian, roaming up Bourke-street, may notice an old man at the corner of Bourke and Stephen streets, and an old woman at the corner of Bourke and Swanston streets. These are the only trotter-sellers that I know of; and I will forbear to particularise – only, should this meet the eye of the old man, he will remember who descended with him into a certain cellar, and may remember also that it is not always expedient to entertain strangers with curious particulars of family history. Trotters are not bad eating at 2d – that is, when they are not too high. Publicans like the trotter trade, and encourage the trotter-sellers. The trotters are salt, and make drinking Bohemia thirsty.

The Cheapest Meal in the World

John Stanley James

Vagabond by name (self chosen) and vagabond by nature, John Stanley James (1843–1896) – or Julian Thomas, as he called himself in Australia – arrived in Sydney in 1875 after two difficult and unrewarding years in America. He began writing 'Notes on Current Events, by a Vagabond' for the Melbourne *Punch* but his real renown came with a series of articles for the *Argus* which depicted, in a straightforward but sympathetic way, the life of the poor and disadvantaged in Melbourne.

The Vagabond Papers, 1877–1878

Most men have to suffer a perpetual combat between their tastes and their exchequer. This is daily brought home to them in the satisfaction of their appetites. Where one has a soul for turtle and ortolans, it is hard to descend to sausages. To feel that a palate educated to appreciate *caviare* should be condemned to boiled ling in a sixpenny restaurant – what an indignity! There you feed like the beasts of the field: it is a mere question of supporting nature. In another sphere one dines, which is a fine art not thoroughly understood by the common herd, and the grossness of feeding is relieved by the poetry of companionship and association . . .

Happily, I have been accustomed to rough it in many parts of the world. I glory in a good dinner, but can eat bread and cheese with an appetite; and so one morning I felt no very great repugnance at the fact of having to make a meagre breakfast, which was forced upon me by the unsatisfactory state of my finances. The day before, I had migrated from a certain hotel where I paid ten shillings a day (very cheap, too, according to London scale) to a small apartment in the suburbs, for which I paid five shillings a week. (In London it would be double.) I had sallied down town with the intention of making a cheap breakfast, and had a shilling in my pocket devoted to that purpose. Although I had been some months in Melbourne, and was aware that the necessities of life were very cheap here, I really had no thought that a breakfast could be got for sixpence. The idea seemed ridiculous, as sixpence appeared to me, up to that time, to be the lowest coin in circulation. I avoided the main thoroughfares, and at last entered a small restaurant in one of the bye streets. 'Breakfast, sir,' said the Irish waitress, 'chops, steaks, sausages, fried fish, dry hash' – 'Stop,' I cried, aghast at this list of luxuries, 'I will have a cup of tea and some bread and butter.' 'What else, sir? there's nice steak this morning.' 'How much is a steak?' I asked, bent on economy. 'Sixpence, sir.' 'And the tea, and bread and butter?' 'All sixpence.' 'Bring me a steak, then,' I said; concluding that I had fully mortgaged my shilling. I was then supplied with a small steak, a roll, and cup of tea, which breakfast I humbly ate with a good appetite. When I had finished I rose, and putting my hand in my pocket, 'How much?' I asked, grandly, and preparing to fling down my shilling as if I had hundreds at the back of it. 'Sixpence for breakfast, thank you, sir,' and I left amazed at the fact of having discovered the cheapest meal in the world. The dinner was even a greater surprise to me. That I could obtain soup, meat, and pastry (no matter of what quality) for the ridiculously small sum of sixpence was a revelation of inestimable value.

After the first day I gathered courage, and have since made a tour through most of the cheap restaurants. In essentials they are all much alike. The dishes appear to be stereotyped, and the cooking is much the same in all. There are generally, and especially in the summer, more flies in the dishes than refined prejudices might fancy. The sausages in all are bags of mystery, and the enormous consumption of these is a convincing proof that faith is strong in the colonies. The stews, which are mostly served at supper time, are not equal to the *pot au feu* of the French peasant, although the ingredients are as miscellaneous. Stewed lamb is a dish often on the supper bill of fare. I wondered for a long time how this was, as lamb is seldom to be had for dinner, till at last I discovered that the multiplicity of dishes consisted chiefly in the names. 'Stewed lamb', with a little curry stirred on the plate, became 'curried mutton'; or, with the addition of a few slices of carrot, was 'haricot mutton' or, again, with a few boiled potatoes mashed in, was 'Irish stew'. Thus, a smart cook will supply a dozen dishes from one base. Rabbit pie and fish are considered extra luxuries, and are generally announced by placards in the windows. What strikes an Englishman as very strange is the fact of eggs being so dear here. These, boiled or poached, are charged 9d. Fowl or chicken is absent from the *menu* of the ordinary sixpenny restaurant; but at some they are to be had for one shilling. It seems to me that one of the best speculations untouched would be a large poultry farm in the neighbourhood of Melbourne.

Sixpenny restaurants vary a good deal in style. There are some in the principal thoroughfares which shine with plate-glass, white linen, and pretty waiter girls. But all this extra display, and the cost of the handbills, which are so freely circulated, causes perceptible diminution in the quantity or quality of the viands. The places where one really feeds best are the smaller restaurants, kept by married couples, who do the cooking themselves. At many of these places the proprietors often work very hard, and are not by any means making rapid fortunes. These are chiefly patronised by working men, who take their dinners there. At one o'clock you will see a tremendous rush, every seat at the little tables being occupied. If one has catholic ideas on the subject of dirty hands, it is amusing to sit down with the crowd and watch the different modes of eating. The waiters are for some twenty minutes under a pressure of orders enough to tire out the intellect of most men. The *habitués* seem to strive to get done first, and he who sits nearest the door may order his 'corned beef and cabbage' a dozen times, on each occasion it being captured *en route* as 'my order'. The great appetites of apprentice boys are something fearful to behold, the soup, steak-pudding, and piles of cabbage and potatoes being assimilated by the consumption of half a loaf of bread. After watching the performance of half a dozen of these embryo 'sons of toil', you feel certain that the proprietor of the restaurant must be bankrupt on the morrow.

A few quiet individuals generally dine after the one o'clock rush is over, and the same number may be seen at supper at seven o'clock, when they will have a chat together. At the restaurant I frequented there was a strange mixture. A negro gentleman from Jamaica, a noted politician in the Yankee sense of the word, who should have emigrated to the Southern States and got into office, instead of wasting his time here, where he is not believed in. A Frenchman, from the Mauritius. Several sons of the sod of various degrees of station and intellect, but mostly banded together under Holy Church in hatred of the Sassenach. A Birmingham mechanic, the best dressed man of the lot, bright, shrewd, and a liberal and freetrader of the John Bright pattern. A stray Chinaman, who is the only epicure, as he grumbles always at the quality of his 'loast beef' or 'cheak and lonions'. A hawker, Hibernian, who orates on every subject. A young man of considerable self-assurance, who was an officer in the Southern army during the American war, and is fond of 'blowing thereon'. A blind beggar, often drunk, who sits near the door. A strange mixture this, truly, but really more interesting than the guests at many a first-class *table d'hôte*.

The blind beggar is a character, not over cleanly certainly, but the presence of this Lazarus at the gate does not affect our appetites. The room is a long one, and he is afar off. Barring his real or simulated blindness, he reminds me of the beggar in *Tom Burke of Ours*. He seems the sort of man to sing a seditious song and humbug a jury. On one occasion he distinguished himself greatly amongst his compatriots by offering to raise a subscription to buy Signor Ricciotti Garibaldi a rope to send to his father.

Now and then a poor vagrant creeps quietly in, and, taking the lowest seat, enjoys a good meal. All through the day miserable-looking dogs, who, according to the Pythagorean doctrine, are transformed vagrants, steal in, and, gliding underneath the tables, pick up scraps and bones. The kind-hearted proprietor often feeds them, and if the dogs fare as well at every restaurant in Melbourne, it is no wonder we see so many ownerless curs.

Restaurant waiters are not a class. They are refugees from all classes. One or two establishments employ young girls, who certainly are efficient in enticing you to order beer, when a bar-room is an adjunct of the place; but men waiters are the rule. They are of all trades and professions – new chums and old hands. Now and then you meet with a smart youth who knows his business. Generally he has graduated at some good hotel, and drink or misfortune has condemned him to this. The cooks at these places, too, are mostly men who have begun with making damper. I know one man, however, thoroughly educated, who has passed years of his life in Parisian society, and is heir to £15,000 a-year, who is now a cook in a restaurant.

Some taverns set up as rivals to the restaurants, by giving 'hot lunches, with pint of ale from twelve to two daily, for sixpence'. The lunch is chiefly a plate of corned beef and potatoes, and instead of a pint of small beer you can compromise for a glass of the best. You get, altogether, about half the amount of food you would at a sixpenny dinner. Still these lunches are very cheap, and are much affected by young clerks, who may be hard up or economical, and who often steal in the back way to these places. Others, too proud, will spend sixpence in beer at an hotel bar, nibbling as much of the 'free lunch' as their shame will allow them. It would be far better for them if they would put their dignity on one side, and take a dinner in a sixpenny restaurant, which, up to this time, I consider to be the most wonderful example of Victorian progress and prosperity which I have met with.

Beef and Bacilli

Anonymous

Despite their penny-pinching personalities, sixpenny restaurants served well the basic needs of the less affluent. By the beginning of the twentieth century, however, ideas on hygiene and sanitation were infiltrating public consciousness; during the 1900s the various states passed Pure Foods Acts. Sixpenny restaurants seem to have been a popular target of those who regarded cleanliness as next to godliness, the testimony of staff with firsthand knowledge adding substance to their suspicions. This piece comes from *Faulding's Medical Journal* published in Adelaide in 1902.

Without doubt the cheap dining-rooms, as the big cities of Australia know them, are a boon to a very large class, but is the control of them sufficiently stringent?

The sixpenny meal is a recognised factor of city life, while the more humble fourpence will even secure a substantial plate of beef, bread and potatoes in some places. It is, perhaps, as well for the diners that in the majority of cases they are not aware of the condition of the food before it is cooked, or the manner and surroundings of the cooking. And yet this is a very important matter, and one in which we are surprised our municipal authorities do not show more interest and interference.

During the cleansing operations in Sydney last year, due to the presence of the plague, the municipal staff had occasion to visit the kitchens of two or three cheap restaurants. The pictures drawn even in the matter-of-fact, unvarnished language of officialism, was enough to turn any stomach. Rats, flies, filth, darkness, and absence of drainage were the leading features of these kitchens, yet will it be believed that nothing has been done to prevent a recurrence of such terrible foundations for the spread of disease? True the places were cleaned up, but that was all, and no doubt they have become as bad as ever underground (for that is where these kitchens were), while the hungry public upstairs goes on unheedingly devouring its beef and bacilli.

It seems to be of no use whatever asking people to protect themselves. They must be protected. Restaurants should be subjected to rigorous inspections so that cleanliness could be insisted upon. Cheap eating houses there are – and in Adelaide we could name one or two – which are admirable, but there are others of which the least said the better. Food prepared amidst insanitary surroundings is a potent factor for evil. Yet hundreds of people never consider the matter until gastric troubles assail them. It may be the result of the food, and it may be the effect of the unhealthy atmosphere of the kitchen or the utensils used. For instance, what are more dangerous than dirty copper cooking pans, and yet if the cook and the proprietor are careless, as they are too apt to be, who is to protect the eater? A system of official control giving security should be established. To some extent our air supply and our water supply are guarded, and why not should some sort of supervision be exercised on the food vended at restaurants and such places?

Resurrection Soup

Sydney Morning Herald, 1910

**A flurry of correspondence to the editor of the *Sydney Morning Herald* was
initiated by this letter from a George Read in August 1910:**

It is a well-known fact that in some places where a person leaves, say,
half his soup it goes back to the pot to be warmed up; meat not eaten
returns to the cook, to be made into stews; and entrees and bits of
potatoes return to the dining table as 'mashed'. You will often hear a
man say, 'I work at such and such restaurant, but I never eat there,'
and it is a well-known and observable fact, the waitresses never take
soup or made dishes. Why? Well, they know. Ask them on the quiet . . .
If a sausage or a saveloy is a mystery, then I contend a steak and
kidney pudding or a haricot is also a mystery.

From restaurateur Edward Magnus, of Paddington, came this response:

Mr George Read states there are places that pour back soup leavings
into the soup-pot, and make stews and entrees from scraps of meat
left on customers' plates. On behalf of my fellow caterers, I deny that
the statement is true. His uncorroborated statements tend to grossly
damage all restaurants, for the uncertainty of the 'places' he imagines
to exist makes the accusation applicable to anyone . . . My experience
as a caterer of long standing shows that the amount of soup left in
plates is so trifling that its value to the soup-pot would be nil, also
that the pieces of meat left on plates would be worthless even in the
largest of cheap restaurants. First-class restaurants with shilling
tariff I presume Mr George Read does not refer to, and the amount of
meat provided on plates at sixpenny restaurants is not of such a lavish
quantity as to permit any to be left.

**From the 'downstairs' side of the industry, however, came a different
opinion. A 'Waitress' claiming some seven years experience in both 'leading
hotels and cafes in the city, and . . . the cheaper line of restaurants' offered
her view:**

I think I can safely say that I can speak from experience as to the accuracy of Mr Read's remarks as to scraps of food left by customers on their plates being duly returned to the chief cook, such as pieces of meat and vegetables, etc, the same being added to make up dishes such as entrees and stews. Of course, I am going to speak with all due respect as to some of the dining-room proprietors of our city. I don't say that they all conduct their kitchens and stock-pots under the same principle, but at the same time a good number of them do. I have often in the course of my duties as a waitress stood at the lifts of restaurants in Sydney's 6d dining-rooms and tried to solve the mystery of why health inspectors under our Pure Food Act could allow such preparations to be placed at the disposal of the public. I have often been told myself by my employer to see that all the girls working under my directions as a head waitress saved all pieces of broken bread left by customers, and return them to the cooks to be converted into puddings. I have also seen vegetables saved the same way. In one particular dining-room in George-street I have seen eggs that I have heard the chief cook say were 'nearly mothers' put into puddings; and I can refer you to dozens of waiters and waitresses who can bear me out in my statements. I know of one other place in the city where the chief cook refused to make 'resurrection soup', and was quietly dismissed over it. I think that it is high time that such places should be put under severe restriction for the health and safety of the eating public. We are all an eating public.

Christmas in Sydney, 1890s

Nat Gould

Nat Gould (1857–1919) was primarily a turf journalist but also the author of more than 120 novels, mostly centred on horses and racing. He came to Australia in 1884 for a visit but stayed for eleven years, writing for a number of different newspapers. His first novel, written under the pseudonym of 'Verax', was published as a serial in the sporting paper *The Referee. Town and Bush* was never intended to be a guide book; by his admission, it was simply a record of his years living in Australia. In similar vein, but with a more particular focus, was *On and Off the Turf in*

Australia (1895) in which he wrote: 'Australia is not a land of gourmands and gluttons, but it is a land of plenty, and, as far as cookery goes, it gives a long start to the horrible messes some people delight in.'

Town and Bush, 1896

What a contrast Australia affords to the old country at Christmas! This festive season is just as much thought of under Australia's burning sun as it is amidst the snow and frost of England. I have spent Christmas in Queensland and New South Wales, and found it thoroughly enjoyable. On first acquaintance with an Australian Christmas, one can hardly imagine it is that season of the year. To indulge in roast goose and plum pudding with the thermometer at over 90 in the shade is making a toil of a pleasure. Christmas in the colonies is a great time for picnics and outdoor merry-makings. As a rule it is brilliant weather at this time of the year, and there is very little chance of being caught in a storm or compelled to abandon an outing owing to the unfriendly nature of the elements.

The Australians can therefore prepare to hold high festival without much fear of a disappointment. And certain it is that great preparations are made to give Christmas and New Year a fitting reception. For weeks beforehand there has been much fattening of poultry and a great making of cakes. Shop-keepers are alive to the fact that Christmas will bring in a lot of ready money, and that they will be able to dispose of goods that cannot be sold at any other period of the year.

One of the first signs of approaching Christmas may be seen in the stationers' shops, where the times of the latest mails to arrive in London before December 25 are posted. Christmas cards for friends in the old country fill the windows, and many of them bring joy and delight when friends and parents receive them on the other side of the world. Some of these cards are of exquisite design. A bunch of Australian wild-flowers painted in true colours forms a fitting souvenir, or perhaps a view of some choice spot in the harbour or up the Blue Mountains. Thousands of these cards are mailed to England about six weeks before Christmas, and reach their destinations before the all-eventful day. Then come the pictures from the London illustrated Christmas numbers, and they arrive in ample time to be displayed before the end of December arrives. Some of these Christmas publications are published a long time ahead, and it would not be at all surprising to read that at Christmas, 1897, the annual for 1898 had just been issued.

If Christmas Day happens to fall on a Friday, the probabilities are no business will be done until the following Tuesday or Wednesday morning. They are wonderful people for holidays in the colonies. An odd day's holiday is not regarded as a special blessing. What the native requires is the day before to prepare for the holiday, then the holiday itself, and then the remainder of the week to gradually get over it. At Christmas time a little extra indulgence is permissible, and most employers of labour are only too willing to extend the holidays after the bustle and worry coming before them.

Of course the grocers make special displays. Mr James Kidman, an ardent sportsman, and likewise an extensive retail grocer, generally manages to collect a crowd round his windows in George Street and Oxford Street. Mr Kidman is great on cheese. He orders a couple from Bodalla, and each weighs two or three tons. These huge monsters he places on a couple of drays, and has them drawn in triumph through the streets by a team of bullocks, with black native drivers to look after them. They are afterwards placed in the shop windows, when it is a case of cut and come again at them by many people, in the hope of securing one or more of the numerous coins that are stated to be buried in the interior. This mode of advertising pays, and Mr Kidman is generally alive to the advantages of publicity.

Whether times are bad or good, there always seems to be plenty of money, and to spare, at Christmas. Most people manage to save up a few shillings for this particular time, and the rejoicing is universal. It is a bustling, busy scene in Sydney on Christmas Eve, but on New Year's Eve the young men of the period are abroad, bent on mischief and mad pranks. There is no busier time of the year than Christmas, and a roaring trade is done in hampers and all the picnic necessaries.

And what picnics they are! Monster organisations, some of them, others on a more modest scale. The harbour resorts are besieged, and picnic parties camp so near to one another that the wonder is they do not amalgamate and combine the contents of their hampers. Somehow they generally keep in separate groups until one party runs short, and then a deputation of borrowers is sent round. The costumes of these merrymakers are in keeping with the climate. The young men start out arrayed in white flannels, and with broad-rimmed hats that would not be unlike Japanese sunshades if they had sticks in the centre. Collars are at a discount, just the usual turndown on the flannel shirt, with perhaps a tie round the neck: A pair of white boots and a sash round the waist, and the male picnicker is complete. And the lady friends who are invited to the picnic are arrayed in the lightest of attire – gauzy looking white or coloured dresses that seem as though a puff of wind would float them away and leave their owners lamenting. And such hats! They would do credit to a florist, so tasteful are the decorations.

The Australian girl at a Christmas picnic is about as fairy-like a mortal as one would expect to see out of a pantomime. They go out in parties of ten or a score, or even more, and the prettiest spots in and around Sydney ring with their merry laughter. There is no shivering in the cold, no fear of getting chilled, no danger of rheumatics from sitting on damp grass. Nature has laid herself out at her best advantage for these Christmas picnics, and if it is a trifle hot – well, it is better than being choked with fog and damp, and half starved to death into the bargain. And if the shades of night fall fast, and daylight quickly fades into darkness, what matters when the evening air is as balmy as zephyr's breezes, and there is not a chill in the night wind? After the glorious sunshine of the day, the shades of night come as a welcome change. As these picnic-parties are homeward bound, the sound of music echoes across the waters of the harbour, and then comes a chorus of song. The day has been merry, and so let the night be.

If ever there was a place where peace on earth and goodwill towards men ought to reign supreme, it is in Australia at Christmas.

Christmas in the Bush

E.S. Sorenson

Born near Casino, New South Wales, Edward Sorenson (1869–1939) began writing short stories and bush sketches in the 1890s, drawing on experiences accumulated since leaving school at the age of 14, working as a stockrider, drover, shearer, wool-classer, gold fossicker and publican. His works appeared in the *Bulletin*, *Lone Hand* and many other turn-of-the-century periodicals, and a collection of essays was later published as *Life in the Australian Backblocks*.

Though lacking the attractions, variety of sights and entertainments, the festivities and general gaiety that the cities offer, Christmas-tide brings good cheer to the denizens of the ranges and forests, and is looked forward to and enjoyed in the humblest places.

On the goldfields the miners take delight in surreptitiously introducing a few small nuggets into the plum-duff – and they do not go round the table after dinner collecting them as some women do the coins. The gold becomes the property of whoever finds it, and it is made into pins, rings and brooches. This habit of salting the pudding induces a good deal of prospecting, and as the prospectors have to eat up the tailings, it is probably the reason that so many people don't feel very well after the Christmas gorge.

Hop-beer, ginger-beer, and honeymead are also made, and stored away in kegs and bottles. 'Sugarbags' are plentiful in many parts of the bush, and a good nest or two is usually left for December, when the trees are felled and the bees robbed. The beer is made from the comb after the honey has been drained out of it. Sarsaparilla is another extensively-made drink, the vines growing plentifully among the ranges. The women and children are fond of these home-made drinks, but father is not always so enthusiastic.

A day or two before Christmas the wanderers return. First comes Jim, cantering up the track with a valise strapped in front of him and a smoke-cloud trailing behind, while the old folks and the little ones are watching with glad faces from the verandah. Towards sundown Bill appears on the hill in another direction, and comes jogging along quietly with a well-loaded pack-horse, and quart-pots, bells and hobble-chains rattling and jingling to every stride. The children run shouting to meet him, and some ride back behind him and some perch on the pack. They help him to unsaddle and carry his pack-bags in; they take his tired horses to water, and lead them through the slip-rails and let them go in the paddock with a gentle pat on the neck. The sun is down, perhaps, when Bob comes plodding slowly along through the trees, carrying his swag, and swinging a billy in one hand, while he shakes a little bush before his face with the other to keep the flies away.

On Christmas Eve the boys go out with guns for scrub turkeys, pigeons and ducks. Often they spend the whole day shooting in the scrubs, and round the swamps and lagoons; and they come home well laden with game. All hands and the cook turn to after tea and pluck the birds. The bushman's table is very rarely without game at this time.

Christmas Day is quiet and generally dull – a day of rest; but Boxing Day makes up for it with a quantum of sport and excitement.

The Ghosts of Many Christmases

Henry Lawson

Henry Lawson (1867–1922) has been acclaimed as one of Australia's greatest writers and the voice of the bush. He was certainly prolific, most of his vast output of short stories, poems, essays and sketches crammed into the 15 years from 1887, when his first poem was published, to 1902 when he returned from England. The nostalgic extract below, written when in England in 1901 and first published in *Children of the Bush*, is like a resumé of his life to that time – travels to Western Australia with his brother in 1890 and with his wife in 1896, in quest of gold; to Bourke and outback New South Wales in 1892; to New Zealand with his wife in 1897, in a vain attempt to overcome his craving for alcohol; and to England with his wife and child in 1900.

Children of the Bush, 1902

Did you ever trace back your Christmas Days? – right back to the days when you were innocent and Santa Claus was real. At times you thought you were very wicked, but you never realise how innocent you were until you've grown up and knocked about the world. Let me think!

Christmas in an English village, with bare hedges and trees, and leaden skies that lie heavy on our souls as we walk, with overcoat and umbrella, sons of English exiles and exiles in England, and think of bright skies and suns overhead, and sweeps of country disappearing into the haze, and blue mountain ranges melting into the azure of distant lower skies, and curves of white and yellow sand beaches, and runs of shelving yellow sandstone sea-walls – and the glorious Pacific! Sydney Harbour at sunrise, and the girls we took to Manly Beach.

Christmas in a London flat. Gloom and slush and soot. It is not the cold that affects us Australians so much, but the horrible gloom. We get heart-sick for the sun.

Christmas at sea – three Christmases, in fact – one going saloon from Sydney to Westralia early in the Golden Nineties with funds; and one, the Christmas after next, coming back steerage with nothing but the clothes we'd slept in. All of which was bad judgment on our part – the order and manner of our going and coming should have been reversed.

Christmas in a hessian tent in 'th' Western', with so many old mates from the East that it was just old time over again. We had five pounds of corned beef and a kerosene-tin to boil it in; and while we were talking of old things the skeleton of a kangaroo-dog grabbed the beef out of the boiling water and disappeared into the scrub – which made it seem more like old times than ever.

Christmas going to New Zealand, with experience, by the SS *Tasmania*. We had plum duff, but it was too 'soggy' for us to eat. We dropped it overboard, lest it should swamp the boat – and it sank to the ooze. The *Tasmania* was saved on that occasion, but she foundered next year outside Gisborne. Perhaps the cook had made more duff. There was a letter from a sweetheart of mine amongst her mails when she went down; but that's got nothing to do with it, though it made some difference in my life.

Christmas on a new telegraph-line with a party of lining gangmen in New Zealand. There was no duff nor roast because there was no firewood within twenty miles. The cook used to pile armfuls of flax-sticks under the billies, and set light to them when the last man arrived in camp.

Christmas in Sydney, with a dozen invitations out to dinner. The one we accepted was to a sensible Australian Christmas dinner; a typical one, as it should be, and will be before the Commonwealth is many years old. Everything cold except the vegetables, the hose playing on the veranda and vines outside, the men dressed in sensible pyjama-like suits, and the women and girls fresh and cool and jolly, instead of being hot and cross and looking like boiled carrots, and feeling like boiled rags, and having headaches after dinner, as would have been the case had they broiled over the fire in a hot kitchen all the blazing forenoon to cook a scalding, indigestible dinner, as many Australian women do, and for no other reason than that it was the fashion in England. One of those girls was very pretty and – ah, well!

Christmas dinner in a greasy Sydney sixpenny restaurant, that opened a few days before with brass band going at full blast at the door by way of advertisement. 'Roast-beef, one! Cabbage and potatoes, one! Plum pudding, two!' (That was the first time I dined to music.) The Christmas dinner was a good one, but my appetite was spoilt by the expression of the restaurant keeper, a big man with a heavy jowl, who sat by the door with a cold eye on the sixpences, and didn't seem to have much confidence in human nature.

Christmas – no, that was New Year – on the Warrego River, outback (an alleged river with a sickly stream that looked like bad milk). We spent most of that night hunting round in the dark and feeling on the ground for camel and horse droppings with which to build fires and make smoke round our camp to keep off the mosquitoes. The mosquitoes started at sunset and left off at daybreak, when the flies got to work again.

Christmas dinner under a brush shearing-shed. Mutton and plum pudding – and fifty miles from beer!

Fasoli's

Louis Esson

Fasoli's was a well-known Melbourne institution in the late nineteenth and early twentieth century, an inexpensive Italian restaurant where, in E.J. Brady's reminiscences, lively minds met to 'share with kindred spirits the feast of reason and flow of soul not to be found at more conventional tables'. It began in Lonsdale Street, transferring to new premises in King Street around 1907 and was sold in 1933. Oscar Mendelsohn describes its cuisine around that time as 'a model of simplicity ... on each of the long tables there were big bowls of potato salad, beans and beetroot and carafes of olive oil. Next ... a dish of spaghetti or other pasta. Then came the meat dish ... on one day a roast, on another a rich Milanese stew or ragout, or a savoury affair of kidney, perhaps on special occasions poultry. Always, of course, a fish dish on Fridays ... [and] good cheese and greens, especially the never-failing supply of spring onions.'

Louis Esson (1878–1943) is better known as a dramatist and a passionate advocate of an authentic Australian theatre, but he also wrote

verse, short stories and journalism, having begun his career as a freelance contributor to the Melbourne magazine *Table Talk*.

Ballads of Old Bohemia, 1980

The Temple of Bohemia, it boasts no golden gate
It flaunts no marble corridor to lure folk on to fate;
But down the pavements dreary, towards one dim lamp's glow,
Fasoli's draws the pilgrims where the good Bohemians go.

Oh! that bottle-laden table! Oh! the mixed and merry scenes!
And oil and garlic mingled with that salami and beans!
Fat macaroni festoons, and pungent, ruddy wines –
Oh! 'tis Bacchus waves his thyrsus where the Latin Quarter dines.

The world is spun of patchwork; and some there are belong
To prayer and holy living, and some to dance and song;
And some explore the cloister to find the key to Truth –
But some prefer the wine-shop and the commonwealth of Youth.

Italian, Swiss and German, French, Chilian and Russ
They fraternise with Cockney, and with Yid and Yank and Us.
They've humped their swags from God knows where, the whirling
    wide world round,
But in old Fasoli's wineshop they meet on common ground.

And there's rich and poor all talking in the tongues of all the earth;
There's dominoes and piquet, and there's long-resounding mirth;
There's every brand of rover making merry at the bar,
And there's smoke, and wine, and strumming of the harp and
    gay guitar.

All creed and caste are buried; there's only man to man –
A strange Australian mixture of the Cosmopolitan.
And there's no bad blood among them, though their arguments
    may roll
From the price of beer in China to the future of the soul.

The world is spun of patchwork, and some there are belong
To prayer and holy living, and some to dance and song;
A rocky road to Heaven, a sloping path to Hell –
But which road is the right road? . . . Good God, it's hard to tell!

The Temple of Bohemia, it boasts no golden gate,
It flaunts no marble corridor to lure folk to their fate;
But song and mirth and mateship; ah, well, 'tis wise to know
That wine-splashed road of Bacchus that the good Bohemians go.

Sucking Pig for Three

Ethel Turner

'Misrule' was the name of the large, rambling house on the Parramatta River in Sydney that was home to the Woolcot family of *Seven Little Australians*, the best-known and most popular of the forty or so children's novels written by Ethel Turner (1870–1958). The success of this book, which sold 5000 copies in Australia alone in its first year of publication, prompted the publishers to request a sequel, *The Family at Misrule*.

The Fresh Food and Ice Company, in addition to its refrigerated transport and ice-making activities, operated refreshment rooms; Quong Tart's was a well-known Sydney café.

The Family at Misrule, 1895

Poppet had been for lunch with Esther or Meg to the Fresh Food and Ice Company, Quong Tart's, and such places on various occasions. But the restaurant to which Malcolm and Martha took her was quite a new experience. She did not know the name of the street it was in, but it was not very far from the Quay, and there was a rather mixed, if interesting, assembly of diners. Not that it was a particularly low-class place; it had a very good name for the excellency of its food and its moderate prices, and its patrons comprised poor clerks who minded fashion less than a good dinner – tradesmen, sailors, and occasional wharf labourers. Martha had asked Malcolm whether, as she had

Poppet with her, they had better go to some place higher up town. Malcolm, who dined there regularly, seemed to see no reason why he should change his custom for a little slip of a girl under ten.

As for Poppet, it was all one with her where she went, and while Martha and Malcolm were studying the bill of fare, she fell to watching some sailors at an adjoining table with the deepest interest.

'Now, Miss Poppet,' said Martha, 'what will you have? Me and Malcolm have fixed on sucking pig, sweet potatoes and baked pumpkin, but I think you'd better have something plainer; there's roast mutton, or corned beef, or beefsteak pie.'

'Why,' said Poppet, 'we have *those* things at home. No, I'll have sucking pig too, please, Martha; I like tasting new things.'

'Did you ever!' remarked Martha, looking troubled; 'it might make you ill, Miss Poppet dear. Have corned beef like a good little girl.'

But Poppet could be firm on occasion. She did not dine at a restaurant every day, and when she did she had no intention of confining herself to ordinary things.

'Sucking pig for two,' said Malcolm to the waiter, and paused for Poppet's order.

'For three,' said Poppet, softly but firmly. While he had gone to execute the order, she occupied herself with considering what pudding she would have. There were five or six down on the list: plum duff, apple pie and custard, treacle roly-poly, stewed pears, and macaroni and cheese. She was wavering between macaroni and plum duff, when the waiter returned with the three great steaming plates of sucking pig and vegetables.

Malcolm and Martha were soon busily occupied, both considering it would be sheer wilful waste, after paying a shilling each, to leave an atom on their plates; but Poppet found a very little satisfying, and fell to watching the sailors again.

She heard them give their orders – five of them, each a different meat and different vegetables; she wondered how the waiter could keep it all in his head, and watched quite anxiously when he returned with the tray to see if he made any mistake.

On Chops

Marcus Clarke

Marcus Clarke was not only a discerning eater, as his restaurant reviews testify, he also knew – or so it appears from this 1874 article – how to cook. The 'so-called cook' whose succinct recipe he roundly rubbishes remains unidentified, but it was neither Eliza Acton (*Modern Cookery*, 1845), nor Isabella Beeton (*Household Management*, 1861), nor Australia's own Edward Abbott (*The English and Australian Cookery Book*, 1864), all of whom recommend a greased gridiron for broiling chops.

Melbourne Herald, 23 February 1874

'The nearest and the dearest things lie close about our feet,' sings a domestic poet, and there are few who are aware that they can obtain from an ordinary butcher, a meal equal to that enjoyed by an Emperor. The CHOP is a national dish. We are accustomed to the word from our infancy. To 'take a chop' is to be on familiar terms with a man. You may sup with a pretty woman; you may dine with a Duke, but you 'take a chop' only with an equal. Yet how is this most pleasant and noble dish, redolent of friendship, honesty, and mirth, maltreated by the ignorant, or ignored by the undeserving! There are human beings, English speaking human beings, who positively have never eaten a chop. They have swallowed lumps of leather, fried – fried, ye powers that smile on virtuous digestion! – in fat, but they have not tasted the simple ecstacy which is the portion of the God-fearing man of chops. Listen to the brutal sentence of a so-called cook – '*CHOPS should be taken from the loin from 1/2 inch to 3/4 of an inch thick. Have a clear cinder fire to broil them. Keep them constantly turned.*' And this is all! All! Why the art and mystery of chop cooking is unknown to this barbarian! '*Broil* them!' But on what machine? 'Keep them *turned*!' But with what instrument? My heart bleeds for the poor palpitating victim, her red and white complexion flushing into uniform brown, with horror, when this monster seizes her for his lusts. *Broiled*, and *Turned* indeed! Ye everlasting doors, shut upon such miscreants!

No, Madam, *we* will proceed in better fashion. First arise on dewy morning, don thy neatest gown – the white one with the pale blue spots, is my favourite – and trip enchantingly fresh from your bath to our faithful butcher. There let your limpid blue eye range over the succulent variety of flaky mutton. Lift a gloved hand – five and three quarters is the size – and point unhesitatingly to yonder group of fleshly roses smothered in milky adiposity. A cabbage leaf shall receive them, and I will carry the basket, while we make for the summit of yonder hill, where lives the *only* man who sells potatoes. Here, again, dear lady, let me advise. A potato is not a yellow monstrosity like Joan's well worn lump of kitchen soap. It is not a hideous white concentration of waxen clamminess. It is – if properly cooked – a ball of flour which melts in the mouth like chocolate and cream. They eat these delicacies in a Warrnambool farmhouse. In all probability your servants have tasted them, but *you* never will unless you purchase them yourself.

But 'tis two o'clock – the fitting time to eat a chop, for then are the gastric juices in full and healthy flow. The walk has made us hungry. Ha, ha. We will soon set *that* right. See, here is a gridiron – not a wire-work abortion, constantly sooty with cinders and oily with lumps of fat – but a fair and splendid fellow, with channelled bars and a spouted cap handle. Take we our chop between these polished tongs. The *coke* fire is briskly glowing. Now – fizz, fizzle, fizzz sh! 'Tis a chop sonata in G. Turn gently with the tongs (he who would basely impale upon a *fork* his chop deserves the burial of a suicide) and collect the gravy, which, bursting from the rosy flesh, rolls down the channelled bars into the receiving cup. Already the fizzling has dwindled to a soft melodious murmur, a tender hum of joy, the swan-song before death. Take this handle, madam, an instant. Does the water boil? So. See here two china plates, affixed to shining pewter dishes. The china has been warmed at the fire, and I pour between it and its pewter bottom some boiling water, replacing the nozzle screw, one plate for you, madame, and one for me. The salt, mustard, *no* sauce, if you love me, only one tiny bottle of that catsup we made last year from our own mushrooms. Two *crusts* of new bread await us. Now pop the hissing splendor on your plate. I have the potatoes here Five balls of flour in a *wooden* bowl! With dexterous jerk, I lift from out the ice-chest – start not, sweet lady – two pots of porter. You eat, you drink, you smile. I thought so. I will cook another one.

The proper finish to a chop is cheese. But not as your respected husband would eat it, Madam. My cheese eating is an art. I hand to you a fair white plate, on which repose four portions of the best Stilton. You take a fragment, and simultaneously I present to you a plateful of hot dry toast and a spoonful of hot powdered ham. A knob of butter is in ice. After which, you will allow *me* to smoke a pipe on the verandah.

What do you say? Your husband prefers a cigar? Precisely, because your husband is not an artist. With a humble chop, the man whose mind perceives the fitness of things smokes a pipe.

Meat Worshippers

Philip Muskett

While Australia grew rich on the sheep's back, its inhabitants earned the dubious honour of being the world's greatest meat-eaters. In the opinion of Dr Philip Muskett (1857–1909), Australian eating (and drinking) habits were completely out of tune with its climate. Though he was not alone in recognising similarities between Australia and the general Mediterranean region, he was the first to suggest this affinity as a basis for dietary (and culinary) reform, particularly in *The Book of Diet*.

The Book of Diet, 1898

The Australian eats annually as much meat as two Englishmen, three Canadians, four Germans, or ten Italians. It would seem, therefore, that an Australian must believe himself to be twice as strong as an Englishman; three times as strong as a Canadian; four times as strong as a German; and ten times as strong as an Italian. But this statement of the amount of animal food consumed by the five peoples in question, has a greater detrimental significance to Australia than appears on the surface. If the climate of Australia, England, Canada, Germany, and Italy were absolutely identical, the matter would be serious enough. But as we all know, Australia and Italy are warm countries – while England, Canada, and the greater part of Germany have a cold climate. So that, whilst living under similar climatic conditions, the Australian eats ten times as much animal food as the Italian. When viewed from this standpoint, the gravity of the meat-eating propensities of the Australian becomes only too apparent.

It is a little difficult to account for this infatuation of the Australian for animal food, and the indifference – if not contempt – he has for the products of the vegetable kingdom. But I have often thought it must be the domineering influence of our Anglo-Saxon heredity at work – an heredity which obstinately refuses to submit to its present semi-tropical environment. There is an old saying, that when you are in Rome, you must do as Rome does. This evidently needs to be altered for local requirements to the following:– 'That when you are in Australia, you must do as England does.' And so, because the roast beef and plum pudding of old England are good, they have to be articles of faith all the world over! If four colonising expeditions were sent out from the old country to four different parts of the globe – of absolutely diverse climates – depend upon it, the new settlement would, in every instance, follow out the food habits of the mother country. It would be so, even were the colonies founded in the polar, the temperate, the semi-tropical and the tropical regions respectively.

It would be interesting to know the exact amount of vegetable diet eaten in different countries. But it is perfectly safe to affirm that the whole civilised world – except the Anglo-Saxon race – consumes much more vegetable, than animal food. In the old country, the scientific proportion of meat to vegetables is considered to be as one to three. That is to say, in the diet there should be three times as much vegetables as meat – irrespective, of course, of other food. Unfortunately, this is not adhered to in the United Kingdom, by those who are in the position to do so, and much more animal food is eaten than is necessary. But if this proportion of three of vegetables to one of meat be proper in the old country, how much the more should vegetables not be required in a semi-tropical climate, like Australia? The most curious feature, in our Australian life, is the anomalous state of our food habits. They have no definite purpose, and nobody appears to know how they have come into existence; in what way they benefit the community; or what they do to promote a settlement upon the soil.

Meat eating in Australia is almost a religion. At any rate the Australian is certainly a meat worshipper.

Curry of Kid

Marcus Clarke

Curry as the basis of a new 'food system' for Australia? Marcus Clarke's 1874 suggestion may be slightly tongue-in-cheek and his recipe unorthodox, but his reforming zeal is sincere: a plea for simplicity, more adventurousness and greater appreciation of local food resources. (He would doubtless have approved the Mendolia family's canned sardines and 'Auschovies' from Western Australia.)

Melbourne Herald, 3 February 1874

In a climate like ours perhaps, a flesh diet is needed, for one cannot work wholly upon vegetables when the thermometer is 150 degrees in the shade, and the air dry as the vapour of an oven. But I am sure that we eat far too much meat. I am sure that we wilfully waste our magnificent fish supply. How often – though crayfish are 2d apiece in the Fishmarket, at six in the morning – do we see salad or fish-curry in the bill of fare at the hotel? How seldom is that most healthy and agreeable vegetable the Tomato, granted that it is rather scarce just now, placed before us? Five tomatoes with pepper, vinegar and oil – Florence oil which has been kept from its birth in a dark bottle I mean, not your fine-drawn nastiness which the grocer sells – five tomatoes, I say, thus judiciously sliced, might lie by an Emperor's side, and command him tasks. For breakfast I know no better dish, 'tis altogether excellent and healthy. The neglect of vegetables is criminal. Who does not know houses where men, women and children live on meat, meat, meat, with perhaps a potato or two; and, so knowing, who wonders at the yellow eyeball, the dirty skin, the slow perception of many well-grown Australian boys. Why do we not eat fruit? . . . There is a dish called a macedoine, which might be served daily in any Melbourne hotel. It is made of all and every kind of fruit, cherries, strawberries, peaches, what not, mixed in a salad bowl and powdered with loaf sugar. Before the man of understanding eats, he pours a tumbler of claret over his portion. But Melbourne cooks are ignorant of these progressive developments.

The simplest food is the best. Away with your Dutch caviar. (Why don't we make it here?) Away with your horrible 'colonial goose', anglice, a leg of bleeding mutton stuffed with reeking onions . . .

Did you know that a good many people live on marinaded pilchards, that is to say, on pilchards which have been split, washed, rubbed with salt, cayenne, spices, and boiled in a jar of bay leaves? Do you know that there is a fortune for anyone who will cure the pilchards which are yearly wasted in Hobson's Bay, and will send them to Italy. No, of course not. Did you ever eat gudgeon pie? I will be bound you never did. Did you ever go across the Yarra below the Falls Bridge, buy an eel from the old man who is always eel fishing there, and cook him (the eel, not the old man) *en matelotte*? Never, I will make oath. Did you ever make a mayonnaise of the common stickle-bat? No. I need hardly pause to remind you that though you have a big pond in your garden you never stocked it with tench or carp as your sensible and civilised Chinese neighbour would do. And you call yourself a civilised being. Pshaw! Go to your burnt chop.

But the base of our regenerated Australian food system must be the curry. A curry of kid, mixed with three eggs, the white of a cocoanut scraped to a powder, two chilis, and half a dozen slices of pineapple, is, as Falstaff said of Dame Quickly – 'a thing to thank God on'. The small river crayfish are excellent material; while he who has never eaten a young wombat treated with coriander seeds, turmeric, green mango, and dry ginger, has not used his opportunities. When I become rich enough to benefit my fellow-creatures, I shall take a shop in Collins-street – say somewhere near the Bank of Victoria – and building a bamboo verandah, will establish a Curry House. Nothing but Curry and Pale Ale will be dispensed, and my waiters will be Chinname [sic] – the best servants in the world – dressed in spotless white robes. Then I will open up the resources of the country, and teach the inhabitants of Melbourne The Art of Feeding.

Dinner, Hotel Australia, Sydney, 1 April 1902

The Kat, April 1902

Consomme Amieux   Crême de tomates

Boiled Schnapper, Sauce Riche

Boiled Chicken and Oyster Sauce   Fillet Lamb, Provençale

Sweetbreads à la Radziville   Petites Boûchees
Fricatelles, Point Asperges

Haunch Mutton, Conti   Sirloin Beef, Parisienne
Wild Duck and Port Wine Sauce

Mayonnaise Salmon, Lettuce

Spinach aux Fleurons, Braised Celery, Green Peas
Baked, Boiled and Mashed Potatoes

Frankfort Pudding.   Vanilla Creamstrips.   Assorted Cake
Compôte French Prunes

Roasted Almond Ice Cream

Albert Sandwiches

English Walnuts.   Almonds.   Muscatel Raisins.
Fruit in season. French coffee.

Bush Cooks

E.S. Sorenson

Edward Sorenson's sketches of bush life around the turn of the century, collected and published as *Life in the Australian Backblocks*, reveal his sympathy, understanding and genuine respect for the people of the bush, their ingenuity and resourcefulness. He is full of admiration for the improvising skills of bush cooks, who could make toasting forks from fencing wire and bread knives from the broken blade of a band-saw.

Life in the Australian Backblocks, 1911

The pioneers were quick to grasp the Aboriginal methods of cooking as being simple and easy, and entailing no carrying of heavy and cumbersome utensils. Men on horseback sometimes carry a frying-pan, but nothing more, excepting, of course, the inevitable billy-cans. The pan does duty for broiling and frying, and also for baking a johnny-cake. The footmen carry only a couple of billies, one inside the other, the smaller being used for tea and the other for boiling meat in. Some have only one, which fulfils the dual office of meat-pot and kettle. This economic person is no epicure in the matter of flavours. His main concern is to get sufficient to 'fill', and as the ultimate fate of everything that goes to that end is to get mixed, a little previous mixing, as he puts it, 'is neither here nor there'. In all other lines of cookery he follows pretty closely the primitive style of Murri – except when he feels inclined for a little pastry, when he boils a lump of dough in the same old billy. 'Doughboys,' he tells you, 'are very filling; you can feel them for a long time after.'

There is very little he cannot cook, and cook well, given firewood and a match. He can turn out a brace of stuffed ducks as delicately browned and juicy as any woman could with her stoves and ovens. And the process is simple. He merely wraps the birds in a sheet of well-greased brown paper and buries them in hot ashes. His damper is mixed up on a sheet of bark or tin, or on the outside of a piece of oil-cloth, if he happens to have such a thing round his swag, and when he has worked it to the required consistency he scoops a hole in the hot ashes, drops it in carefully, and covers it over, first with ashes, and then with red coals. When baked it is stood on end to cool. It has a sweet, delicious flavour that is peculiarly its own.

When bread is wanted for immediate use a few johnnies are baked on the coals. In cooking a rich currant cake the batter is also wrapped in brown paper, and from its appearance no one could tell that it had not been cooked in a brick oven; but the brownie (which is simply a damper with currants and sugar added) is placed in the naked ashes. A pigeon-pie is baked in a casing of stiff clay, obtained round the margins of water-holes. When lifted out of the ashes the baked clay is broken off by tapping the top with a stick. Many a good pie is made in turtle-shells, and even in stones having a concave surface.

It is surprising what a lot of things can be cooked, and what excellent cooking can be done, in bare ashes and on coals. Steak and chops are thrown on the latter and grilled, but in fixed camps various appliances are used. A gridiron is made by zigzagging a piece of hoop-iron, which is stood on the coals; another is made by twisting and plaiting pieces of fencing-wire together. Shearers use a barrel-hoop, covered with wire netting and having a wire handle, so that it can be hung over a fire, in preference to any modern invention. Sufficient meat can be grilled on this at once to serve a dozen men. A traveller's duff is made by mixing the batter in a billy-can with a stick. It is then poured into a handkerchief or into the sleeve of a shirt or something equally convenient, tied with a bootlace, and boiled in the same vessel.

The implements and appliances of the bush-whacker are in keeping with his surroundings. His rolling pin is a bottle; his toasting fork is made out of fencing wire; and his skimmer is a piece of perforated tin tacked on to a stick about two feet long. An old billy or pint-pot, with holes punched in the bottom, makes a serviceable colander; and the bread knife and carving knife are made from the broken blade of a hand-saw, with two flat pieces of wood riveted on one end for a handle. His dishcloth is a piece of moleskin tied on the end of a stick and cut in strips. It is an effective weapon in the hands of a cantankerous and pugnacious cook in silencing a complaint about the tucker. A sudden and unexpected swipe across the mouth with it (and it laps and clings beautifully) has a remarkably depressing effect on the average grumbler. It is a handy, useful instrument; with it Slushy can wash the tinware and pots without greasing or even wetting his hands.

Then, again, he has his own self-made tongs – a piece of iron hoop bent double. Iron hoop and fencing-wire have a wonderful range in the matter of utility in the bush. So has greenhide. This triumvirate figures in every hut and camp in the back country, and in the home or in the paddock it is the settler's everlasting standby.

Despite all inconveniences, the average far-back cook is generally a smiling, happy-go-lucky individual, who looks upon flies, dust and smoky chimneys as part and parcel of his profession, with a cheery 'Sit in, mate' to every chance traveller, and views everything with an optimistic eye.

Paddy's Market, 1910

Louis Stone

Described as the first great novel of Sydney, *Jonah* captures the city in vibrant images – its colours and flavours, smells and sounds – and depicts the larrikin gangs of the early 1900s. Jonah and Chook's stamping ground was the inner-Sydney suburbs of Redfern, Surry Hills and Waterloo, an area Louis Stone (1871–1955) knew intimately. After arriving in Australia in 1884 with his parents at the age of thirteen, Stone spent most of his adult life in Australia as a teacher.

Jonah, 1911

Chook was standing near the entrance to the market where his mates had promised to meet him, but he found that he had still half an hour to spare, as he had come down early to mark a pak-ah-pu ticket at the Chinaman's in Hay Street. So he lit a cigarette and sauntered idly through the markets to kill time.

The three long, dingy arcades were flooded with the glare from clusters of naked gas-jets, and the people, wedged in a dense mass, moved slowly like water in motion between the banks of stalls. From the stone flags underneath rose a sustained, continuous noise – the leisurely tread and shuffle of a multitude blending with the deep hum of many voices, and over it all, like the upper notes in a symphony, the shrill, discordant cries of the dealers.

Overhead, the light spent its brightness in a gloomy vault, like the roof of a vast cathedral fallen into decay, its ancient timbers blackened with the smoke and grime of half a century.

On Saturdays the great market, silent and deserted for six nights in the week, was a debauch of sound and colour and smell. Strange, pungent odours assailed the nostrils; the ear was surprised with the sharp, broken cries of dealers, the cackle of poultry, and the murmur of innumerable voices; the stalls, splashed with colour, astonished the eye like a picture, immensely powerful, immensely crude.

The long rows of stalls were packed with the drift and refuse of a great city. For here the smug respectability of the shops were cast aside, and you were deep in the romance of traffic in merchandise fallen from its high estate – a huge welter and jumble of things arrested in their ignoble descent from the shops to the gutter.

At times a stall was loaded with the spoils of a sunken ship or the loot from a city fire, and you could buy for a song the rare fabrics and costly dainties of the rich, a stain on the cloth, a discoloured label on the tin, alone giving a hint of their adventures. Then the people hovered round like wreckers on a hostile shore, carrying off spoil and treasure at a fraction of its value, exulting over their booty like soldiers after pillage.

There was no caprice of the belly that could not be gratified, no want of the naked body that could not be supplied in this huge bazaar of the poor; but its cost had to be counted in pence, for those who bought in the cheapest market came here.

A crowd of women and children clustered like flies round the lolly stall brought Chook to a standstill; the trays heaped with sweets coloured like the rainbow, pleased his eye, and, remembering Ada's childish taste for lollies, he thought suddenly of her friend, Pinkey the red-haired, and smiled.

Near at hand stood a collection of ferns and pot-plants, fresh and cool, smelling of green gardens and moist earth. Over the way, men lingered with serious faces, trying the edge of a chisel with their thumb, examining saws, planes, shears with a workman's interest in the tools that earn his bread.

Chook stopped to admire the art gallery, gay with coloured pictures from the Christmas numbers of English magazines. On the walls were framed pictures of Christ crucified, the red blood dropping from His wounds, or the old rustic bridge of an English village, crude as almanacs, printed to satisfy the longings of the people.

Opposite a cock crowed in defiance; the hens cackled loudly in the coops; the ducks lay on planks, their legs fastened with string, their eyes dazed with terror or fatigue.

A cargo of scented soap and perfume, the damaged rout of a chemist shop, fascinated the younger women, stirring their instinctive delight in luxury; and for a few pence they gratified the longing of their hearts.

The children pricked their ears at the sudden blare of a tin trumpet, the squeaking of a mechanical doll. And they stared in amazement at the painted toys, surprised that the world contained such beautiful things. The mothers, harassed with petty cares, anxiously considered the prices; then the pennies were counted, and the child clasped in its small hands a Noah's ark, a wax doll, or a wooden sword.

Chook stared at the vegetable stalls with murder in his eyes, for here stood slant-eyed Mongolians behind heaps of potatoes, onions, cabbages, beans, and cauliflowers, crying the prices in broken English, or chattering with their neighbours in barbaric, guttural sounds. To Chook they were the scum of the earth, less than human, taking the bread out of his mouth, selling cheaply because they lived like vermin in their gardens.

But he forgot them in watching the Jews driving bargains in second-hand clothes, renovated with secret processes handed down from the Ark. Coats and trousers, equipped for their last adventure with mysterious darns and patches, cheated the eye like a painted beauty at a ball. Women's finery lay in disordered heaps – silk blouses covered with tawdry lace, skirts heavy with gaudy trimming – the draggled plumage of fine birds that had come to grief. But here buyer and seller met on level terms, for each knew to a hair the value of the sorry garments; and they chaffered with crafty eyes, each searching for the silent thought behind the spoken lie.

Chook stared at the bookstall with contempt, wondering how people found the time and patience to read. One side was packed with the forgotten lumber of bookshelves – an odd volume of sermons, a collection of scientific essays, a technical work out of date. And the men, anxious to improve their minds, stared at the titles with the curious reverence of the illiterate for a printed book. At their elbows boys gloated over the pages of a penny dreadful, and the women fingered penny novelettes with rapid movements, trying to judge the contents from the gaudy cover.

The crowd at the provision stall brought Chook to a standstill again. Enormous flitches hung from the posts, and the shelves were loaded with pieces of bacon tempting the eye with a streak of lean in a wilderness of fat. The buyers watched hungrily as the keen knife slipped into the rich meat, and the rasher, thin as paper, fell on the board like the shaving from a carpenter's plane. The dealer, wearing a clean shirt and white apron, served his customers with smooth, comfortable movements, as if contact with so much grease had nourished his body and oiled his joints.

Chook elbowed his way to the corner where Joe Crutch and Waxy Collins had promised to meet him, there was no sign of them, and he took another turn up the middle arcade. It was now high tide in the markets, and the stream of people filled the space between the stalls like a river in flood. And they moved at a snail's pace, clutching in their arms fowls, pot-plants, parcels of groceries, toys for the children and a thousand odd nameless trifles, bought for the sake of buying, because they were cheap. A babel of broken conversation, questions and replies, jests and laughter, drowned the cries of the dealers, and a strong, penetrating odour of human sweat rose on the hot air. From time to time a block occurred, and the crowd stood motionless, waiting patiently until they could move ahead.

In one of these sudden blocks Chook, who was craning his neck to watch the vegetable stalls, felt someone pushing, and turning his head, found himself staring into the eyes of Pinkey, the red-haired.

"Ello, fancy meetin' yous,' cried Chook, his eyes dancing with pleasure.

The curious pink flush spread over the girl's face, and then she found her tongue.

'Look w'ere ye're goin'. Are yer walkin' in yer sleep?'

'I am,' said Chook, 'an' don't wake me; I like it.'

But the twinkle died out of his eyes when he saw Stinky Collins separated from Pinkey by the crowd, scowling at him over her shoulder. He ignored Chook's friendly nod, and they stood motionless, wedged in that sea of human bodies until it chose to move.

Chook felt the girl's frail body pressed against him. His nostrils caught the odour of her hair and flesh, and the perfume mounted to his brain like wine. The wonderful red hair, glittering like bronze, fell in short curls round the nape of her neck, where it had escaped from the comb. A tremor ran through his limbs and his pulse quickened. And he was seized with an insane desire to kiss the white flesh, pale as ivory against her red hair. The crowd moved, and Pinkey wriggled to the other side.

'I'll cum wid yer, if yer feel lonely,' said Chook as she passed.

'Yous git a move on, or yer'll miss the bus,' cried Pinkey, as she passed out of sight.

When Chook worked his way back to the corner, little Joe Crutch and Waxy Collins stepped forward.

'W'ere the 'ell 'ave yer bin? We've bin waitin' 'ere this 'arf 'our,' they cried indignantly.

'Wot liars yer do meet,' said Chook, grinning.

The three entered the new market, an immense red-brick square with a smooth, cemented floor, and a lofty roof on steel girders. It is here the people amuse themselves with the primitive delights of an English fair after the fatigue of shopping.

The larrikins turned to the chipped-potato stall as a hungry dog jumps at a bone, eagerly sniffing the smell of burning fat as the potatoes crisped in the spitting grease.

'It's up ter yous ter shout,' cried Joe and Waxy.

'Well, a tray bit won't break me,' said Chook, producing threepence from his pocket.

The dealer, wearing the flat white cap of a French cook, and a clean apron, ladled the potatoes out of the cans into a strainer on the counter. His wife, with a rapid movement, twisted a slip of paper into a spill, and, filling it with chips, shook a castor of salt over the top. Customers crowded about, impatient to be served, and she went through the movements of twisting the paper, filling it with chips, and shaking the castor with the automatic swiftness of a machine.

When they were served, the larrikins stood on one side, crunching the crisp slices of potato between their teeth with immense relish as they watched the cook stirring the potatoes in the cauldron of boiling fat. Then they licked the grease off their fingers, lit cigarettes, and sauntered on. But the chips had whetted their appetites, and the sight of green peas and saveloys made their mouths water.

Men, women, and children sat on the forms round the stall with the stolid air of animals waiting to be fed. When each received a plate containing a squashy mess of peas and a luscious saveloy, they began to eat with slow, animal satisfaction, heedless of the noisy crowd. The larrikins sat down and gave their order, each paying for their own.

'Nothin' like a feed ter set a man up,' said Chook, wiping his mouth with the back of his hand.

Nationhood and Eating

Anonymous

It might seem remarkable to find a newspaper editorial on the philosophy of cookery in 1903, but perhaps this reflects the influence in Sydney of Dr Philip Muskett, a vigorous champion of the art of cookery. The writer – indubitably male, in view of his flagrant dismissal of women – ends with a call for the establishment of a chair of cookery at Sydney University; but several years earlier, in Melbourne, Rita Vaile had put forward the idea of a chair of, or a minister of, Gastronomy. And in the same vein, 'Lois' of the *Sydney Morning Herald* had suggested in 1900 that a French recipe book be set as a text for students of the French language.

Sydney Morning Herald, 2 September 1903

Recent proceedings in the Arbitration Court have given food for thought. That is the literal sense of the expression. A procession of chefs has been explaining to an astounded Bench for the edification of all how Sydney has its food cooked. The personal proclivities of some of the artists to whom is entrusted the task of pleasing the palate of the diner have had some sidelights thrown upon them, but there has been on the whole an air of frivolity in this handling of a grave and solemn subject.

For after all eating, and its necessary complement drinking, is an all-important function of life. The fate of an empire may easily depend upon a good meal. In fact Napoleon, who was something of an authority upon such matters, held that an army travelled upon its stomach, and it was to his attention to the internal requirements of his soldiers that he owed much of his martial success. At the present day no portion of the equivalent of a force for the field receives greater consideration than the commissariat. But apart altogether from greater issues everyday social relations depend largely for their cordiality upon respectful and reverent attention being devoted to the preparation of food. Conceive what the world would be if there were no bad cooks! Envy, hatred, and malice, and all uncharitableness would disappear, for all these attributes and sentiments find their primary cause in indigestion. The lion would lie down with the lamb, and labour, after discussing a dream of a dinner with capital, would catch the latter's eye, rise solemnly with glass uplifted, and propose with thankful deference 'The Cook'.

It is because, as a nation, we are not yet out of our swaddling clothes that the art of dining has not received in Australia the consideration which is undoubtedly its due. In the old world and in the civilised parts of America a great culinary artist has the position and the prestige and the emoluments which are the meed of those who achieve distinction in the other arts. That is as it should be. The man who presents a chaste and well-balanced dinner does not merely appease a material craving. He satisfies the demand which is latent in all of us for something which appeals to the spiritual and poetical part of our being, and a good dinner well served is as much a creation as a picture by Rubens or a composition by Mozart. There have been few women poets, and none of them in the first rank. That is why it is that no woman can cook. She has not the imagination, the taste, or the judgment.

The art of cookery is full of mysteries. Not merely the sinister mysteries which are hidden in the basements of the cheaper class of restaurants, but matters of much higher import. Is there a man who has not wondered what is the name of the benefactor of mankind who discovered that horse-radish was essential to the enjoyment of roast beef, and that without mint sauce lamb was a vain thing? Monuments have been erected to men who have merely sacked a city or who have ruled or misruled a country, but where is the stately statue raised to the discoverer of the Bombay duck or to the splendid intellect that created caviare? Democracies are said to be proverbially ungrateful, but the charge of ingratitude in this respect lies at the doors of monarchies and democracies alike. It is a stigma upon the nations that a Columbus of the kitchen, the first master mind that discovered that there was something more in cookery than poking a stick through a piece of meat and holding it over a fire, has been allowed so long to rest:– 'Unwept, unhonoured, and unsung'.

Different countries, different customs. The French consider that the Britons are barbarians in the matter of eating. The Italian flavours everything with garlic, and many races drown their viands in oil. Perhaps the lower class Chinese is of all the eater of the plainest food. There is no false fastidiousness about him either. In Peking the street leading from the Hatamen is fringed on both sides by eating booths which are open to all the winds that blow. It is always blowing there, and the Pekinese have the dust-storm with them all the summer. Not the poor half-hearted thing we have here occasionally, but a dust-storm which whirls acres of the surface soil of the province of Chih-li in the air and deposits it upon the just and the unjust and their belongings alike. The food in these booths, bowls of rice with a symptom of meat, naturally becomes encrusted with dust, as of course it never occurs to John to cover the food over. Yet the coolies eat their dust and rice unabashed and unfearing and with a cheerful countenance withal. Which would show that our well-meant endeavours to raise China from her coma have been wrongly directed. Until the Chinese are taught the grandeur and nobility of well-considered eating they will not be brought to desire the Higher Life.

By your eating shall ye be known. When we have learnt to appreciate the true importance of eating and the paramount necessity of educating our cooks to tread in the paths in which they should go, the Commonwealth will begin to take a foremost place among the nations of the earth. And to achieve that end a chair of cookery should be established at the University, and the highest honour that the State has in its gift should be bestowed upon the chef who achieves success in his benignant mission.

Tea and Suppers

Henry Handel Richardson

Set in the second half of the nineteenth century, the three novels that make up the *Richard Mahony* trilogy are the best known of the books by Henry Handel Richardson (1870–1946), nom-de-plume of Ethel Florence Lindesay Richardson. Richard Mahony is an Edinburgh-educated doctor who practises at the Victorian goldfields: his wife, Mary, is the daughter of a Geelong innkeeper. The first extract describes the meal served at the inn on Mahony's first visit in the mid-nineteenth century, when he meets Mary; the second the supper at a party Mary arranges several years after their marriage. In the third extract, Richard and Mary Mahony have returned to the English village of Buddlecombe, and the generosity of

Mary's Australian supper table stands in stark contrast to the parsimony of English hospitality.

1

They got home from the cave at sundown, he with the ripe Jinny hanging a dead weight on his arm, to find tea spread in the private parlour. The table was all but invisible under its load; and their hostess looked as though she had been parboiled on her own kitchen fire. She sat and fanned herself with a sheet of newspaper while, time and again, undaunted by refusals, she pressed the good things upon her guests. There were juicy beefsteaks piled high with rings of onion, and a barracoota, and a cold leg of mutton. There were apple-pies and jam tarts, a dish of curds-and-whey and a jug of custard. Butter and bread were fresh and new; scones and cakes had just left the oven; and the great cups of tea were tempered by pure, thick cream.

To the two men who came from diggers' fare: cold chop for breakfast, cold chop for dinner and cold chop for tea: the meal was little short of a banquet, and few words were spoken in its course. But the moment arrived when they could eat no more, and when even Mrs Beamish ceased to urge them.

2

The climax of her evening was fast approaching. Excusing herself, she slipped away and went to cast a last eye over her supper-tables, up and down which benches were ranged, borrowed from the Sunday school. To her surprise she found herself followed by Mrs Devine.

'Do let me 'elp you, my dear, do, now! I feel that stiff and silly sitting up there with me 'ands before me. And jes' send that young feller about 'is business.'

So Purdy and his offers of assistance were returned with thanks to the card-room, and Mrs Devine pinned up her black silk front. But not till she had freely vented her astonishment at the profusion of Mary's good things. ''Ow do you git 'em to rise so? – No, I never did! Fit for Buckin'am Palace and Queen Victoria! And all by your little self, too – my dear, I must give you a good 'ug!'

Hence, when at twelve o'clock the company began to stream in, they found Mrs Devine installed behind the barricade of cups, saucers and glasses; and she it was who dispensed tea and coffee and ladled out the claret-cup; thus leaving Mary free to keep an argus eye on her visitors' plates. At his entry Richard had raised expostulating eyebrows; but his tongue was of course tied. And Mary made a lifelong friend.

And now for the best part of an hour Mary's sandwiches, sausage-rolls and meat-pies; her jam-rolls, pastries and lemon-sponges, her jellies, custards and creams; her blanc and jaune-manges and whipped syllabubs; her trifles, tipsy-cakes and charlotte-russes formed the theme of talk and objects of attention. And though the ladies picked with becoming daintiness, the gentlemen made up for their partners' deficiencies; and there was none present who did not, in the shape of a hearty and well-turned compliment, add yet another laurel to Mary's crown.

3

Another thing that sent people's eyebrows up was the supper to which Mary sat them down as the clock struck ten. At this date she had not been long enough in Buddlecombe to know it for an unalterable rule that, unless the invitation was to dinner, a heavy, stodgy dinner of one solid course after another, from which, if you happened to be a peckish eater, you rose feeling as though you could never look on food again; except in this case, the refreshment offered was of the lightest and most genteel: a biscuit, a jug of barley-water for the gouty, or lemon-water for the young – at most, a glass of inferior sherry, cellars not being tapped to any extent on such occasions. But Mary had gone at her supper in good old style, giving of her best. And Mahony was so used to leaving such matters entirely to her that it had never entered his head to interfere. Not until the party was squeezed into the little dining-room, round a lengthened dinner-table on which jellies twinkled, cold fowls lay trussed, sandwiches were piled loaf-high – not till then and till he saw the amazed glances flying between the ladies, did he grasp how wrong Mary had gone. A laden supper-table was an innovation: and who were these new-comers, bailing from God knew where, to attempt to improve on the customs of Buddlecombe? It was also a trap for the gouty – and all were gouty more or less. Thirdly, such profusion constituted a cutting criticism on the meagre refreshments that were here the rule. He grew stiff with embarrassment; felt, if possible, even more uncomfortable than did poor Mary, at the refusals and head-shakings that went down one side of the table and up the other. For none broke more than the customary Abernethy, or crumpled a sandwich. Liver-wings and slices of breast, ham patties and sausage-rolls made the round, in vain. Mrs Challoner gave the cue; and even the vicar, a hearty eater, followed her lead, the only person to indulge being the worthy gentleman who had caused half the trouble – and *him* Mahony caught being kicked by his wife under the table.

The Proper Time for Cake

Rita Vaile

Rita Vaile was the woman's editor of the Melbourne *Herald* in the 1890s and author of *Cottage Cookery: Hygienic and Economic*. A strong advocate of domestic education for girls, she helped establish the Australian Institute of Domestic Economy in Melbourne in 1904. Her pronouncements on the proper time and place for cake echo the subtle distinctions hinted at by Dame Mary Gilmore (page 39).

Cottage Cookery, 1892

People who give their children cake between breakfast and lunch, or as the chief part of a lunch, should note the following. It is a vulgar thing to do. I am quite sure people would stop the practice if they understood that, and that other people knew it, much quicker than for any considerations of health. When sweet cakes first appeared in cookery they were used exclusively as a sort of 'bonne bouche'.

A 'bonne bouche' is a dainty mouthful, and, as the name implies, is eaten in small quantities; also, towards the end of a course, or a meal, as the crowning point, so to speak. In that way it is not so unwholesome, so sweet cakes were used, as what Mr Pecksniff calls 'a little light refreshment', that is, with wine for visitors, and in place of afternoon tea. But the only meal that sweet cakes were served at was tea. They were then eaten after scone, bread and butter, etc, and strictly as a 'bonne bouche' – a finale to the meal. They were all right in that place. They never were, and never are, served in good houses before lunch, or as chief part of a lunch, and often not at afternoon tea. A visitor would think a hostess a savage if she offered sweet cake at eleven o'clock.

Why train children in a way that is recognised as vulgar by gentle people, because incorrect from the health point of view? The only reasons that occur to me as the probable ones are these. From the mere fact that sweet cakes – mind, oat cakes and various other cakes made without sweetening were, and are, used for breakfast – were regarded as a delicacy, people, directly they begin to live comfortably, think that they are having things in good style if they have plenty of cake right through the day. Another thing is the cheapness and quantity of factory made cake that is obtainable. So the indolent are saved the trouble of thought or cooking. Many women think they are encouraging a nice, refined style by doleing out cake before or at lunch. It is all very vulgar. The same rule applies to eating sweets ('lollies') in the morning. These, taken as a 'bonne bouche', after dinner, are more wholesome than eaten before the meals. When cake is used for lunch, let it be a plain light cake, not over sweet, and do not use it as the chief part of, or at least half the meal.

When afternoon tea is taken, pastry, scones and sweet cake should not be eaten with it. A little thin bread and butter is preferable. Whatever is eaten should be used in small quantities. Also, afternoon tea should not be taken just before dinner. The average person who dines at six, half-past six, or seven o'clock, should remember that fashionable people in the old world, who have established the custom of five o'clock tea, dine at 8 and 8.30. What they take at five o'clock has time to digest. They do not create confusion by taxing their stomach to digest dinner, with the tea in a half digested state. So let a reasonable time elapse between the afternoon tea and dinner.

Party Supper

Louis Stone

Betty Wayside was Louis Stone's second novel. Like *Jonah*, it was set in the inner Sydney suburbs – here, Paddington and Woollahra – in the early years of the twentieth century. The party was a surprise to celebrate Betty's twenty-first birthday; its supper could have come straight from 'Aunt Mary's' recipe pages in *The Australian Home Journal*.

The party was in full swing when Betty and Freda slipped from the room. In half an hour they came up to announce that supper was ready, and the young men, pairing off with the girls, trooped downstairs to the kitchen. It was transformed. The humble utensils had been swept out of sight, and coloured fairy lamps, distributed about the room, threw a soft light on the walls. The table was a sight to make the mouth water. Gay with flowers and fairy lamps, it was loaded with dainties. There were piles of sandwiches – ham, tongue, sardine, lettuce, and cheese; cakes of all shapes and sizes – rock cakes, seed cakes, currant cakes, and Swiss roll; jellies coloured like the rainbow; bowls of fruit salad and cream; fruit piled in pyramids; lollies neatly packed in boxes, date creams, cocoanut ice, walnut creams, almond rock, and Turkish delight. Freda stood ready to serve coffee and claret cup from the small table near the door.

It had been agreed that nothing should be bought from the shops, and the girls, proud of their handiwork, pointed out their contributions, secretly pleased to show that when the time came to be serious they were as much at home in the kitchen as in the drawing-room. The young men, seizing the opportunity, declared their intention of eating nothing but that made by the hands of their girl. They sat down at the table, a lady to each gentleman, but two girls were left together.

High Tea

D.H. Lawrence

D.H. Lawrence (1853–1930) visited Australia in May 1922 and stayed for just over three months, renting a cottage, 'Wyewurk', on the edge of the Pacific Ocean at Thirroul south of Sydney. In his novel *Kangaroo*, written in just six weeks, Somers and his wife, Harriett, are thinly disguised versions of Lawrence and his wife Frieda. Victoria and Jack are friends met in Australia. In Australia the book was praised for its descriptions of the landscape, but it also includes interesting depictions of Australian middle-class manners.

Victoria said she would prepare the high tea which takes the place of dinner and supper in Australia, against his return. So Harriett boldly invited them to this high tea – a real substantial meal – in her own house. Victoria was to help her prepare it, and Jack was to come straight back to Torestin. Victoria was as pleased as a lamb with two tails over this arrangement, and went in to change her dress.

Somers knew why Harriett had launched this invitation. It was because she had had a wonderfully successful cooking morning. Like plenty of other women Harriett had learned to cook during war-time, and now she loved it, once in a while. This had been one of the whiles. Somers had stoked the excellent little stove, and peeled the apples and potatoes and onions and pumpkin, and looked after the meat and the sauces, while Harriett had lashed out in pies and tarts and little cakes and baked custard. She now surveyed her prize Beeton shelf with love, and began to whisk up a mayonnaise for potato salad.

Victoria appeared in a pale gauze dress of pale pink with little dabs of gold – a sort of tea-party dress – and with her brown hair loosely knitted behind, and with innocent sophistication pulled a bit untidy over her womanly forehead, she looked like a magazine cover. Her colour was very warm, and she was awkwardly excited. Harriett put on an old yellow silk frock, and Somers changed into a dark suit. For tea there was cold roast pork with first-class brown crackling on it, and potato salad, beetroot, and lettuce, and apple chutney; then a dressed lobster – or crayfish, very good, pink and white; and then apple pie and custard tarts and cakes and a dish of apples and passion-fruits and oranges, a pine-apple and some bananas; and of course big cups of tea, breakfast cups.

Emerald Jellies

Hal Porter

This novelist and autobiographer's recollection of Sunday tea in the early years of the twentieth century, and the table laden with sponges, cream puffs and diverse sweet delicacies, seems to fly in the face of Rita Vaile's

strict rulings on the place of cake. But then, Sunday was not like other days; as Hal Porter (1911–1984) suggests, it was the one day of the week when daydreams could be indulged.

The Watcher on the Cast-Iron Balcony, 1963

The house contains many indications of Empire: small silk Union Jacks, a red-blotched map of the world, Pears' Soap, Epps's Cocoa, Lea and Perrin's Sauce, a chromo-lithograph of Edward VII and Queen Alexandra, Beecham's Pills, Mazzawattee Tea canisters and, stamped in purple inside wardrobes and drawers, the assurance *Manufactured by European Labour Only*. The house contains also many indications of a lower middle-class lavishness Australians regard as bare necessities. In the meat-safe are a sirloin, pounds of rump steak and cutlets. In the pantry are a case of apples, a pineapple, peaches, oranges and bananas. The shelves are lined with bottles of jam, with sauces, pickles, chutneys and jars of Rose's Marmalade. On top of the crammed vegetable rack lies a crescent of pumpkin on the cut surface of which is some large back-to-front lettering sucked from the newspaper it was wrapped in. This may be, for all I know, the heading from the news of the Czar of Russia's assassination. It is curious that these mundane and humbly lavish still lifes of food should be so clearly remembered for, never having experienced what hunger is, I have no recollection of ever performing, at that time, the act of eating anything except mandarins, strawberries and asparagus. There is my wooden egg-cup, my own egg-spoon with teeth-dents in its silver bowl, and no memory of egg-eating. There is the Sunday tea-table: white damask glossily starched, and bearing, as the table-napkins stiff as cardboard do, a design of swans and bulrushes; the salad bowl, cake-stands, jam dishes, pickle jars, sugar-castor and celery vase all of cut glass; the tiered electro-plated cruet; the silver trumpets of sweet peas; the butter knives, cake knives, jam spoons and Sunday bread knife with mother-of-pearl handles, and silver-gilt blades and bowls engraved with florid scrolls and curly acanthus leaves – all the glitter and gleam of the setting for an Australian Sunday tea. I recall seeing the emerald green jellies inside whose fluted trembling are suspended grapes and strawberries and banana slices; the pink-iced sponge-cakes flavoured with rose-water, the cream puffs, macaroons and lamingtons piled up; the ham coated in breadcrumbs and stuck with cloves at Father's end of the table and, at Mother's end, the highly peppered Sargasso of sliced cucumber, tomato, lettuce, onion and radishes sodden in Champion's Malt Vinegar which Mother imagines is a salad.

Saturday afternoon is for baking. This is a labour of double nature: to provide a week's supply of those more solid delicacies Australian mothers of those days regard as being as nutritiously necessary as meat twice daily, four vegetables at dinner, porridge and eggs and toast for breakfast, and constant cups of tea. Empty biscuit-barrels and cake-tins being as unthinkable as beds not made before eleven am, Mother, therefore, constructs a great fruit cake, and a score or more each of rock cakes, Banburies, queen cakes, date rolls and ginger nuts. These conventional solidities done, she exercises her talent for ritual fantasy, for the more costly and ephemeral dainties that are to adorn as fleetingly as daylilies the altar of the Sunday tea-table. Now appear three-storeyed sponge cakes mortared together with scented cream and in whose seductive icing are embedded walnuts, silver *cachous*, *glacé* cherries, strawberries, segments of orange and strips of angelica. Now appear cream puffs and éclairs, creations of the most momentary existence, deliberately designed neither for hoarding against a rainy day nor for social showing-off. Sunday tea is the frivolous and glittering crown of the week; there is the impression given of throwing away money like delicious dirt; there is the atmosphere rather than the fact of luxury; Sunday tea is, above all, my parents' statement to each other and their children that life is being lived on a plane of hard-earned and justifiable abundance.

An All-Australian Dinner

Anonymous

From cocktails to coffee (and the post-prandial cigar), this proposed 1925 Christmas menu, from 'a writer who has dined in most parts of the civilised world', is proudly Australian – even if pleasure has been subordinated to patriotism.

Now that America has gone dry, and theoretically anyhow, is producing no wine or spirits, Australia may claim to be the only country on earth that can supply itself with a first-class dinner complete from cocktails to coffee . . .

Our vegetables – peas, brussels sprouts, asparagus, beans – are incomparable. The best of the fish is naturally to be found in the cold water States – Victoria and Tasmania – but connoisseurs have pointed out that there is no choicer boiling fish known than the turbot-like black rock cod of New South Wales, while the schnapper, the black bream, the Botany sole and the flounder all have their places in the memory of thousands of gourmets. An Australian shoulder of lamb is equal to any that came out of Wales, and the fabled roast beef of old England is in no sense superior to that of Queensland. Britain beats us for variety in game; though an Australian pheasant is easy enough to come by we have no partridges, and nothing to compare to that Northern monopoly, the grouse. On the other hand we beat the world in the variety and perfection of our fruits. The best of Scotland's whisky is no doubt superior to ours, but we are already turning out a very fine article, and our beer is equal to England's best. The local wine industry – *pace* Prohibition – is destined to be one of our greatest and most stable money-earners and population-bringers, and the quality of the stuff turned out is improving out of all belief. A generation ago no affluent Australian drank the wine of the country; today no Australian household that drinks anything is complete without a stock of Australian wine, and the movement has little or nothing to do with considerations of price. It is a sheer tribute to merit.

With these few words of introduction I now come to my ideal dinner – a poor thing, perhaps, in the opinion of many critics, but my own. A cocktail can be composed of almost anything in the liquid line, but the basis of most cocktails is gin or vermouth, and both of course are made here – as are all the liqueurs which ordinarily go to the manufacture of cocktails. That settled, let us take up the card and consider the position. Here it is in English as plain as the influence of an alien race in the art of cooking will allow:–

Salted almonds. Olives.

Oysters on the shell.

Beche de Mer soup.

Fresh water Blackfish. Maitre d'Hotel.

Fillet of Beef. Pique: Sauce Bearnaise.

Roast Teal. Port Wine Sauce. Orange Salad.

Ice Pudding.

Devilled Prawns.

Dessert.

Coffee.

Sauterne or Chablis. Burgundy.

Champagne. Cognac.

A little heavy, perhaps, and the bird course might well have been utilised to sustain the whole burden of the meat theme in the composition, but it may stand. Both almond and olive are South Australians.

The oysters should come from Moreton Bay, which produces the finest in Australia. A squeeze of lime – if you can get it – and a suspicion of red pepper; have them on the deep shell, and beware of over-icing.

Beche-de-mer soup, like liquid golden velvet, with two or three pieces of the blue-black 'fish' floating in it, is one of the most delicious compounds known. Australia grows its own turtles in bulk. Beche-de-mer is preferable in the writer's opinion. A score of fishes may be preferred by different readers to the Victorian blackfish, though old-time Melbourneites regarded it as a king among food fish. The Victorian or New South Wales fresh-water trout is a great fish. So are the Hobart trumpeter and the John Dory – a magnificent fish which the trawlers re-introduced to Sydney some years ago. However, as already mentioned, my choice is the blackfish, served up simply with the concoction of butter and chopped herbs that goes so well with other sorts of fried or grilled fish.

The fillet, with its tiny points of fat and its garnishings of peas, carrots, potatoes, etc, will be accompanied by the burgundy, preferably a dry, light type, such as the Hunter River vineyards produce to perfection.

The teal has been chosen as, possibly, even more delicate than our black duck, which has an international reputation. Mark Twain considered the latter equal to America's canvas back duck. Be sure, by the way, that the teal comes from fresh inland waters, and do not cook him too much. The fat juicy breast should gape faintly pink when the knife is plunged into it. But see he is not too raw. The old idea of cooking wild duck by carrying it on a plate through a hot kitchen is nowadays frowned on. And it should not be too high. The custom of 'hanging' a teal for ten days has gone into general disfavor. Salads run in all shapes, but the conventional orange one goes best with any member of the duck family. If a lettuce salad is preferred the lettuces should come from Victoria and the oil and vinegar from South Australia.

All the materials for the most ornate kind of ice pudding may of course be got in any of the States. As for the sparkling wine which would have been opened with the appearance of the bird, the choice would probably lie between South Australia and New South Wales, though Victoria also does very well in this line.

Any dulling of the palate may be banished by the next course of devilled prawns. The sweet, perhaps, has brought a touch of surfeit – these delicate, pink morsels, in their golden bath of fire will refresh eye and appetite alike.

Australian fruits are so many and delicious, from the tropical grenadilla and pine-apple, and the Hunter River grapes and melons, to Victorian peaches, nectarines and oranges and Tasmanian cherries and apples, that it is hard to make a choice. But the dinner should not forget to include the paw-paw, that wonderful natural aid to a good digestion, without which the most perfect of meals is either a nightmare or the prelude to one.

For coffee let us take the fresh, un-chicoried product of the foothills behind Cairns in North Queensland. It should be made in Turkish fashion by pouring hot water on the coffee in an open pot. Bring it three times to the boil, settle the grounds with a dash of cold water, and pour, frothing hot, into the warmed cups. Then, with a glass of South Australian or Victorian cognac, square the jaw firmly, and select and set fire to an Australian cigar. There need be no false patriotism on this question. The local cigar is emphatically not a rival to the product of Havana – yet. It stands, as a matter of fact, in about the same class as Australian claret did, relatively to the claret of France, half a century ago. But at the worst it is no more dreadful than some of the outrages that are smoked appreciatively on the European Continent.

The Victoria Markets Recollected in Tranquillity

Furnley Maurice

Furnley Maurice was the pseudonym of Frank Wilmot (1881–1942), poet
and champion of Australian literature. His Melbourne odes, published as
a book in 1934, take as their subjects events (such as the Royal Show) and
places (such as Victoria Markets) that would have been familiar to most
Melburnians, and are said to represent the first attempt by an Australian
poet to portray city life.

Melbourne Odes, 1934

---

i

Winds are bleak, stars are bright,
Loads lumber along the night:
Looming, ghastly white,
A towering truck of cauliflowers sways
Out of the dark, roped over and packed tight
Like faces of a crowd of football jays.

The roads come in, roads dark and long,
To the knock of hubs and a sleepy song.
Heidelberg, Point Nepean, White Horse,
Flemington, Kellor, Dandenong,
Into the centre from the source.

Rocking in their seats
The worn-out drivers droop
When dawn stirs in the streets
And the moon's a silver hoop;
Come rumbling into the silent mart,

To put their treasure at its heart,
Wagons, lorries, a lame Ford bus,
Like ants along the arms of an octopus
Whose body is all one mouth; that pays them hard
And drives them back with less than a slave's reward.

When Batman first at Heaven's command
Said, 'This is the place for a peanut-stand.'
It must have been grand!

ii

'Cheap today, lady; cheap today!'
Jostling watermelons roll
From fountains of Earth's mothering soul.
Tumbling from box and tray
Rosy, cascading apples play
Each with a glowing auriole
Caught from a split sunray.
'Cheap today, lady, cheap today.'
Hook the carcases from the dray!
(Where the dun bees hunt in droves
Apples ripen in the groves.)

An old horse broods in a Chinaman's cart
While from the throbbing mart
Go cheese and celery, pears and jam
In barrow, basket, bag or pram
To the last dram the purse affords –
Food, food for the hordes.

Shuffling in the driven crush
The souls and the bodies cry,
Rich and poor, skimped and flush,
'Spend or perish. Buy or die!'

Food, food for the hordes!
Turksheads tumble on the boards.

There's honey at the dairy produce stall
Where the strung saveloys festooning fall;
Yielding and yellow, the beautiful butter blocks
Confront the poultryman's plucked Plymouth Rocks.
The butcher is gladly selling,
Chopping and slaughtering, madly yelling.
A bull-like bellow for captured sales;
A great crowd surges around his scales.
Slap down the Joint! The finger point
Wobbles and comes alive,
Springs round to twenty and back to five.

No gracious burbling, nor arts to please,
No hypocritical felicities.
Buy and be damned to you! Sell and be damned also!
Decry the goods, he'll tell you where to go!

To him Creation's total aim
Is selling chops to a doubting dame.
And what will matter his steaks and joints,
The underdone and the overdone,
On the day when the old Earth jumps the points
And swings into the sun?

Along the shadows furtive, lone,
The unwashed terrier carries his weekend bone.
The old horse with a pointed hip
And dangling disillusioned under-lip
Stands in a harvest-home of cabbage leaves
And grieves.
A lady by a petrol case,
With a far-off wounded look in her face
Says, in a voice of uncertain pitch,
'Muffins' or 'crumpets', I'm not sure which.
A pavement battler whines with half a sob,
Ain't anybody got a bloody bob?'
Haunted by mortgages and overdrafts
The old horse droops between the shafts.

A smiling Chinaman upends a bag
And spills upon the bench with thunder-thud
(A nearby urchin trilling the newest rag)
Potatoes caked with loamy native mud.

Andean pinnacles of labelled jam.
The melting succulence of two-toothed lamb.
The little bands of hemp that truss
The succulent asparagus
That stands like tiny sheaves of purple wheat
Ready to eat!
Huge and alluring hams and rashered swine
In circular repetitive design.
Gobbling turkeys and ducks in crates,
Pups in baskets and trays of eggs;
A birdman turns and gloomily relates
His woes to a girl with impossible legs.

When Batman first at Heaven's command
Stuck flagstaffs in this sacred strand . . .
We'll leave all that to the local band.

Rabbits skinned in a pink nude row,
Little brown kidneys out on show;
'Ready for the pot, mum, ready to bake!'
Buy them, devour them for pity's sake
(Trapped, 'neath the moon in a field of dream,
Did anyone hear a bunny scream?)

'Cheap today, lady, cheap today.'
Slimy fish slide off the tray.
Women pondering with a sigh –
'Spend or perish, buy or die!'
Packed with babies and Brussels sprouts,
It's a rickety pram for a woman to shove –
But tell me, lady, whereabouts
Is the long leisure of love?

Multicultural Melbourne

Hal Porter

The Watcher on the Cast-Iron Balcony, the first volume of Hal Porter's autobiographical trilogy, is a minutely detailed and vivid account of his boyhood in a Victorian country town and his teenage ardour for life in the metropolis of Melbourne. Porter's semi-detached style allows the older narrator/interpreter to observe, as if in slow-motion playback, his younger self, the third-person 'he', with all the sophisticated pretensions of youth.

The Watcher on the Cast-Iron Balcony, 1963

The meal, paid for by Uncle John, is invariably – partly affectation, partly because it sounds a sophisticated meal, partly because he loves it – Consommé Julienne, Chicken Maryland, Lemon Pancakes and, stealing a trick from past and Nurse Mawdsley, tea with lemon. This last he does not absolutely enjoy but it is as 'different' – deliberately – as a black tie, hatlessness, streaming hair and nigger-brown cigarettes. He whips up a little contempt for the 'suburban' tastes of the others: Tomato Soup, Roast Lamb, Apricot Tart, and black coffee. Really, I think now, what he likes most about these gatherings are the trickling and splashing noises from the fountain, the thick carpets, the frilled and diaphanous aprons of the lavender-clad waitresses, and the orchestra of three women in brown taffeta palpitatingly playing 'La Paloma', 'Rendez-vous', and 'In a monastery garden', melodious muck he thinks he prefers to the Grieg and Handel he conversationally pretends to love and understand.

Shirking the roast lamb, mint sauce three vegs, apple pie and custard restaurants, he takes to eating and drinking in foreign cafés of which Melbourne, in 1928, has far fewer than today, more authentic places not at all frequented by the general Australian who, in those times, prefers such places as Ambassadors, The Wild Cherry, The Oberon, and The Lattice which is then famous for its enormous wedges of cream-stifled sponge cake and its décor of copper vessels, and piled-up gourds and Turk's Cap pumpkins. He is, indeed, happy to be the one conspicuously blond Australian drinking ouzo or scented Metaxa brandy and eating vine-leaf-wrapped meat-balls at the Greek Club, or shrimps fried in batter at the Japanese *Hoi San Café*. He goes with Max Meldrum and George Bell students to the *Chung Wah Café* in Heffernan Lane, a place not then touristised and, sitting among prostitutes and their Chinese pick-ups, learns to become glib about Chinese menus, adept with chopsticks, and suspiciously knowledgeable about Chinese teas. It needs hardly be stated that his unsuitable choice as favourite is Jasmine Tea. Happy country boy acquiring innocence sip by scented sip!

Always seeking for what, when he was the little watcher on the cast-iron balcony, he knew lay beneath the endless roofs spread before him, some magic place behind the million minute golden panes oiled by the sunset exploding over the ridge of Kensington, he wanders past the florists' shops of the Eastern Market and the shops that sell waiters' white monkey-jackets and chefs' caps and butchers' aprons and the brass pins, hook-and-heart, for grocers' aprons; he wanders Exhibition Street, and comes to the *Café Latin*, and thinks he finds, at the top of the narrow stairs, what he seeks.

At least he is in love again.

He is in love with a café, and for what he can buy – Life – for half a crown. What does he buy that he calls Life? Jazzy frescoes, already dated, even to him. The smell of garlicked salad bowls. Rectangular looking-glasses edged by hat-pegs. A plump and queenly poofter called Flo who sips Strega between the cheap sad tunes he plays on the upright piano from a railed-in platform at the head of the stairs. Vast spotless table-napkins of coarse linen. *Grissini, antipasto, minestrone,* grilled whiting, chicken or lobster *mayonnaise*, Limburger or Gorgonzola, and a bottle-green half-bottle of red or white wine poured from the wickered stoneware jars that line the corridor to the lavatory. Half a crown! Two and Six!

Sydney Grillrooms

Kenneth Slessor

There were good restaurants in Sydney, too, in the 1920s and 1930s, as poet and journalist Kenneth Slessor (1901–1971) recalled. By all accounts Slessor not only enjoyed good dinners but was a very competent cook. In *A Man of Sydney* (1977), Douglas Stewart praised his hospitality, his manners and his table. 'His cold turtle soup in summer or hot toheroa with a dab of cream on it in winter were flawless; his roast beef was cooked to just the right shade of rareness; the ice-cream that followed was found to be swimming luxuriously in maraschino; and, after the assorted cheeses, there were walnuts, in the best English tradition, to bring out the full flavour of his port. He did all this not only because he appreciated good food; ... but also because, in dining as in poetry, he always strove for perfection.'

Bread and Wine, 1970

For those who could afford them, the three hotels offered other pleasures besides those of drinking beer at 6d a glass and enjoying the succulent free counter lunches. In Pfahlert's and the Café Français there were dim religious grillrooms of a kind no longer seen in Sydney, filled with the smoke and splutter of mutton chops and T-bone steaks, sizzling over red-hot charcoal which now and then burst into flame as the fat fell down. The tables were large and solid, the chairs leather-padded, the napkins snow-white and folded into intricate frills, and in the centre of each table there was a circular mahogany cruet-stand which spun when you revolved it, presenting a merry-go-round of Worcester sauce, anchovy sauce, mushroom sauce and other pungencies.

For luncheon at the Café Français, you entered the grillroom, your appetite already honed by the almost unbearably tempting smoke and smell, and selected your chops or steak from the meats laid out before the fire. You left instructions for the cooking and then passed through the swinging half-doors to the adjacent main bar. However, the 'back bar' boys seldom tasted these delights, even though the best beefsteak dish cost no more than five or six shillings. They preferred the beer and counter-lunch (sausages, pies, brawn, pigs' trotters, pickled onions) of 'The Lane'.

In spite of its vestigial flamboyance, for all the survivals of its native sauciness, King's Cross is not the King's Cross I remember from the 20s and 30s. Its people, certainly, are noisy, irreverent, crackpot and emotional, but they are not the kind of people who used to charm and horrify and puzzle me when I lived in Old Hampton Court. Where have they gone? Where has my digestion gone? Where has my hair gone?

Last week I dug up an old book of jingles which I wrote about 'Darlinghurst' over 30 years ago. In those days, Darlinghurst meant nothing but King's Cross –

> Where the stars are lit by Neon,
>> Where the fried potato fumes,
> And the ghost of Mr Villon
>> Still inhabits single rooms,
> And the girls lean out from heaven
>> Over lightwells, thumping mops,
> While the gent in 57
>> Cooks his pound of mutton chops . . .

and also:

> Where the Black Marias clatter
>> And peculiar ladies nod,
> And the flats are rather flatter
>> And the lodgers rather odd,
> Where the night is full of dangers
>> And the darkness full of fear,
> And eleven hundred strangers
>> Live on aspirin and beer.

The fried potato has given way to deep freeze or instant food, all mutton has become 'lamb' (just as all fowls have become 'chicken'), the Black Maria seems to have disappeared with its nickname, and the 1100 strangers living on aspirin and beer have proliferated into 11,000 strangers living on aspirin and beer and also on smoked eel, metwurst, goulash, salami, Vienna schnitzels, benzedrine and tranquillisers . . .

As for the food, it has been said that the postwar influx of Europeans has widened our taste and improved our cooking. This strikes me as boloney in the full sense of the Bologna sausage. It is true that King's Cross is crowded today with restaurants and cafés of a dozen nationalities – Dutch, Hungarian, German, Russian, Indian, Italian, Swedish, Indonesian and others – but this is no evidence of better food. Since the only two great cuisines of the world are French and Chinese, both of which flourished in Sydney before the war, the new tides of Slavs and Balts and middle or southern Europeans have merely imposed the exigencies of their sparse national larders on the Australian menu. They have contributed a number of sausages as well as a number of ways of disguising veal. But anyone who believes they have improved Australian eating is clearly ignorant of the state of Sydney's restaurants in the first quarter of the century. The claim is preposterous to anyone who remembers the glories of Monsieur Lievain's Paris House, Stewart Dawson's Ambassadors, the first Romano's, Pearson's fish-café and Watson's Paragon, the Cavalier in King Street, the Café Français in George Street, Petty's Hotel and a dozen more dining-rooms, all now vanished. I find little compensation today in walking through King's Cross and looking at the spaghetti-bars, the hamburger-counters and the lines of electrically 'barbecued' chickens rotating in their glass coffins.

Steak and Eggs

Lennie Lower

Still in the 1930s, at the other end of the spectrum were the 'greasy spoons', low-budget cafés (frequently with milk bars) often run by Greek families. These were the favoured dining-out choice of 'suburban battler' and unashamed chauvinist Jack Gudgeon, a character created by humorist and journalist Lennie Lower (1903–1947). In this episode from *Here's Luck*, Jack tells the story of how he and his son, Stan, met the two girls who, known simply as Steak and Eggs, feature in their subsequent adventures.

Where in this world will you find anything more sustaining, more inspiring, more satisfying, more invigorating, more absolutely culminating and fulfilling than steak and eggs? Nowhere.

As I said to Stanley at the Greek restaurant, after we had given our order: 'Stanley, when the poor sailor returns from foreign lands, from long, lonely cruises, from sleepless nights and toil-filled days; when at last he sets foot in his home port – what does he do?'

'Gets drunk,' said Stanley.

The boy was right.

'What does he do next?' I asked.

'Father, I'm surprised at you talking about that. You know very well what – '

'No,' I cut in firmly. 'I don't mean that. I mean, well damitall he orders steak and eggs, doesn't he?'

'Yes, of course.'

'Well, why didn't you say so at first? Trying to confuse your poor old father!'

'What,' I continued, 'does the explorer do when he returns to civilisation after long months in the jungle – what does he crave?'

'Steak and eggs.'

'Right. When the starving wanderer, lost in the desert, first starts to lose his reason; what does he see?'

'Steak and eggs.'

'What does the acquitted co-respondent rush for as soon as he leaves the divorce court?'

'Steak and eggs.'

I was satisfied. I leaned back in my chair and gazed around me. Two young women of the gimme type were gazing with bright, lizard eyes at our table.

'Who are those girls over there, Stan?' I asked.

'Steak and eggs,' replied Stan in a flat, toneless voice.

Dockside Eating

F.E. Baume

F.E. (Eric) Baume (1900–1967) wrote several novels, but he was more successful and certainly better known as a Sydney journalist and newspaper editor. An outspoken and typically controversial radio and television commentator, he became a household name in the 1950s and 1960s. This extract from F.E. Baume's *Burnt Sugar* describes a dining scene vastly different to that of Melbourne and Sydney. At the north Queensland port of Eulaville, nationalistic Irish and Italian workers each patronise their own culinary cultures, at the same time maligning and mistrusting the other's foods.

Burnt Sugar, 1934

Eulaville regarded the sea as its natural outlet and friend; and the sea did a service to the community by separating Australian from foreign, sheep from goats. Walk out to the smaller cane holdings within a mile of the towns and you found another country, other tongues, strange food and oaths, strangely weak when compared with the meatier Australian product. But take the tiny two-foot gauge train from the town (which was inland, on the river) to the port (which was eight miles down, sheltered by great green hills, faced by a rambling estuary), and you were, somehow, back under the Flag. That is, you found yourself at the Port restaurants and eating-houses which could (and did) put on the following bill of fare – three courses for a shilling:

Soup
Irish Stew or Lamb's Fry
or
Corned Beef and Carrots
Roast Mutton
and
Apple Pie or Steamed Pudding
Bread. Butter. Tea. Coffee 1d extra.

In such eating places you sat comfortably and smoked a pipe without finding the blue smoke, oily, sour and rank, of an Italian cigarro. You found opposite you a Bill or a Patrick or a Wullie, eating comfortably from the back of a knife, finishing Irish stew with great slabs of bread laid flat on the plate so that the last skerrick of gravy, or the tiniest slice of parboiled potato, should not be lost. On two tables you would find card games alive after the evening meal. There would be crib or euchre; perhaps an odd game of five hundred, if the tally clerks – the social side of the Port – happened to be eating out.

Usually the proprietor was his own waiter. His voice at the slide was a tonic and an appetiser; his dealing with drunks or non-payers an art in itself. Yet he was always good-natured, and his own private slate for Tims or Denises or Macs was elastic-sided and certainly run at a discount of, say, forty per cent.

Here men discussed the last race and the next; the proprietor was the arbiter and the worst tipster; here a man's conversation with his eating partner was carried on as etiquette, with the proprietor listening and leaning purely as a matter of politeness.

Here cotton singlets and dungarees were as good as white collars and tweed, or pith helmets and ducks; here was the comfortable smell of boiled flesh and roast flesh and fatty stews and venerable butter. Here a man could ask for more pastry than pie – fruit – and get it; or insist that the potatoes were not brown enough and be answered in friendly argument.

Here men talked of wages and ships; of old-time prize-fights and present Commonwealth policy. Here there were no women; no artists or musicians, bank clerks or poets. A man walked outside to blow his nose in his own way with his fingers, but he would not spit on the homely floor.

He ate what he craved and believed in. Mrs Cassidy, for six years the cook, knew what he wanted, as she had known what three husbands, now shriven with bell, book and candle, had eaten and insisted on eating before they passed to Purgatory (from where they left for Heaven, she said, on the first Saturday after their death).

When a woman has genuflected before the death-beds of three hearty labouring husbands (wharf or road) she knows something of the lining of the stomach of each and of all men.

Thus the watersiders fed (if they had no homes, which few of them had) at the Port.

Over the way from Burke's Meals Three Course a shilling, Domenico Pura set up his cafe for the Others. But there was not the trade for him in the Port. In the two streets and on the wharves it was difficult to hear a tongue different from English. Domenico served canalone, long meat-filled cubes of pasta; gnocchi, and risotto, minestrone and octopus. Often the Irishmen of the village would pass and sniff loudly as they ambled by the restaurant.

The blue smoke of burnt olive oil, the faint stench of garlic, the aroma of veal fried in egg, upset them. Their distaste was real. They were the last ditch, they said. Old Padrais Finnehan, who had second sight and would go into trances when drunk, so long as he was able to anticipate more whisky from his audience, assured the boys in Burke's that only the Irish, and boiled bacon, and cabbage (Mick Burke's special that night, which had created a satisfying flatulence in twenty ample-girthed wharf labourers) could withhold 'thim Eyetalian oilburners' from ownership, not only of Australia, but of the Irish Free State.

His audience, rumbling with cabbage, agreed vociferously, yet without ill-feeling.

Had not young Merro climbed down Central Wharf and held Bernard Dowd safe from the drowning death which faced him until help had come? Was not old Mother Sarti the finest midwife outside County Clare? Weren't Timothy Clark's twins alive only because she knew how to stop a bleeding?

Here at the Port the Italians and the rest talked and mixed as friends. Only had they been forced to eat together would there have been Notes, Ultimatums and War.

Tomato Sauce

Angela Thirkell

Trooper to the Southern Cross is a fictionalised account of the 1920 voyage to Australia on board a troop ship taken by Angela Thirkell (1890–1961) with her new Australian husband, George Thirkell. It is George's fictional counterpart who is speaking in this extract. Angela Thirkell eventually returned to England in 1939 and produced a string of successful novels with English settings. Crocheted sauce-bottle covers similar to the ones described here can still be found in Australian country museums and historic houses.

Trooper to the Southern Cross, 1934

It was near the end of the war, and Celia and I got married and were living in Leeds. We have never had a quarrel yet. Sometimes we both get a bit nervy, but we'd always make it up before things got too far. The nearest we came to a quarrel in those days was about the tomato sauce. Of course at home the Mater used to make ours, dozens of bottles, and it lasted us right round the year. Many's the good meal I've had when I was a kid, chops, or sometimes a parrot pie if we boys had been shooting, and plenty of the Mater's tomato sauce. Of course we lived quite simply up on the station, and it wasn't till I grew up and went to Sydney that I found you oughtn't to put tomato sauce in the soup. But a few meals at the Australia, when I could afford it, soon showed me that for soup you should use Worcestershire sauce. I've not much use for this etiquette myself, but there are a few things it's useful to know.

They don't seem to understand etiquette so much in England. I naturally like things nice about the house, so after we had been in our lodgings a few days, I asked Celia for the tomato sauce. You would have thought I was asking for the Bank of England, the way she took it. She never seemed to have heard of it and said you only had it with veal cutlets. Of course I know things are a bit different in England; for instance the way you get your mustard mixed in the cafés. I know the cafés and the tea-shops in Sydney pretty well, and they always served their mustard just as it comes out of the tin. The other way seems to me extravagant and not half so tidy. But anyway, Celia got me a bottle of sauce, and we had chops one night and some nice fried steaks of fish the next night, and what with that and the bacon and eggs at breakfast, the bottle was finished. So we had to get some more. Celia soon got the hang of it, and she makes it herself now, and it's nearly as good as the Mater's.

My Aunt Minnie at Pott's Point is a splendid worker, and she gave Celia some lovely bits of crochet work she had done. There was a cover for a tea cosy, and some doilies for cake, all beautifully crocheted, but the best of all was a white crochet cover for the tomato sauce bottle. You put the bottle in, and pulled it tight round the neck and tied it with a piece of ribbon, and it had the words 'Tomato Sauce' worked into the crochet. I must say Celia did appreciate it enormously, and she put it away for fear of getting it dirty. So Aunt Minnie worked her two or three more. They can be boiled with the laundry on Mondays, and just give that artistic touch to the table that I like. And Celia deserves it all. She is the best little pal a man could have.

Pudding for Christmas

Ruth Park

Swords and Crowns and Rings won for Ruth Park the prestigious Miles Franklin Award for 1977. It spans the period from 1907 to 1930, when the depression had just started. Ruth Park describes scenes in the Sydney Domain when as many as 400 would stand in line on Sundays for free soup, bread and coffee, and evokes the humiliation of families evicted from their homes, their household belongings sold from under them. This is the Sydney that greets Jackie Hanna, a dwarf, and his stepfather Jerry MacNunn ('the Nun') in the final part of the novel.

Swords and Crowns and Rings, 1977

As Christmas neared, various religious and civil charity depots dispensed Christmas cheer to the needy. There were haunting scenes of crowds queuing in the sun for five or six hours waiting for a depot to open. Jerry had stood in a few of them. He was embarrassed to do so, but his wistful longing for a shirt with an unfrayed collar was too much for him. Sometimes he thought he might even land a pair of boots.

He sincerely enjoyed the deplorable hassle when a mob, driven wild by heat and impatience, rushed a depot and caused a ton of potatoes, four hundred cabbages, and nine hundred pumpkins to vanish in seven minutes flat.

'I timed them,' said Jerry to Jack. 'There was not a bloody thing left but the do-gooders, and they woulda snitched them if they coulda eaten them. But they was all wire and gristle.' He added, 'I could do with a toothful of Christmas duff, couldn't you, me old Jack? Crikey, your mum used to make a corker pudden.'

So they walked all the way out to Glebe Town Hall, where a Christian Ladies' Guild was giving out Christmas puddings to genuine cases.

They arrived good and early, and Jack thought it was a bit unnatural that there were no more than twenty or thirty people around the door.

A curdled-looking fellow looked over Jerry and Jack's susso cards penetratingly, hoping to find that they were out of date or fraudulent. At last he said reluctantly, 'I can only give you single men's puddens, you know.'

'Go on, show us the married men's puddings,' urged Jack, who was beginning to feel a bit of a devil. 'We want to see what we're missing.'

The clerk sneered, and thrust two muslin-wrapped black grapefruit across the counter. They were as hard as boulders.

The clerk chopped out a few words. 'You boil 'em up,' he said.

'Merry Christmas,' said Jack, but the man made no answer.

'Ah well,' said the Nun forgivingly, 'maybe he's a Jew.'

They walked down towards Broadway, through the old wide streets bordered with crumbling houses, shops squeezed between them, run-down-working-class hotels. The Nun felt wambly. They had had no breakfast but a cup of tea.

'Might have a gnaw at me pudding,' he said. 'Just a taste, like.'

'Has to be boiled up,' said Jack. 'Smiley said so.'

The Nun peeled off the muslin. 'Smells good,' he said. 'Spice or something.' He took a sacramental mouthful.

'Single men's puddings!' scoffed Jack. 'Did you ever hear such damned rubbish?' He turned around. 'How's the Christmas cheer, Dad?'

'Like a gobful of black kack,' said the Nun. He spat it out, and bowled the remains of the pudding over a wall. 'Flaming sod!' he barked with irrational rage. 'They think anything is good enough for us, even if it would drop a pig in its tracks.'

'Ah, knock it off, Dad,' said Jack. 'It's only a bloody old spotted dick. Don't do your block.'

'It's not only the bloody old spotted dick,' cried the Nun, looking wild. 'It's everything. I'm fed up, boy!'

'On the wing!' said Jackie swiftly, and he showily passed his single man's pudding to his father, who caught it automatically and drop-kicked it down the street.

So they toed it down the footpath, Jack fancily dribbling it, the Nun occasionally getting in a neat one with his better foot, both of them letting out yips and cheers which made a passer-by say reproachfully, 'Yous unemployed don't appreciate nothing.'

The pudding survived for a couple of hundred yards, and then Jack skilfully punted it through the door of a fish-and-chips shop. There were brays of panic from within, as though the wrecked and wobbling comestible were horse dung. Jackie and his father discreetly vanished up an alley.

Table Talk

Norman Lindsay

Best known as an artist and illustrator, Norman Lindsay (1879–1969) was also a prolific writer, with eleven novels to his credit plus critical essays and children's books – most notably, *The Magic Pudding* (1918). *Pan in the Parlour*, from which this extract is taken, expresses many of Lindsay's ideas on the connection between sexuality and creativity and contrasts the prim and pedantic Gilbert with the pleasure-loving Tarran who 'in the character of a gourmet ... refused to annoy his throat with a stiff collar, and wore a soft shirt with his dinner suit'.

Pan in the Parlour, 1934

Dinner was served in the smaller dining room off the verandah, with doors open to a background of blue night beyond the gold-shaded candles which illuminated only a circle of polished table sparkling with glass and silver. In this charming setting all were aware that life was about to become perfect; all except Gilbert, who endured with difficulty the way everybody settled down at table as if they intended spending a week there. Like all people of a fanatic industry in one métier, he was incapable of patience with any other. Eating was an intolerable nuisance to him. He either talked and ate nothing, or ate with gastric recklessness to get the job over.

But a dinner designed by Irene was no ten-minute affair of snatching a few mouthfuls to talk on. At the very hors-d'oeuvre, Gilbert groaned to think of the synthetic sequence of dishes to follow, and got up to open bottles. By opening enough wine to last the company a week he dodged the oysters and the soup, making a nuisance of himself to the two girls who served dinner. 'Leave that,' he said sternly, if one offered to lay hands on a bottle.

Glances of despisal from these minions left the office of butler to him . . .

'This Vouvray is delicious,' said Tarran. 'Where did you get it, Gilbert?'

'Oh, picked it up somewhere, I suppose.'

'It came from Paris,' said Irene. 'I can always follow Gilbert's movements abroad by the books and bottles he sends home. They are the two things he can't resist buying, and he never stays here long enough to read the books and he never drinks anything but whisky which he buys here.'

'There's a dream of leisured ease behind it somewhere,' said Tarran. 'Booze and books. But he'll never attain it while he drinks whisky; spirits are a slovenly trick for getting the job done in a hurry.'

It was notable that these comments on Gilbert were indulged in his presence with the effect of discussing him behind his back. Guests caught that inflection from Irene, who annotated Gilbert's personality in the tone of an indulgent mother talking about a precocious child. Beyond a bothered glance in her direction Gilbert never acknowledged this gratuitous service to the revealing of his being. Perhaps he was unaware of it. Just at present he urgently desired to analyse the destructive effect of abstract nouns. Sentences in smoke faded to shapelessness in the chatter about him. How may the spoken word clarify itself in a gabble of spoken words? On his right Olga was saying to Reggie,

'How does that man do it gravely solemn always with a fresh affair and quite undaunted when found out you heard about the earring?'

'No, what was that?'

'Found by Mrs Frampole coming home from Sydney in Peter's bed and instantly recognised the housemaid's and held under Peter's very nose he calmly said, "A careless slut, you never know what bed that girl's been sleeping in."' . . .

Gilbert's powers of attention withered under such talk. He fiddled with knives and forks, pushed plates about, ate olives and salted almonds and any other trifle that looked least like food, lit cigarettes and let them go out on his plate, appeared always about to burst into talk and was dammed up again by chatter.

They exasperated him, these people who tricked life of its need for torture. By what superior cunning had they acquired tolerance for a system under which he squirmed? Somewhere under their disarticulated nonsense there must exist the conviction of a concrete earth, to be sought and feared. Not that he really wished to tear off their masks and find what real entity between desire and disgust lurked there; all he required was the flat surface of their attention on which to project his own.

The dinner went on and on and Gilbert went round filling glasses to try to push it on a little faster. An empty glass was the only thing that abstracted his abstraction from dining. From such a blank he now emerged to hear Tarran saying,

'Have you tried braising them with raisins, prunes, young carrots and shallots, a head of garlic and of course bacon?'

'Yes, but I rather think I prefer them cooked in cream, served with salsify,' said Irene.

'The only really beastly way of cooking chicken is with olive oil,' said Laurence. 'In my opinion the perfect method is to grill them – '

Gilbert bit savagely at a stalk of celery and demanded attention.

'You people are the limit. Not content with eating food you talk about it too. A wretched subject of conversation.'

'Nonsense, it's almost as fascinating as the only other fascinating subject of conversation,' said Laurence.

'Oh, one's a decent lust and the other isn't.'

'All lust is decent,' said Tarran.

'Guzzling isn't.'

'Why not! Guzzling absorbs the lesser desires, mental, moral and physical.'

'Exactly; the belly is an abyss which destroys all energy. The Greeks knew that.'

'Yes, the Greeks built their entire effort on indigestion. They destroyed the stomach in order to set up an anxiety neurosis about work.'

'Fat is – ' began Gilbert; but Irene said smoothly, 'Gilbert's dream is to live on cheese and water biscuits. He did live on them once: for nearly three days.'

'– the death of intellect, as you damn well know, Tarran,' said Gilbert.

'I hope so,' said Tarran. 'Nothing like a padding of adipose deposit to absorb pinpricks. I look forward to guzzling myself into a thoroughly silly old man.'

Gilbert charged an opening in the defences of drivel. 'Look here, Tarran, you know that all overdone sensualities destroy their mental image. That explains why no guzzler can have an intellect. The abstract noun is –'

'Gilbert dear, I beg you to make yourself at home,' said Irene sweetly.

Gilbert swallowed a denunciation of the abstract noun and drowned it in whisky. As a meal, it sufficed him. He went to the sideboard for another bottle. By that device he reached the door to the verandah and thereby escaped to the library.

Etiquette Without Tears

Lennie Lower

Humorist Lennie Lower proposes a larrikin's version of etiquette, making fun of seemingly senseless table rituals. This is one of the many pieces he wrote in the 1930s and 1940s for publications such as the *Australian Women's Weekly*, *Telegraph* and *Smith's Weekly*.

The Illustrated Treasury of Australian Humour, 1988

There has been some talk about the deplorable manners of the present-day male. Also the lack of etiquette displayed in Australia. I intend to rectify all this. If the ignorant and boorish reader will get these few points off by heart, he or she will be able to hold his or her head or heads up in any company.

It is the little details that count. At table, for instance, it is not good form to jam the lid down tight on the golden syrup after you have used it. Someone else may have to struggle with it later.

The careful hostess will see that the jam is tastefully displayed. A little crêpe paper around the tins will easily fix this. She will also avoid having peas for dinner if possible. Peas are very annoying, and, if they are a bit hard, one can only fork two or three at a time, and the mental concentration necessary and the monotony spoils a good dinner. If one is dining out, and one is given peas and mashed potatoes, one is fairly safe. Give the peas a good coating of mashed potato before forking. They stick much better. Take care, however, not to run out of potato before the peas are finished.

Many people are confused by the multiplicity of knives, forks and spoons set before them, and are inclined to make a haphazard selection, thus making goats of themselves. Remain calm and do the thing systematically. First of all, use up the spoons; secondly, go through the forks; then wind up on the knives. In the case of wine glasses and so forth, select the biggest and stick to it. I do this myself invariably, and have never been tossed out of a dining-room yet.

If you are asked to pass the butter, always remember to pass the plate as well.

When eating fruit such as watermelon, the seeds should be removed from the mouth with the hand and placed in the pocket or handbag. At important functions it is best to swallow them, as it saves mucking about.

At the conclusion of the dinner the hostess gives the signal to rise. I am not sure how this is done, but I should think that a green flag waved two or three times above the head should be sufficient, or at an informal affair, just a cheery remark, 'Now, come on! You've had enough,' would suffice.

I forgot to mention that where the guest of honour is a man, he should take the hostess's arm when entering the dining-room. If the hostess is very far gone, another gentleman may hold the other arm, a third gentleman going in front with the legs.

Rum should not be drunk with fish, as it spoils the taste of the rum. (Not that I've ever had a drink with a fish – don't run away with that idea!)

Now for the other odds and ends of etiquette. A gentleman should not talk to a lady with his hands in his pocket – unless she's his wife, in which case it's unavoidable.

Best Dinner Ever

Norman Lindsay

In *Age of Consent* Norman Lindsay continues his discussion of sensuality
and creativity, its chief character being an artist, Bradly Mudgett. Podson
is an ex-bank clerk who arrives, unexpected and uninvited, at Bradly's
beachside shack – and stays. Miss Marley is a solitary neighbour at
Margoola Beach. An opportunistic idler, Podson nevertheless epitomises
the principle so abhorred by Gilbert of the previous Lindsay piece, that
talking about food and drink enhances the pleasures of the table.

Age of Consent, 1938

She came in now, breathless, to announce dinner, her apron discarded
for a toilet confessing to elbow sleeves and a chaste expanse of bare
neck to enhance her pearls. Much attention had been given to the
elaborate coiling-up of her hair, in which, with trepidation, Miss
Marley had impaled an imitation red rose.

But Podson was only an appendage to his belly just then, and was
goggling beatitude at the table, set with the best of Miss Marley's
glass and silver on a spotless cloth, and under a pink lampshade, a
bottle of Sauterne, oysters served, and soup in its tureen. He made
a luscious sound of sucking, seating himself and rubbing his hands to
sustain impatience while Miss Marley took her chair. For the moment
speech failed him, so active were his gastric juices. The belly god in
him was passionately aroused. The pink glow of the lamp gave an
apostolic and holy air to his meek whiskers and his brushed-back
hair, a little sprouting at the ends, through misadventures of clipping.
Peppering and lemon-juicing at speed, he forked up an oyster, absorbed
it, ejaculated, 'Exquisite,' and instantly forked up another.

That was the key of his chanting all through dinner. He concentrated attention entirely on the food, talking about it while guzzling
it, on the hedonistic principle of enhancing felicity by announcing it.

Whitebait followed the soup, roast chicken the whitebait, served
with bacon, crisp roast potatoes and green peas. Podson ate three-
quarters of it. The sweet was a caramel custard and the savoury pâté
on toast.

Miss Marley pecked at her food, too agitated to eat after the strenuous anxiety of cooking, and now excited by Podson's extravagant appreciation of her art as cook, at which she simpered a modest depreciation.

'I'm terribly afraid that the chicken could have done with a tiny bit longer in the oven.'

'Absolutely *no*. Cooked to the minute. Best cooked chicken I ever ate.'

'The potatoes are *hardly* crisp enough.'

'Crisped to *per*fection.'

'I was so worried about the peas. So hard to get young peas at this season.'

'Peas are *per*fection. Melt in the mouth.'

In the front room at last Podson reclined his over-stuffed belly on the over-stuffed couch, and loosened the top button of his trousers, and oozed repletion, while Miss Marley made coffee. When that arrived, there was a box of fifty cigarettes on the tray too, and Podson made the gesture of one who accords reverence to a final benediction. 'I might have known you'd do the perfect thing,' he said, and rose, and took Miss Marley's hand and solemnly kissed it, so fluttering her at this regal act of courtesy that she could hardly hold the coffee-pot steady. Podson lit a cigarette and got his belly back on the couch and there confessed that life had no more gifts to bestow.

'Exquisite,' he said. 'First decent smoke for a month. Best dinner I ever ate in my life. And mind you, I've eaten dinners . . . best that money could buy.'

Chinese–Australian

F.E. Baume

Eulaville, the setting for F.E. Baume's *Burnt Sugar,* is a fictional north Queensland port town serving the mining and sugar cane industries of the hinterland and home to an odd assortment of nationalities – Irish, Italian and Chinese among them.

Cora Wong Yip announced her betrothal to Henry Kee that night after supper, and Mario felt frozen and afraid. He had been the only one present, except the family. For minutes at a time old man Wong Yip had spoken Cantonese instead of English, pausing from time to time to pick some delicacy from a centre dish for Mario. Otherwise he treated Mario exactly as he would have treated Charlie, except that he spoke to him in English. Mario, well versed in the Chinese fashion of eating, was unafraid of the food. Noodles swimming in soup; duck – boned and roasted – in a side dish; soy sauce, brown and pungent; succulent Northern Queensland barramundi, fried and swimming in a rich sauce of pineapple chunks, bamboo shoots and mushrooms brought preserved from China; tea in tiny cups scented with roses; prawns done in a batter as only Cora could do them. Mario could never forget, later, the picturesque comfort of the Chinese home set in a European's country, the food looking fantastic in a room in which the pictures were photographs of Australian beauty spots, and the calendar, high over the low, grateless mantelpiece, from a firm of stock and station agents. Sometimes old man Wong Yip would find a morsel of food tasteless on his chopsticks (which Mario tried always, if unsuccessfully, to use). He would turn from his soy sauce to a jar of Australian mustard; and he would fill his long pipe with its tiny bowl, after the meal, with tobacco grown almost within sight of Eulaville's main street.

On the wall facing the old man was a decorated Anzac scroll he had obtained during the war; near it hung a photograph of William Morris Hughes.

Punch cartoons of the Kaiser and Little Willie were neatly framed; a pigtail, cut off in 1911, was here as an everlasting relic in a long glass case, backed with sandalwood, which the old man had had made for him in Townsville after Sun Yat Sen had cut off the strength of the Manchus by lopping off the queues of their Chinese subjects. An harmonium, treasured gift and remembrance of his long-dead wife, who had saved her soul once she found she could live in comfort with a Chink, stood near the door; Cora's golf clubs lay idly in a corner; Charlie's tennis racquets Anglicised another corner; yet above them were long strips of paper, letters received from numerous and entirely indigent relations from China's middle country, who seldom, if ever, failed to receive some gift or other when they wrote to their relative

The Man Who Owns The Earth. And around the cosy, cool room was evidenced the woman-presence of Cora. She was there in every fold of a curtain, every set of an armchair, every poise of a vased flower.

The Barbecue

Colin Thiele

Much has been said about the Australian barbecue and its pride of place in our national culture, but few writers have managed to convey its sounds and smells as realistically as Colin Thiele in this extract from *Labourers in the Vineyard*, set in the Barossa Valley of the later 1930s.

Labourers in the Vineyard, 1970

The barbecue was already sizzling when he arrived in the Lindners' yard. Sudden flares of fire shot up under the iron grill, and the air writhed with the hiss and hot squirt of flame and fat – a furious rushing together of sound, half gurgle, half gas, an explosion of sausages bursting their skins, oozing and flowering red-grey mince from fork-holes and dripping tacky gobbets of it over the wire mesh. Ossie Grope stood by with a huge homemade wire fork in his hand, prodding and worrying the little inferno. Under the thrusts of flame and fork the chops slowly curled and blackened, the sausages twisted, swelled, bloated, contorted and shrank, till Ossie was able to skewer them dexterously and flip them on to huge slabs of buttered bread. The tang of fat and smoke and grilling meat hung in the air, tingled the nostrils of the little crowd who cried and jostled, juggling hot chops from hand to hand, dribbling red sauce down their chins, gnawing and sucking at bones, and wiping the sticky slick from their fingers on to their tongues, handkerchiefs, and trousers.

Ossie saw Kurt arriving. He transfixed a big leg-chop on one of the wire tynes and, couching the long fork under his arm like a tournament lance, rushed at Kurt with a great yell.

'Have a chop, old man! Straight in the bread basket!'

There was a general shout of welcoming laughter. Young Vic, a hero-worshipper of Kurt's since the last great Festival ride, danced and held himself in excited delight as the two men tussled good-humouredly for a second until Kurt wrenched off the chop and hastily clapped it between two hunks of bread.

'I like it in the bread-basket, Os,' he said. 'But I generally chew it first.'

Another shout of laughter went up, and with everyone offering him salt, sauce and advice he was quickly carried into the mill of movement and revelry.

Fried Mutton Chops

Patrick White

The characteristically Australian odour of grilled chops – the appetising aroma of charred flesh tempered by the acrid pungency of burnt fat – hangs around the novels of Patrick White (1912–1990) almost as if part and parcel of the Australian environment. Perhaps it was; in her autobiography *I Sang for My Supper* (1999), food writer Margaret Fulton tells of her experience in the late 1950s, descending towards the coast while driving back towards Sydney, and being greeted by the collective smell of Sunday lamb roast from hundreds of suburban households.

The Eye of the Storm, 1973

'What do you want for breakfast?'

'There you've got me. Whatever they have.'

'Men eat charred chops,' Dorothy reminded him with every sign of gravity.

She even produced from out of a fly-proof cupboard a dishful of drought-fed, mutilated chops, and held one up, not for him to laugh at, mercifully he realised at the last moment. 'Rory himself does practically all the outside work,' Dorothy said; and let the chop fall back on the pile.

'Well,' he said, 'I'll have a chop, if that's what you advise. Or two.'

The Princesse de Lascabanes actually knew what ought to done. Not only was she grilling the chops, so the stench told him, she was melting a lump of dripping in an enormous blackened pan, to fry up a mound of grey cold potato laced with ribbons of pale cold cabbage.

The blue fumes, the spitting, then the revolver firing a blank at memory, brought the image jerking to life. 'You know – ' he wanted somebody to share it, 'we might be on our – in digs up north – doing for ourselves. Before anybody knew we existed.' Encouraged by the fug of sentiment, he moved in on her and squeezed a buttock.

The princess did not like it. 'Watch the grill!' she shouted. 'See if the chops are far enough gone.'

They looked infernal. 'They should be. They're writhing.'

In her irritation, she pushed him aside, to stoop, to peer, to frown: her recently contracted partnership with life made her as damn humourless as she had been when a girl. 'A tough chop is easier to swallow if frizzled,' she announced with bossy assurance.

Her opinion of him was probably as low as Sheila's or Enid's. Faced with his trio of contemptuous women, what he desired most, as ageing man and precarious actor, was respect rather than admiration.

Dorothy at least handed him a plateful of food, all the better for being primitive and mountainous: he tucked in, devouring with particular appetite the charred fat round the edges of the chops and those bits of the fried-up veg which had stuck to the pan. He had forgotten something, and Dorothy pushed the bottle at him to test his reaction to ritual. She stood watching obliquely, and only turned away, whether hissing or sighing it was difficult to tell, on seeing him consecrate amorphous matter, first with a turgid clot or two, followed by an ejaculation of authentic, plopping red; while the act transformed him into a boy, greedy for life as much as food, as he watched an old rain-soaked drover still sitting in this same kitchen chewing the greasy mass of tucker a boss's cook had doled out as charity.

Sauce and Seduction

Ross Campbell

This piece on the aphrodisiacal properties of tomato sauce is taken from *An Urge to Laugh*, the autobiography of journalist and humorist Ross Campbell. Campbell is familiar to generations of Australians through his regular features in the *Australian Women's Weekly* in the late 1950s and

1960s describing life at Oxalis Cottage and the adventures of Theodora, Lancelot, Little Nell and Baby Pip.

An Urge to Laugh, 1981

His wife, who was also of stately appearance, kept a maternal eye on the boarders. Though generally benign, Mrs Littlejohn caused dismay by banishing tomato sauce from the boarders' dining room. The reason she gave was that it 'heated the blood of the boys'.

Tomato sauce was a traditional item on Melbourne tables. The most popular brands were Rosella, which had a gaudy picture of a parrot on the label, and White Crow. When helping myself to White Crow tomato sauce I wondered what was the connection between this bird and the red liquid in the bottle. Possibly the rarity of white crows was meant to suggest that the sauce was of freakish excellence.

Nobody dared to ask Mrs Littlejohn why she believed tomato sauce to be an aphrodisiac. Perhaps one of the senior boarders, inflamed by an overdose of White Crow, had made lascivious advances to a house-maid. Or Dr Littlejohn himself may have been too pressing in his conjugal demands after looking on the Rosella when it was red.

Her ban on the popular condiment had the opposite effect to what she intended. I was told that dissolute boarders would take a furtive swig of tomato sauce before going to romantic assignations in the back seats of the local picture theatre.

Dinner and Dancing

Michael Terry

It is unusual that in 1939 a magazine devoted to marine matters, *The Trident*, should feature an extensive survey of Australian restaurants – albeit only Sydney and Melbourne restaurants. Given the rarity of such accounts, Michael Terry's piece is even more valuable, not only for details of menus and prices but also for tips on coping with the draconian licensing laws: 'one has to "bring in" or risk getting "taken in" to the arms of the law.'

You may be told we have to dine at 6.00 pm in Australia or go hungry? Don't you believe it – that's as dead as the diprotodon. I ought to know, having been a lad about all the Australian cities for twenty years. A little bent and broke now I admit, I'm still able to take a good dinner and evening up to 2.00 am.

Of course as drinks may not be sold after 6.00 pm, or with your meal after 8.00 pm, a little staff work has to be done in advance of the party. A supply can be ordered in – but I think it best not to go into all that. A short time in Australia makes one proficient in certain directions and able again to refute the nation-wide drought which is supposed to set in promptly at closing time.

The main 'pub' of Sydney is the renowned Hotel Australia. It has the longest bar in the world, a new wing completely air-conditioned, a radio in each room; an old wing also, which savours of Bloomsbury; and a high ceilinged dining-room, ballroom and numerous special places for private functions.

The place has great pillars, gold facings and all the 'tone' of a first-class hotel . . . but where it outstands is in its flowers. People don't 'say it with flowers' in Sydney – they live with them. Huge bowls of enormous blooms make the first floor of the 'Pig and Whistle' remarkable.

There's no doubt Sydney is lavish with its delicacies and for a mere song. Oysters. You've never had them till you've reached 'Our Harbour'. I have tried them in several countries, but none is within a mile for size, flavour, succulence and price of the famous 'Sydney Rock'. You remember what the Romans thought of the Britons? A poor crude people – but they possessed the finest oysters. That made the gourmandising Emperors think quite kindly of the islanders. My hat, wouldn't they have sped their galleys to the great continent down under if they had learnt of 'Sydney Rock' at 1s 6d a dozen.

Dinner without oysters is hardly a meal – fried, Mornay, in soup or plain raw. And 'tis curious that in far away Adelaide they should be sold for only 1s 3d a dozen, although practically all the oysters eaten in Australia come from Sydney. But not from the Harbour as you might think. They are infected. North in the Hawkesbury River, south at Cronulla, the beds are thick.

Even over at Perth, on the Swan River, 2262 miles by sea from Sydney, they have re-planted 'Sydney Rock'. The oyster gardens at

Fremantle, and a dash there in a car on a hot night, highlight the visits of many to the capital of Western Australia. And still for 1s 6d a dozen, which, being Australian currency, would work out at about 1d each in London.

In the private houses, pineapples, mangoes, paw-paw, custard apples, sweet corn, and all usual fruits can be put on the tables of the poorest. No luxury prices control them.

And then if you are tired of ordinary cooking and sumptuous places, come with me to King's Cross, the flat-life centre of Sydney. Come to 'The Clermont' where, for 2s 6d, you can have soup, fish, a choice of thirty dishes, sweet and coffee. Here is Austrian cooking par excellence. Richard Tauber remarked on the Paprika Schnitzel; I, too, never miss that or the Goulash Hongroise. I've never had as nice in London.

A short way along Darlinghurst Road from 'The Clermont', you enter 'The California', a typically American coffee shop, holding say, 300 people, busy with steak or omelette or salads. It is a buzz of life in the evening: Jazz orchestra playing and – when the tune is popular – people singing cheerfully. And all sorts mixed together . . . the gunman and his blonde . . . society from a cocktail party . . . bathers, obviously straight from Bondi . . . long-haired arty people . . . short-haired business men . . . laughter . . . the roving eye . . . scurrying waitresses . . . clinking cups. That's 'The California'. And so is it the 'Santa Barbara' over the road, where a huge fat fellow croons into a microphone and looks a real double of Paul Whiteman.

Melbourne differs a great deal from gay, effervescent Sydney. Radically, it would be English if only to oppose the rapid Americani-sation of its northern neighbour. One dines at home in Melbourne . . . Sydneysiders want to be up and about and of course, out. Melbourne, however, has in Collins Street probably the best restaurant in the Commonwealth – 'The Australia' – which, although its orchestra plays till after nine, does not provide dancing. Its speciality is epicurism. Chicken à la King, Toheroa soup from New Zealand, are unforgettable memories. The boiled Murray cod, and fried Schnapper, make the place famed as London's Simpsons is for English joints. The Peach Melba is, naturally, being the home town of that great singer, superlative.

Below the street level they have a second-grade small restaurant, where plainer dishes are offered cheaply. It is the 'Vienna', a cheery place with quaint murals showing the making, the taking and the results of their special cocktails. A three-course dinner costs 2s 6d.

If you go up Collins Street, turning left at Exhibition Street, then halting at Bourke Street, you'll be in our southern Soho. Mario's, Café Latin, Italian Club, Florentin and Ricco's sell table wine, minestrone, spaghetti, a choice of many dishes, and fruit for 2s 6d . . . Here there is beer and good company and sometimes adventure. Ricco's is a similar sort of place, only more cheerful, as they sing there. An Italian tenor takes our thoughts to the colours and warmth of southern Italy, and we all join in his popular choruses.

Not far away, as well as the St Kilda Palais de Danse and similar places, is Melbourne's chief upstage counterpart of Romano's – 'The Embassy'. Personally, I have enjoyed being there, for the food is quite good, the high ceiling keeps the air clearer than most places of this kind, and the band can do a very good job.

I must not forget 'The Ritz', in Little Lonsdale Street. I think it is my favourite small restaurant in the city, being quiet, comfortable and so intimate. It is the place to dine slowly and privately. No music, never a crowd, and waiters who do not seem to think of time. Never can I forget the evening 'me and my girl' – the current one I mean – celebrated a cable that one of my books had been accepted in London. We went in at eight, ordered the best to eat and drink that Monsieur had, took them leisurely . . . and then it was just 11.30. I cannot think of a better *tête-à-tête*. And this mark you, in a country infamous for its extraordinary *heure de diner*.

Spaghetti, Steak and Chicken Paprika

Geraldine Halls

Born in Adelaide in 1919, Geraldine Halls achieved literary success initially as a writer of thrillers published under the name Charlotte Jay. She also wrote 'straight' novels, including *The Last Summer of the Men Shortage*, which was first published in London in 1976. The story of two young Adelaide women working in war-time Sydney in 1945, it treats the quest for love and pleasure with delicate irony.

At the bottom of the hill were shops on either side of the road, a picture theatre, three restaurants and a hotel. A few men lingered around the closed hotel looking at passing girls with greedy eyes but not much expectation since the advent of Americans with better manners and a lot more money. Couples drifted towards the restaurants.

It was an area that attracted, in Dinah's view, extraordinary people who aimed at looking eccentric and bizarre. Women not to be seen in more conservative suburbs wore clothes that Dinah would never have dared to be seen in and dyed their hair crimson or glittering yellow, sweeping it back from their foreheads in fat scrolls that were stuffed to make them fatter with a woolly substance and that looked as hard as brass. The most tempestuous wind would not have disarranged them. European refugees, many of them Jews, spoke languages Dinah had never heard before, or had strong guttural accents. And in spite of the War, some people seemed to be rich and do nothing.

The first restaurant they passed was called 'Maxim's' and, with its red shades over electric candles dripping with imitation wax, was too expensive for them or for anyone they had got to know, with the exception of Spike. He could well have faced the bill but was not a gourmet, preferring dancing when he discovered Claudia and, previous to that, when he knew Dinah, sandwiches and coffee.

They stopped at the next restaurant, which had a large window through which people could be seen dining within. It was called 'Dino's' and was the most exciting restaurant Dinah had ever encountered, being famous and yet sufficiently inexpensive for them to he able to afford a meal there now and again. Artists, actors and ballet dancers – some of them Russians from the de Basil Company, which had come to Australia in 1939 – had signed their names in big, sprawling writing on the walls, and the menu comprised exotic dishes like goulash and chicken paprika, served, not with vegetables, but with French salad mixed with vinegar and oil.

In Adelaide the two most favoured restaurants were called 'The Quality Inn' and 'The Wentworth', where you could have fried whiting and lamb chops served with peas; and for afternoon tea, hot buttered scones and slices of cream cake. The women who frequented them – no man would have been seen dead there – wore white straw hats, white gloves and stockings, or in winter, green or brown felt hats decorated with pheasants' feathers, pigskin gloves and brogues to go with their tailored coats and skirts made from Scottish tweed. But at 'Dino's' people wore anything that came into their heads; and hats and stockings never. And far from being a place for women only, you felt rather conspicuous if you didn't have a man to accompany you . . .

Andrew chose a table by the wall and drew back chairs in a courtly way. 'Darling,' he said to Claudia, still being Noel Coward, 'I love you in that frock. You look like a plum tree in spring.'

So it was 'darling' already after two weeks. And a married man . . .

After a short silence, Andrew said, 'So this is Dinah about whom we have heard so much. Such a neat little thing, like a bird. But with rather cumbersome tail feathers. Can you fly? Or are you one of those birds that spend their time on the ground pecking away?'

'I don't know what you mean,' said Dinah, understanding only that he had meant to be unkind.

'What I mean is, why are you angry?'

'I'm not angry,' said Dinah. 'What on earth makes you think that?'

'Goulash,' chanted Claudia. 'Spaghetti, steak, chicken paprika. Oh God! Chicken paprika!'

'You know, Dinah,' said Andrew, 'Claudia has told me a lot about you. About your brains, beauty and charm. You have had considerable advance publicity. But what she failed to tell me, perhaps because she has never noticed, is that you are a little bird who has never learned to fly. And perhaps never will, unless you can shed some of the weighty disapproval that is keeping you on the ground.'

Dinah realised now that Andrew was not only perceptive but cruel as well. Struck with terror, she shrank into silence. She looked about her at the silhouetted shapes of people sitting by the window, with cars and people outside moving behind them. At a table in a corner four American officers looked superior and exclusive. Dinah felt they had been to Harvard or Yale and had no girls with them because they would never consider taking a girl to dinner who had not been formally introduced. Their uniforms were gala with decorations and glittered with polished brass; it was difficult to believe that they were fighting the War, not attending a fancy dress party.

Seated alone, a fat man, so dark you might almost call him 'coloured', ate spaghetti with a fork. In Adelaide you simply couldn't have got away with shoving into your mouth a forkful of spaghetti, the ends of which trailed on your plate. In Adelaide spaghetti, never more than two inches long, came out of a tin. And in Adelaide everyone aimed at an intermediate complexion as though determined to be safe. Here they were either too dark, like that Jew over there, or too fair, like the Major's girlfriend with her metallic yellow hair. Here they chose their line and went just as far as they could . . .

At last a waitress turned up and stood restlessly by their table.

'Dinah, what are you having?' Claudia shivered with excitement and began reading the menu for the fourth time.

'I think I'll have steak,' said Dinah. Steak, at three and sixpence, halfway between spaghetti at two and sixpence and chicken paprika at five shillings, seemed safe, not putting you in the position of being too diffident or mercenary.

'She doesn't want steak,' said Andrew. 'She wants chicken paprika, but she'll enjoy her fast. Tell me Claudia, does she keep whips and knives in her bottom drawer?'

Galah Pie and Emu

Jock Marshall and Russell Drysdale

Journey among Men, by zooloogist and explorer 'Jock' Marshall (1911–1967) and noted artist Russell Drysdale (1912–1981), is an account of their travels and adventures in north-western Australia. Like all diehard bushies, they lived off the land as much as possible, but they were honest enough to admit a preference for the usual fare of civilised society.

Journey among Men, 1962

We built our fires and soon had cooking a splendid meal of galah. Most people will not believe that galah cockatoo makes good food. Although one-third of the population of Australia live near cities, the bush and its traditions are always very close and almost everybody is a reasonably efficient camper and a self-confessed authority on bush cookery. But

Pitt and Collins Street bushmen will never believe that the big pink cockatoo makes good meat. The fact is that the meat of tolerably young galahs is little, if at all, inferior to that of pigeons. This great truth is not new. As early as 1801 Grant of the *Lady Nelson* said: 'Nor is the flesh of the parrot disagreeable, having very much the same taste as our pigeon.' Most people, of course, have never eaten parrot; nor (in Australia) pigeon either, for that matter.

So the old recipe for galah persists as follows: *Take one galah, Prepare it carefully, and cook with one piece of quartz over a slow fire. When the rock is soft, the galah is fit to be eaten.*

A variation of the old bush joke is: *When the quartz is soft, throw the galah away.*

When we had time, we simmered our birds in a shallow pan for about half an hour. Often we curried them, with delicious results. Ivan, the kangaroo shooter, was engaged in this rewarding pastime when the other party found us under the white gums and the baobabs. We were well pleased. Soon there was a rush for pannikins, for Dom had let the moths out of his pocket at Broome and was brandishing a bottle of Scotch.

These days we dined well, for there was plenty of meat, including emus. Once, at a pleasant camp on the banks of a timbered creek that still held large pools of clear water, Tim shot a young hen emu that turned Dom Serventy's bigger scales at seventy pounds. At a later camp we were cooking steaks from its heavily muscled legs, and lounging about the fire with some rum, when a truck pulled up. Out jumped a pleasant young station owner. He had a noggin with us. He told us that his property was about ten miles further down the road. Time passed, and we invited him to stay and eat with us. He hesitated. Then he heard that we were about to eat emu.

'Jesus!' he said.

We gave him polite attention.

'You can't eat that stuff!' he cried, 'It's bloody muck. My blackfellas eat it. Lord, you can smell it on 'em for days after. I just couldn't come at it, thanks all the same.'

Nor would he. As he downed another large rum he watched us, fascinated. After a while he hauled himself to his feet. He invited us all to call in for lunch tomorrow at the homestead when, he said, he'd see that we got some real tucker.

He was an exceedingly pleasant chap but, like a lot of country people today, just could not accept the thought of eating emu. In the pioneering days bush tucker of necessity formed the main diet in many places and, as recently as a little before the turn of the century, kangaroo chops and 'roo-tail soup figured on the menus of city hotels. With increased production of cheap mutton and beef, bush foods disappeared from 'good' tables.

One old country dish, and a very good one too, was galah pie. But most people today have never heard of it, let alone tasted it. As a result the great majority have come to regard the eating of 'roo or other bush tucker as putting oneself on the subsistence level of tribal Aborigines. This is all to the good. It means that wild ducks are almost the only animals that Australians shoot for food, although in the settled areas Italian migrants have begun to put themselves on the wrong side of the law by eating willy wagtails, jacky winters, kookaburras ('ha ha pigeons') and, in fact, almost everything in feathers.

Because we could not hang our emu meat and had to eat it comparatively fresh, we cut the steaks thin and fried them in the pan. They tasted like beef steaks. Properly cooked, almost any animal makes a good dish. Even the goannas, or bung-arrows, as the Western Australians call them, can be made into reasonable food. On Cape York Peninsula one of us was fascinated to see white stockmen almost invariably confine their diet to salt beef, damper and bush pickles. In the Aboriginal camps nearby the menu consisted of barramundi speared in the rivers, wild sucking pig, geese and ducks, scrub turkey and squatter pigeon. One wondered who really were the savages – the white or the black? Bush pickles, according to the old recipe, are made by stirring a bottle of Worcester sauce into a large tin of plum jam. This can be varied to suit individual tastes.

The emu was eaten from the earliest days of colonial settlement. Captain John Hunter, the Scot who succeeded Phillip in 1795 to become the second governor of New South Wales, left record of its edibility. Those days the bird was generally called either a cassowary or an ostrich in confusion with birds of the East Indies and Africa respectively. 'The flesh of this bird,' wrote Hunter of the emu, 'although coarse, was thought by us delicious meat; it had much the appearance, when raw, of neck-beef; a party of five, myself included, dined on a side-bone of it most scrumptuously . . .'

It could be said, of course, that the reduced state of the infant colony sharpened Hunter's appreciation of emu flesh. 'The pot or spit received every thing which we could catch or kill, and the common crow was relished here as well as the barn-door fowl is in England.'

A mature emu may weigh as much as 120 pounds and a kick from its powerful legs can disembowel a dog. After the female lays her eight or ten dark green, twenty-ounce eggs, the male takes over. He broods and guards them for about two months. The emu is essentially vegetarian. It eats mostly fruits, berries and grasses, although it also likes caterpillars. It would seem, then, that here is an animal that could never become a pest. Yet mobs of them sometimes break into ripening wheat fields, devouring much grain, but trampling and destroying more than they eat.

And so the usual situation arose: farmers bawling for the blood of an attractive animal, and harassed protectionists trying to discover a means by which both crops and emu could be saved. Dom, as ardent a conservationist as anyone, told us that he has no doubt that the farmers had a grievance, however sympathetic one might feel towards the apparently harmless bird which appears as the left supporter on the national emblem.

The problem was reduced by the removal of the emu from the protected list north of a certain latitude, and the payment by local boards of a shilling, or sometimes half-a-crown, per head or beak. The government rabbit-proof fences that stretch hundreds of miles across the land helped to protect the wheat fields. During the droughts, mass movements of emus were halted by these fences and their skeletons bleached in hundreds along the wires . . .

As the years passed, the big birds were checked in the wheat belt by the bounty, or by the distribution of free ammunition to farmers. By neither method is the emu likely to be extinguished. It still breeds within thirty miles of the state capital. We never saw them in great numbers but Dom says that hordes of them still periodically converge on the wheat farms from the dry areas beyond.

We accepted the young station man's invitation to lunch the next day. We found his house set back from the road amidst tall trees and green lawns, a charming oasis miles from anywhere. His wife fed us as though we were starving schoolboys. They plied us, too, with great mugs of cold beer. The repast was, in fact, better than rum and emu.

Parrot Pie and Curried Wattle Birds

M.J. Pearson

Mrs Pearson's recipes for parrot pie and curried wattle birds, from her book *Cookery Recipes for the People*, might serve to justify Jock Marshall's claim that galah pie is actually a very good dish, though the addition of one pound of fillet steak and half a pound of bacon could well overwhelm eight rather small birds. An English-trained domestic science teacher, Mrs Pearson gave public lectures on cookery and taught in Australian schools in the 1880s and 1890s.

Cookery Recipes for the People, 1894

Parrot Pie

INGREDIENTS
8 paroquets
Teaspoonful of lemon juice
4 eggs (boiled 10 mins until hard, and then put in cold water)
1/2 lb of bacon or ham
little good gravy or stock
1 lb of fillet of beef cut in thin slices
Rough puff paste

MODE
Cut the birds in two, and rub well with butter, place the slices of beef in pie dish, and place on them the birds and slices of ham, cut in neat pieces the hard boiled eggs and add, then pour in cup of well seasoned stock; cover with rough puff paste (see paste), decorate with cut leaves, etc, from the paste, and stick the legs and feet well cleaned and blanched in centre.

Curried Wattle Birds

INGREDIENTS

10 or 12 wattle birds

1 sour apple

1/2 pint of good stock

1 dessertspoonful of flour

1 tablespoon of cream

1 tablespoon of curry powder

1 onion

MODE

Clean and cut birds in two, dry well and dredge with flour, put little butter in stew pan, and when hot fry minced onion, then brown the birds nicely, add minced-up sour apple and curry powder, then add stock; allow to boil up and simmer gently till tender, before serving add lemon juice and cream. Note – There should be just sufficient good gravy to coat the birds; serve in a border of rice.

The Ritual of the Pig

Colin Thiele

According to Angela Heuzenroeder, author of *Barossa Food* (1999), some German families in the Barossa Valley of South Australia still make their own wursts and sausages and smoked meats, using every single scrap of the slaughtered pig. Colin Thiele, who was born in Eudunda, just north of the Barossa Valley, was clearly familiar with the annual ritual and the various tasks involved.

The Sun on the Stubble, 1961

As soon as he'd finished breakfast he had to help with the pig. Dad had killed it with his usual dexterity, and now he, Oscar, and Herbert were busily scraping off the bristles. Now and then Dad went over to the nearby copper, seized the dipper, and splashed boiling water over the carcase. Then he spread a piece of hessian over it and drenching that splashed more boiling water all over the place. Oscar and Herbert stood back at a safe distance, afraid they might share the pig's fate. For a moment Dad stood too, critically eyeing the smoking carcase.

'Keeps the heat in all right,' he said; 'nothing better!' Then he flung off the hessian and the three of them assaulted the pig again with their scrapers, the black bristles flying and the sharp blades flashing in swift arcs. Bruno felt it was a miracle that somebody's arm didn't get the same treatment as a trotter. Come to think of it, Dad's hairy paw looked more in need of it than the pig's.

'Steady the swingle on the gallows, Bruno!' Dad said at last.

The pig, white and gleaming, was carried across by the three of them and hung by the back legs. Victor tugged at the block and tackle to set the carcase at just the right height for Dad to work on, and Oscar and Herbert steadied it while he dressed it with fierce skill. Then, washed and bagged in calico, it was hoisted to the top of the gallows into the cold wind.

Dad pointed to the gruesome collection of basins, filled with intestines, heart, head, knives and blood, that surrounded him. 'To the kitchen with all this, and help Mum with the wurst.'

He waved a gory hand. 'Victor, put up the big mincer on the table. And Bruno, bring wet chips for the smokehouse. Better look sharp if you want all this finished by dinner-time.' . . .

Mum worked at the head of the kitchen table, supervising the sausage industry. As each dish arrived she directed it methodically to its proper place in the production line, then set up her divisional overseers – Victor on the mincer with Little Anna as his feeding assistant, Herbert at the copper, and Bruno on the sausage casings. Normally it was a job with a lot of fun in it, but today Bruno found it something to be endured with chafing impatience.

'Here are the runners. Outside with them and through each one the water pour,' Mum directed him.

Bruno took up the big basin of intestines.

'Warm water, and salt in it – inside and outside,' she added.

For once Mum seemed calm and self-assured, despite the gore that surrounded her. It was as if some ancient awareness made her distinguish between bloodshed that provided food, and other forms of violence.

'This is meat!' Her tone was almost reverent.

Bruno took the basin outside and gathered together a bucket, a dipper and a funnel. Then he stood on a box, fished out a long intestine from the dish at his feet, and poured water into it through the funnel. The long runner, full and tight, swung and raced about in the grass like a snake. Saw-Ears, the old tom-cat, crouched, and watched it with fascination. When Bruno took another one from the dish, the cat, his tail lashing, stealthily advanced on it as it flung itself about in the grass.

'Saw-Ears!' Bruno warned. 'You put your claws through that, and I'll give *you* the same treatment.'

The cat paused, crouching, but when the next runner suddenly turned and dashed straight at him, he leapt back hastily and fled.

When Bruno had finished all the runners, he turned each one inside out and started all over again. Then he took the whole dish inside to Mum.

'Here you are; they're done!'

'Then to Victor for the wurst to start,' said Mum. 'And straight into the copper if it boils already.'

'It's boiling,' Herbert yelled from outside, stoking diligently.

Victor turned the handle of the mincer mightily until the whole table throbbed and hopped, the mince pouring out unendingly from the special funnel that was clamped to the face-plate. And Mum, with marvellous skill, swung each casing upwards in an arc as it filled, curling it round like a ringtail until it completed the circle and she could tie it off with string. Periodically Bruno loaded the finished sausages on his arm like quoits on a pole and took them out to the copper.

The morning slipped away quickly. Blood-wurst and leber-wurst, frying-sausages hanging from the cellar ceiling, white puddings stuffed and flattened between two boards under the colossal press of Dad's downward thrust . . .

It was all done efficiently enough, but it did take time. Finally, while Dad set the fire in the smoke-house, Bruno wheeled up a great barrow-load of wet chips and sawdust to keep it going when the hams and bacon went in for curing.

'Good!' Dad stood on the verandah and stretched himself prodigiously. 'Dinner-time!'

'I will fry sausage,' said Mum. 'It will take ten minutes only.'

'And then maybe I can get to my traps,' said Bruno feelingly. 'At this rate I'll never get them home today. I don't . . .'

Then he caught a glimpse of Dad and left the rest of his complaint unlodged.

Yorkshire Pie

A.E. Martin

Born in Adelaide, A.E. Martin (1885–1955) grew up in the outback town of Orroroo, which may well have provided him with the small-town setting for his novel *Sinners Never Die*. The Yorkshire pie he describes is no fiction; *Traditional Foods of Britain* (1999) reports that in the eighteenth century Yorkshire Christmas Pies, filled with spiced poultry and game birds boned and stuffed one inside the other, were sent from Yorkshire to London at Christmas time. The narrator is the small town's sanctimonious postmaster.

Sinners Never Die, 1944

I got to the hotel one midday to find myself dragged into the commercial room where an unusual drink was thrust into my hand, while Dr Hansen proposed a toast.

I had never tasted such a beverage before but I know that, temporarily at least, it eased my mind and even gave me a sense of well-being in addition to a tremendous appetite. I discovered later that it was two parts of sherry to one of brandy mixed with the yolk of an egg and two spoonfuls of sugar, the lot strained and dusted over with nutmeg or cinnamon, or maybe both. Somehow Mrs Marven had managed to keep it icy cold (they were the days before crushed ice came to the country towns), and I observed that tongues were noticeably loosened almost immediately we had drunk the stuff, Price in his boisterous manner declaring that our hostess should be recognised by the queen in the next birthday honours.

We drank twice, during which Mrs Marven told us with frank delicacy that the concoction was called a 'bosom caresser', and Price made some risqué allusion that embarrassed me greatly.

We went in to luncheon, the others laughing, and all of us hungry, and that was just as well, for Helen, it appeared, was of Yorkshire descent, and Mrs Marven had been up early to do justice to the occasion. We sat down to a Yorkshire pie such as I had never seen before. A goose and a fowl had been sacrificed on the altar of gastronomy, and both boned, the latter stuffed with minced ham, veal, suet, lemon peel, various spices, sweet herbs and goose liver, with onion and a little cayenne worked into a paste with the yellow of two eggs. Mrs Marven had then sewn up the fowl, trussed it, and stewed it with the goose for twenty minutes in some beef and giblet stock mixed with a small glass of sherry and in a closed stewpan.

After that the fowl had been popped inside the goose and the latter placed in a pie mould lined with short paste. The goose had rested on a cushion of stuffing in the middle of the liquor in which he had been stewed, and was surrounded in the pie with slices of semicooked hare and wild turkey (the latter taking the place of the Yorkshire pheasant and partridge, Mrs Marven explained) alternating with more seasoning. Butter was spread before the pie was roofed in, and, I believe, the whole lot had then been baked for three hours.

It was served to us cold and as I ate I imagined myself at the head of my own table as host at just such a meal, but prepared, of course, by servants. It was all right for Mrs Marven in her capacity as hotel-keeper to do her own cooking, but I could not see my own wife engaged in a task so menial. No, I thought, as the birthday luncheon progressed, the meals in my home would be prepared by our domestics, and the cook, no doubt, duly complimented after we had bidden good-bye to our guests.

Corned Beef Again

Marjorie Barnard

Marjorie Barnard (1897–1987) is best known for her short stories but, in partnership with Flora Eldershaw, she also wrote books under the name of M. Barnard Eldershaw. In this short story, 'The Dressmaker', Miss Simkins is an itinerant dressmaker doing a day's work in the stolidly middle-class Bowker household (which I always imagine to be in the Sydney suburb of Cremorne). Her inferior status, in the eyes of Mrs Bowker, is made perfectly plain at the lunch table but Miss Simkins has her revenge, of sorts. She, too, has known love, and she, too, can enjoy the pleasures of life.

'I suppose you haven't got "Vogue"?'

'Well, no, Miss Bowker. I don't get "Vogue". You wouldn't believe how much those books cost.'

'I do think "Vogue" is so chick.'

She looked intently at the illustrations. Would she really look like that if Miss Simkins copied the dress? She was always filled with an agony of hope when the dressmaker came, but she had never got exactly what she wanted. Not exactly.

'If,' she said dreamily, 'I could only have a little feather hat like that.'

'We might see,' said Mrs Bowker. 'We'll price them. Mr Bowker,' she explained, 'thinks the world of his girlies. He likes them to look their best. What I say to him is, he won't have the privilege of buying their clothes for long. Edna's as good as engaged now.'

'Mother,' cried Edna, 'you shouldn't say that, there's nothing fixed.'

'I only said "as good as".'

Edna plunged down among the fashion books. She tried not to hear her mother. She couldn't imagine why she felt so uncomfortable.

Mrs Bowker lowered her voice, presumably that the spirit of romance, now hovering over the house, might not take fright. 'Such a nice young fellow. He'll have plenty by and bye. He's got his car and all that now.'

'How nice,' said Miss Simkins.

'Edna's had plenty of chances, but this time it's serious. Alan is mad about her. Everybody has noticed it. So you see we want to make a special effort with her clothes.'

Miss Simkins saw perfectly. She bit off a length of cotton.

The maid brought in morning tea. 'I think morning tea is a mistake,' said Mrs Bowker. 'It spoils lunch.'

Miss Simkins couldn't help hoping there would be something worth spoiling. Her early breakfast had been a very ghostly affair. For the present there was thin captain biscuits, buttered but rather soft.

'Do mind the butter,' cried Mrs Bowker in an agony of anxiety.

Edna wandered out into the kitchen and returned with a slice of cake in one hand, and a tart in the other.

'I'm always eating,' she said, laughing it off.

The machine whirred, Mrs Bowker ran in tackings, Edna still sat hunched over the fashion books. She was looking at wedding dresses, and her lips moved as if she were telling herself a story. 'There's some finishing you can do, Edna,' said her mother. 'U-um – half minute,' answered the girl.

Miss Simkins was turning the Bowkers over in her private mind. She supposed they were a happy family. They all thought a lot of one another. But she really couldn't see why. They weren't very exciting, were they? She had seen Mr Bowker. He had a brick red face and very thick, red eyebrows. She supposed Mrs Bowker had been romantic about him once. Edna's young man they were so pleased about, was probably ordinary too.

Really, some people got everything very easily. It didn't matter a bit that Mrs Bowker was stout and stupid and rather mean too, or that Edna was spoilt and affected, or that everything about them was utterly, overwhelmingly commonplace. They had one another, they had Mr Bowker, a man, to fend for them. It made all the difference.

Mrs Bowker went on talking. 'My son says . . . My husband . . . Our girlies . . . Edna . . . Joycie . . . My son . . . My hubbie . . .' It wasn't necessary to listen. Miss Simkins knew all that – from the outside.

Then it was lunch time. Miss Simkins gave two pokes to her hair, shook the cottons from her skirt, and they went into the cold, rather dark, dining-room. Miss Simkins looked round the table and her heart sank. It was corned beef and carrots. Miss Simkins had noticed that it was always either corned beef or sausages – never a roast or fillet steak or boiled chicken or fried sole – but it was a mistake to think of these things for they made the corned beef, with its rind of thick, yellow fat and its mottled, brownish flesh (bought ready cooked at the smallgoods shop, she knew) and the hot carrots, smelling of earth, lying beside the cold meat on the warm plate, seem even more unappetising than it was. People must think that dressmakers liked corned beef and sausages above everything else. No, it wasn't that. People didn't think at all, that was the hardest part to bear.

Edna, it appeared, was not going to have corned beef. She had a chop instead. She explained that it was left over from last night, and it would be a pity to waste it. It did not look at all left over, but was fresh and juicy with a rich gravy mottling the plate. It smelt most appetising too, and when Edna put a lump of butter on top of it, peppering it well, that chop fairly took hold of Miss Simkins' imagination.

Neither, it turned out, was Mrs Bowker going to have corned beef. She never took meat more than once a day, and they were having a nice little stuffed shoulder for dinner. The corned beef, it was obvious, had been bought entirely for Miss Simkins – a quarter of a pound. Mrs Bowker had lettuce, and cheese, and brown bread, and some stewed apple with the cream off the milk. She needed, she said, something nourishing, she ate so little. They ought to be glad they had their appetites. Edna said mother ate nothing, and she was glad Miss Simkins was there because often she felt such a beast, eating a hearty lunch while mother just pecked. Mrs Bowker's delicacy did not show, however, unless it was in her habit of looking intently and rather suspiciously at every piece of food before she took it on her plate.

Miss Simkins' heart rebelled against the corned beef. She longed to say that she didn't eat it, but she was hungry, and there did not appear to be anything else. Besides, it would be rude. Mrs Bowker would probably remember it against her, and not send for her again. She put a small piece of meat in her mouth. It lay cold and dead on her tongue. It seemed utterly alien. It was very stupid and very gross to feel so keenly about food. But she did. She could have wept.

Lunch over, Miss Simkins felt more cheerful, despite herself. Also the sun had reached the glassed-in verandah and it was now bright and pleasant. The warmth brought a familiar, friendly, oily smell out of the sewing machine and the light was better. Edna had a fitting. She disliked being fitted, because Miss Simkins had cold hard fingers, and because she stood so close that she could feel her breath on her neck, her bare arms, her cheek . . .

The dress was finished and Miss Simkins had gone before Joyce came home from school. She was a fair, leggy girl, lull of vitality and curiosity. Even the advent of the dressmaker seemed to her an incident out of which some excitement could be squeezed. She began to pester her mother with questions. 'How did Miss Simkins get on! Did she bring some nice fashion books? Did she have any news!'

'Well, she talked a lot,' said Mrs Bowker.

'What did she say? What did she say?' cried Joyce, jumping up and down.

'She told us the story of her life,' answered Mrs Bowker, beginning to smile.

'Did she have an exciting life?'

'I'm afraid not.'

'What happened?'

'The usual thing,' Edna cut in. 'She nearly got married, but not quite.'

'She talks too much,' said Mrs Bowker. 'I don't think we can have her again.' . . .

Miss Simkins went home happy. Always when she had told her story she had a sense of exaltation. She had had romance, even if she hadn't been able to keep it. She couldn't help thinking that there was something fine about her tragedy. It was more beautiful than the commonplace happiness of mediocre people.

Tonight she was going to give herself a little treat. She bought a portion of steamed chicken, a paper bag of potato crisps, a punnet of strawberries, and a little carton of mixed nuts.

'Why not?' she asked herself, defiantly.

Scones and Friendship

Patrick White

The Tree of Man by Patrick White is a powerful and poignant epic of Australian life in the first half of the twentieth century. The brief exchange of this extract illustrates the gulf between mother and daughter, and in a more general sense the distance between two generations and their values.

The Tree of Man, 1956

The second visit that Amy Parker received that winter was of a different nature altogether. It did not rend, though it disturbed. It was unexpected, and Amy Parker no longer liked that, unless she played the unexpected turn herself. Even to be caught out by her own face unexpectedly in mirrors she did not care for. Am I like that? she asked, and would then try to remember how she had been, but this was always indistinct.

Anyway, Thelma came down, drove down in the afternoon, and this was usual.

Thelma came in and said, 'How are you, Mum dear?'

As if she were expecting her mother to be sick.

'I am all right, thank you,' said the old woman, and began to sharpen.

Thelma was dressed well. Thelma's dress was never noticed, it was rich but too discreet. Now it was her mother looking, though, who saw that Thelma was dressed extra well.

'I have brought a friend,' said Thelma Forsdyke, 'who is most anxious to meet you.'

This is a most dishonest friend, the old woman felt.

'What friend?' she asked incredulously.

'It is a lady,' said Mrs Forsdyke. 'It is my friend Mrs Fisher.'

A dishonest lady, this was worse. And the old woman began to get up, out of the deep chair in which, unwisely, she had been sitting. To get up would have been terrible, if it had not been imperative. And so she heaved.

'There, you need not worry,' the daughter said, and would have had her mother in a strait jacket, she liked people under control, then to be authoritative and kind.

'I have brought a box of little cakes. There need be no fuss,' she said.

'In my house,' said Amy Parker, 'I will have to make a batch of scones. Do you think the pumpkin ones, or does she like them plain?'

'I am sure I do not know,' said Thelma Forsdyke. 'It is unnecessary.'

'But she is your friend.'

'Friendship is not fed on scones, Mother. We have interests in common.'

It was puzzling. It was evident also that Mrs Fisher was approaching, at leisure, though with confidence.

'Am I to come in?' she asked.

She did.

Aunt Ollie's Kitchen

David Malouf

Generations of Australian women claimed the kitchen as their domain, while the men found refuge in the back shed. Aunt Ollie's kitchen, in novelist David Malouf's description, is as disciplined and orderly as any male workshop with shadow-board walls.

Harland's Half Acre, 1984

My Grandmother's beauty was a powerful legend that continued to convince people of the present fact. All three of my aunts saw themselves in the light of it. As an ugly duckling in the case of my Aunt Ollie, who had always thought of herself as her mother's shame, and in the case of the younger ones, 'the girls' as they were called, as timid but not always passive rivals. Their mother, in the early days, had quite simply stolen their men.

Aunt Ollie in fact was not an ugly duckling and never had been, but she had no confidence in her beauty, and I suspect my grandmother from the beginning may have implanted the notion of plainness in her as a way of making certain, once the other children began to arrive, that she would always be there to nurse them. Aunt Ollie had taken this as being the point of her lack of charm. She was to devote herself to the family. That, rather than marriage or children of her own, was to be her fate. She accepted it cheerfully, and so far as one could tell, entirely without question. She had mothered each of her brothers and sisters, and was, when it came to my turn to be mothered, a large, pale, fair creature, as soft as a cloud and with arms that were always powdered with flour.

Her province was the kitchen. With its big central table of scrubbed pine, its marble slab for pastry, its chopping-blocks, knife-drawers, canisters, and the rack on the wall where all Aunt Ollie's saucepans and frying-pans were hung, it was a place of continuous messy activity and perfect order. Sacks of potatoes and onions were stacked in an alcove; jars of melon and lemon jam, marmalade, mango chutney, tomato relish, all carefully dated and labelled, glowed on pantry shelves. The salt-box was of wood and had a thistle motif. There were two stoves. One was modern and enamelled, its legs set in tins of dessicated ants. The other was a range for baking. Very low and black, it was housed in a corrugated-iron recess and fed from a pile of stove-lengths that Uncle Gil would cut – if he was in the mood for it and could be trusted with an axe.

Aunt Ollie's kitchen had its own routine, to which only the privileged were admitted. I spent long hours there on Sunday mornings and in the afternoons after school, watching the miracles Aunt Ollie could whip up in her theatre of sieves and whisks and earthenware bowls of eight different sizes; licking the sugared white off egg-beaters, scraping out bowls, and being told, when I enquired what went into some favourite dish, 'Oh, a little bit of this and a little bit of that,' which was Aunt Ollie's only recipe for a dozen kinds of biscuits, and for whole-meal, pumpkin and marmite scones, treacle tarts, sago plum-puddings boiled in a basin with a clip-over lid, and the two kinds of dumpling that went into the various soups and stews for which Della, wielding a little bone-handled knife or an ancient cleaver, did the donkey-work of peeling and dicing vegetables.

Della was a shapeless girl of Aunt Ollie's age – that is, over forty – with hair so wispy that she might have been balding and odd stumps of teeth. She came from a farm across the border and had been part of my grandmother's household for nearly thirty years.

She and Aunt Ollie were a pair. Aunt Ollie, in her modest view of herself, saw Della as a kind of twin, closer and more like her than her flashy sisters. Della cut up vegetables, washed pots, pans and dishes, which gave her nails in the puffy fingers a horn-like texture, dealt with butcher-boys, bottle-os, ice men and grocers' assistants, fed the fowls that were kept at the bottom of the yard with soaked bread and scraps, and with her skirt hiked up and a pail of sloshy water before her, scrubbed each morning, before the rest of us were up, the worn tiles of the kitchen, the back steps and all the boards of the verandah. She spoke only to her chooks and in a toothless, incomprehensible gabble to the iceman.

She had an understanding with this wiry, red-headed fellow that allowed her to be rough with him.

'Gawn yew!' she would say in a burst of sudden hilarity, and give him a shove that might have overbalanced him altogether, he was so stringy-looking in his shorts and singlet, if there hadn't been the compensatory weight of the ice.

The occasion would leave them both chuckling and shaking their heads as they moved off in opposite directions; the block having been lowered by then into its chest, and beginning to melt, and the iceman, the lighter for the encounter, bouncing a little on his toes.

It was the iceblock that occupied the centre of this daily drama. Glittering there at the end of hooked claws and leaving a wet trail all the way from the gate, with a puddle where the two figures had crossed beside the mint patch halfway up, it gathered to itself whatever heat these meetings contained, so that it might have been the iceman's foxy attempts to catch her hand, or Della's feelings when she turned things over in her little cubbyhole by the stairs, that reduced the great block to liquid, and some understanding between them that the relationship would continue, but not necessarily develop, that created that void in the ice-chest that had each morning to be filled.

Communications between Della and Aunt Ollie were also silent. Words did crop up in them, as monosyllabic requests or directives, but they were not essential. The real dialogue was that set of exchanges by which vegetables, the same ones each day, and chuck-chops and steak, became stews, broths and thick winter soups, and whisks, sieves, bowls, ladels passed from Della's hands to Aunt Ollie's and so on through a complicated process of beating and churning and patting and pricking till the dishes were produced that we would later consume at my grandmother's table; after which, they went back into Della's hands to be washed, dried, restored to brightness and hung again on the kitchen wall.

These utensils, clean and in place by eight o'clock in the evening, when Della closed the kitchen door and retired to her room to listen to the serials on the mantle radio we had given her, were the elements of a lifelong discourse that could for the moment be dropped but would be taken up again in the morning when all these things would come down from their hooks and be gathered back again into the world of use. Even Della and Aunt Ollie's quarrels had no words. They could be guessed at only by the higher level of noise they produced when Della went to work with her hacker, or by the banging down harder than usual of an iron pot.

Wattle Flowers, Mud Crabs

Mabel Edmund

Mabel Edmund is an artist as well as story-teller. Her grandmother, on the maternal side, was Aboriginal and her grandfather German; her paternal grandfather came from the New Hebrides. After her marriage to Digger Edmund she moved from a pastoral station to his South Sea Islander community on the central Queensland coast. This extract from her memoir, *No Regrets*, describes her adjustment to a new life, learning to choose firewood, catch prawns, and cook scones and sponges.

No Regrets, 1992

Soon after I moved to Joskeleigh I found out that cutting firewood was one of my duties as a wife. I remember my first trip to Scenty Gum Ridge with the womenfolk to cut firewood. I didn't know my trees and I was cutting anything and everything. I soon had my spring cart full and loaded up with nice lengths of wood and I thought I was great, when someone looked in my cart and called out to the others to come have a look too. They all burst out laughing and started throwing out all of my wood. I just stood there stunned. Then my mother-in-law showed me the logs that I should have been cutting up. My sister-in-law, who was the same age as me and pretty good with an axe, helped me to re-load my cart with decent wood.

I learnt which type of tree was suitable for the stove and what was best for the open fire to boil clothes. Ironbark was the best of all for baking. Quinine had good heat too and didn't leave any soot, but it would soon crack the inside of your stove if you used it all the time. Gum was OK if you liked cleaning out the ashes. Mahogany, teatree, stringybark and similar varieties were only good to boil up the copper boiler as they were too smoky and had less heat.

Collecting firewood was a part of the community life. It was a day of fellowship with each other, each family of women working side by side cutting wood up in the ridges, the huge scented gum trees with their clean smooth red trunks standing tall and beautiful. We used to take our lunches and boil up the billies for tea, and make the babies' bottles, though most of the babies were breastfed and strong and healthy and fine little specimens. We didn't have to cut down any trees, just cut the dead limbs lying around the place. There would be a lot of laughter and storytelling about what had happened during the week.

As I walked the long distance home from Scenty Gum Ridge on my first visit, my thoughts went to my mother and how much I was missing her. It was only twelve months since she had died and my life had changed so much. Here I was, sixteen years old, still dressed in my navy blue school uniform of box-pleated pinafore, leading my horse that was pulling the cartload of wood, with my baby girl tied onto my back in a sling made from a strip of old sheet. I was in a completely different environment. I have always loved the bush and I would rather be there than anywhere else. But my mother had always done the hard work around our home and now I was paying for it. Just one of the lessons that I was to learn.

The first home Digger and I ever had, we built it ourselves, just the two of us. We worked hard. It was in Joskeleigh about a mile from Digger's family. It was nothing flash, anything but that. Digger stayed up in Rocky at his sister's place during the week and on weekends when he was home we worked on our house. It was built from bush timber, we cut the iron bark beams and all timber we needed up at Scenty Gum. Digger built a wooden sledge from the trunk of a large tree. He would harness his horse to it and pull the logs down from the ridge.

Our home was always neat and tidy. It had one bedroom, a kitchen and living room. The walls were made from opened-up sack bags stitched together with a bag needle. We got the bags cheap from Walkers Bakery. When they were nailed up, Digger painted the outside walls with wet cement and I whitewashed the inside.

The war was over, but there was still a shortage of all materials and we were unable to buy iron for the roof, so Digger compromised and nailed on malthoid, a stiff black rubbery-looking material. It kept out the rain and the wind. We carted bags of mud from the saltpan near the beach, mixed it with shell grit and packed it on the sand floor. It made a nice hard floor like cement and was easy to sweep, except when it was cloudy or rainy, when the salt would become damp.

Life at Joskeleigh was very different from what I had experienced in Rockhampton. My mother-in-law and most of the womenfolk were excellent seamstresses and made their children's and their own clothing. I could never sew anything straight and Digger's grand-mother would make me unpick my sewing and start all over again. I used to think that she was doing that because she didn't like me, I didn't realise then that Granny did it because she was a very neat worker and she couldn't bear to look at shoddy workmanship.

I stitched material scraps on sack bags for mats and laid them on the floor. In the winter time our blankets were made from opened-up flour sacks, covered with colourful scraps of material on one side and a cotton blanket stitched on the other. We were never cold, and too poor to be proud.

My mother-in-law and her sisters taught me to cook. They always had new recipes to try out. We had no bread delivery through the week, so we made our own bread and prepared our own yeast. I learnt to make great big dampers, pumpkin scones and tarts. I loved cooking in those days. Digger used to love a dish made with grated sweet potato, shredded coconut, and dried apples, baked in the oven and served with cream and custard. The Islanders called it *nullong*. I added my own ingredients to make it taste the way I liked it.

Norah Mallamoo, a friend of my mother-in-law, was great cook. She made the lightest sponges I had ever tasted and her chocolate cakes and tarts were out of this world. She also grew the sweetest watermelons I had ever eaten. Norah's husband, Charlie Mallamoo, was one of the original Islanders brought to Queensland to cut cane. He was a lot older than she was. She had to go out and do all the fishing and hunting while he sat under his mulberry tree at home, keeping the fire in the stove going and the kettle hot. Charlie must have been close to one hundred years of age when he died, he was a great person, I could sit for hours and listen to him talk. When he was a very young man he worked on building the swinging bridge that spanned the Fitzroy River. That bridge has been demolished many years now and replaced by another one that my father worked on when it was being built.

Huge paperbark trees grow along the banks of the swamps down home at Joskeleigh, many of them one hundred years old. Some of the big limbs are hollow and they make good places for the English and Italian bees to build their hives in. There are so many flowering trees in the area and the swamps are always filled with flowering hyacinth that it doesn't take long for the bees to fill their hives with honey.

One year, the folk decided to rob a big hive, laden with honey, that was hanging out of a hole in the side of the tree. Down they all went, women, kids, everyone who was there at home went down to help.

Old Charlie Mallamoo was going to quieten the bees down, while some of the stronger women and young boys chopped the tree down. He lit a fire with some wood he'd gathered and instead of throwing green bushes on it to create some smoke to make the bees dopey and harmless, he threw a whole packet of sulphur on it and the fumes from the sulphur rose up and killed all the bees.

Everybody just stood there suddenly silent, all the excitement was gone from their adventure as they stood and watched all the bees dropping dead all around them. After the shock wore off, they got to work and cut down the tree and collected all of the honey. We still laugh about the time Charlie killed all the bees.

A few years later the women found another good hive in a smaller tree, and they came to get my dad, Jack Mann, to cut the tree down for them. We all went up the swamp, women carrying young babies and toddlers. When we got there, Dad made the fire and built up a good smoke and started cutting down the tree. But the bees weren't affected much by the smoke and they started getting angry. By the time the tree hit the ground the bees were really stirred up and they were getting stuck into Dad. He dropped his axe and started running to where we were all hiding behind a couple of big trees, Everyone was yelling, 'No Jack! Don't come this way, don't come here!' but he kept coming with a big swarm of angry bees behind him, so we all took off too, flat out in all directions. He finally outran the bees, but not before he got heaps of stings from them.

Going fishing with a group of women was always an experience. The day before we went we would check the moon and from it could work out how the tides were making and which creeks would be best to fish. Catching our bait was also worked out to a fine art. We knew right down to the last five minutes how much time we had to scoop the creek for prawns. You had to stand in water and mud almost waist deep and hold a round hoop with your bait net tied to it and hold it in the channel of water. As the prawns were coming down there would be dead silence and if you so much as coughed and frightened them you could be sure of being most unpopular for the rest of the day. After catching enough bait to last us for the day we would head for our chosen fishing spot.

I loved those days, there was a closeness and friendship and also competition to see who would catch the biggest fish. I shall never forget the day that I caught the big one that got away. I hooked a real big salmon and I couldn't handle him so my husband grabbed my rod from me and when he took it he let the line go slack and gave the fish a chance to throw the hook. When he looked at me and said 'He's gone,' I just fell down in the mud and I kicked.

There were a few old Islander beliefs too, whenever you went fishing. They were a sort of unwritten law. You weren't expected to take an elaborate lunch or have money in your pocket. Damper and syrup were sufficient or maybe fried scones and baked peanuts. The Lord would not send fish along to bite on the lines of someone sitting on the bank with money in his pocket and eating cakes.

Another belief that has always proved to be true is that when the wattle trees are in bloom the mud crabs are fat. When I see a wattle tree in flower I always think of home and I can almost smell those beautiful crabs cooking.

Strawberry Fête

Colin Thiele

The strawberry fête was an annual community event in rural South Australia, particularly popular in the early twentieth century. Colin Thiele's novel *Labourers in the Vineyard* is set in the easily recognisable Barossa Valley just before the second world war.

Labourers in the Vineyard, 1970

The Strawberry Fête was a flummery of people. Loaded tables stood everywhere and jostling bodies heaved and surged between them. Strawberries lined the shelves on the walls and spread over boxes and trestles; strawberries with noses like nipples peeping from punnets and plates, strawberries in glasses, jars, saucers, and cartons; strawberries sunk in syrup, soused in castor sugar, buried in clots and gobs of cream; strawberries finally mashed in saucers, bulging unswallowed in children's cheeks, squashed under their feet, and oozing between their fingers. The whole hall was sticky with them – sight, smell, taste, and tacky touch. A gluey bath of strawberries and cream.

Roland and Cecilia, having earlier opened the function, had just made their escape and the crowd was wallowing in an enthusiastic fervour of food and drink.

'By God,' Martha Fiedler said, compressing her huge rubbery behind between a bench and the wall as she squeezed past; 'there ain't much room in here.'

'Worse than last year,' August agreed, slipping along adroitly in her wake.

They came to Ossie and Edna, hemmed in by a hundred gourmands all pelicanning into their dishes or scraping, sucking, and smacking their lips over the last sticky licks on their spoons. Ossie held one of their children on his hip and led the other by the hand. A third, again the inevitable product of his virility and Edna's eagerness, and due to be born within a week, Edna still carried hugely before her.

'Better be careful in here,' said Martha matriarchally, 'or they'll trample you under their feet.'

'We're just trying to get out,' Ossie said, bucking about in the waves of the crowd. 'They're a rough mob.'

'Let me go first,' Martha said.

'Yes,' August agreed proudly, 'Martha'll soon clear a track!'

His wife turned to Edna. 'You better stand by me and face the opposite way.'

'What for?'

'Protection. My bottom and your belly are just about the same size, I reckon. Same shape too.' She rollicked with laughter. 'But my bottom is tough enough to take any amount of thumpin' and pushin', and your belly ain't.'

She moved forward and thrust aside a bow-wave of bodies like a rotund barge in a swell. 'Come on, Edna! Hold it in both hands and bring it after me.' On the way they met Kurt and Helga.

'Come on, Kurt,' bellowed Martha, 'Join in. With your shoulders, my bottom, and Edna's middle, nobody will be able to stop us.'

They reached the door eventually and she waddled gratefully out into the fresh air, 'Whew! Strawberry Fête they call it! Only needs a barrel of cream tipped over 'em, and they'd be eating each other!'

Birthday and House-Warming

George Johnston

After ten years on the Greek islands, George Johnston (1912–1970) returned to Australia with wife Charmian Clift in 1964 after his semi-autobiographical novel *My Brother Jack* won the Miles Franklin Award for that year. The first of a trilogy, it offers a richly detailed image of life in Melbourne between the wars. This extract contrasts two very different parties and their foods, the generous, old-fashioned cornucopia of his family's table and the contrived modernity of his wife Helen's supper.

My Brother Jack, 1964

The room had been rather hideously decorated with twisted paper streamers and coloured bells and lanterns of frilly paper, and pleated collars of coloured crêpe-paper had been arranged around the ferns and the flower-pots and what Mother always called the 'jarderneers', and in the centre of the table was a frosted birthday cake with no candles but a centrepiece of marzipan violets and a sugar '60' (later to be preserved with all the other memorable fragments under the glass dome on the pianola) and the words 'Happy Birthday to Mum' flowing over the almond-flavoured glaze in pink hard icing; and Mother and Jean and Marj kept coming up from the kitchen with still more dishes to add to the prodigious bounty on the big table. My sisters, I suddenly realised, must have been baking and cooking and preparing for two whole days! There were dishes of cold chicken and ham and corned beef and brawn and pork sausage, there were salads and beetroot and radishes and spring onions, there were sandwiches of cheese and of egg-and-lettuce and meat and of lemon-butter for the children, there were plain scones and fairy scones and sultana scones and date scones, there were Banbury tarts and apple tarts and jam tarts and pikelets and queen cakes and rock cakes and éclairs and napoleons and lamingtons, there were sliced Madeira cake and sliced plain cake and sliced caraway seed cake, there were mince pies and sausage rolls and coffee scrolls, there was a plain cream sponge and a chocolate sponge and a coconut sponge and an orange sponge, there were jellies and wine trifles and neapolitan blanc-manges and fruit-salad-and-cream, there were bananas and passion-fruit and pineapples, there were cheese straws, and there were milk arrowroot biscuits and rusks for the babies.

There was no organised point at which the party began, for in a sense it was a family gathering and not a party at all, but suddenly everybody was in the room at once, and seated, and passing dishes around, and Jack, the eternal barman was pouring the drinks, and Jean was saying to her kids, 'You just sit there where you are and keep quiet and wait till the grown-ups are served.'

I think I saw them all more clearly on that birthday afternoon than I had seen them for years: I suppose it was that I was instinctively scrutinising them for the faults or merits that I felt Helen might find in them . . .

With Helen, there was to be no commingling of the old life and the new. There was, I believe, a certain forceful integrity about her determination never to return to the surroundings of her past in that she set herself just as obstinately against her own family and background as she did against mine. It was quite extraordinary after our marriage to observe the almost ruthless way in which she cast off everything that had gone before . . .

At any rate, instead of the 'house-warming' we had cocktails and a buffet supper for twelve more fastidiously chosen guests – the elect of Helen's new 'set', the Turleys, two other young reporters from the newspaper and the assistant social editress, and one of Rene Farley's burly, polo-playing cousins from the Western District, who was visiting the city at the time on some matter concerning stud service for a pedigreed Aberdeen Angus.

Helen went to immense pains to get everything right. She was up at dawn and she happily worked all day with the same unruffled and practical poise that she applied to almost anything she ever put her mind to, including copulation. She spent hours in the kitchen, wearing the red rubber work-gloves which had become almost a talisman of her domesticity (she had a repugnance for touching raw meat or fish or any tuberous vegetables, and, in any case, she always took the greatest care of her fine and beautiful hands), indefatigably busy and every now and then referring to an illustrated article in the *Ladies' Home Journal* entitled 'Sixteen Savouries With a Difference'.

The result of all her labours was lavish and striking. Colour, she had decided, was to be her theme. I recall that each person's table napkin and tumbler was of a different colour, that colour glittered in gherkin parings and maraschino and pale cheese and purple olives and blushing carrot gratings on the varied dishes of savouries (I suppose there were sixteen of them; certainly they were all with a difference!); I remember mounds of grapefruit and oranges curiously porcupined by coloured pickled onions stuck there on toothpicks; there were oysters Kilpatrick and chicken patties and bacon slices served with fried apple and baked ham with grilled pineapple rings.

She must have known that she had carried off a real *tour-de-force* when, in a wave of general compliments, Miss Kirkwood, the gaunt and crane-like assistant social editress, conferred on her the professional accolade of 'imagination, my dear, originality, and *excellent* taste'. Helen accepted this commendation with a composed smile and a winning, self-deprecating little curtsy, but I knew that she really felt as if someone had pinned a medal to her breast.

The Lamb and Pickles Dinner

Tim Winton

The Lamb and Pickles families of *Cloudstreet* end up sharing – with strict respect for the dividing line, and all it represents – a large house in Perth around the late 1930s. Later, much later, Rose Pickles and Quick Lamb marry, living in the same house with both families until they establish their own home. *Cloudstreet* is probably Tim Winton's best-known and best-loved novel, especially since its adaptation for the stage and, subsequently, for film.

Cloudstreet, 1991

The night before Rose and Quick's trip, Oriel put on a dinner in the big room where Lester slept. The bed was taken out and two tables were laid end to end, draped in a great white cloth that stank of mothballs and the *Reader's Digest*. It was getting stupid, Oriel decided, the way Rose and Quick wandered from kitchen to kitchen, not knowing who they were supposed to eat with, and besides, if they ate with the Pickleses it was a sure bet that poor Rose'd do all the cooking, and on the night before her first holiday in years, it wasn't right that the girl should cook. Anyway, it would save all kinds of embarrassment if a gesture was made, a compromise sealed, and they ate together. Oriel had a headache the moment she conceived the idea. But it had to be done. Someone had to take the initiative. Also, and she could barely admit it, the prospect of not having Harry and Rose and Quick in the house depressed her. After their holiday, now that their new house was finished, they'd be leaving Cloudstreet for good. It was weakness this silly dinner. It was hanging on to them, but Oriel considered she had the right to a bit of clinging.

When the big room was full of noise and laughter, Sam and Dolly came knocking. Red let them in. They looked overscrubbed and shaky. Fish was rolling soup bowls, Lester was giving the accordion a bit of a hiding, and Lon was telling a joke that no one could possibly approve of.

Come in, come in! said Oriel, brightly signalling them in and avoiding their eyes.

The stove roared, gusting hot air into the room beyond, where the riotous mob was milling.

Welcome below deck! called Lester as they went through.

Geez, it's like the engine room, orright, said Sam to no one special.

Sit down, Mum and Dad, Rose said, trying not to bite her lip. Geez, you're all got up.

Dolly trod on Harry who had crawled under the table and there was pandemonium. Dolly nearly fainted with guilt and embarrassment.

It's alright, said Rose. Relax, Mum.

Sam sat next to Fish who said: Who's got your fingers?

Lester insisted on singing 'The Wild Colonial Boy'. He sounded terrible, but everyone was grateful for the break and while he was singing and squeezing, Oriel brought out the food with Elaine who passed hot plates that took the prints off a few fingertips. Out came roast lamb, cauliflower cheese, mint sauce, a tray of roast potatoes, parsnips, onions, pumpkins, cabbage, slabs of butter, hot white bread and Keen's mustard. There was a chicken stuffed with leek, cold ham, beetroot, and a jug of lemonade the size of an artillery shell.

Everyone passed and grabbed. Plates disappeared beneath it all.

For what we are about to receive, Lester said, stopping them all dead with his mild voice, we are truly thankful.

Amen, said Sam.

Christ Almighty, look at the food, Dolly murmured. She's tryin to kill us.

They ate and passed and picked while Lester told them all stories that could only have been the weakest of lies, until there was steampud with jam, custard and cream. A pot of tea was hauled in, cups brought, chairs snicked back a little to allow legs to be crossed. Fish and Harry played under the table with Pansy's girl Merrileen.

I hear you're thinkin of sellin, Mr Pickles.

Our Own National Dishes

W.P. Thornton

As with the Christmas menu proposed in 1925 (page 99), oysters were still among the favourites for an all-Australian menu in 1953 (and again for Oscar Mendelsohn's 1968 dinner – page 185). This one is noteworthy for its championing of indigenous ingredients: kangaroo, graylings, quandongs and macadamias.

Sydney Morning Herald, 20 June 1953

A visitor to this country recently claimed that Australians had no national dishes of their own – not even a national drink.

He is wrong, of course, although you will have to journey outside the cities to sample most of our original drinks and dishes.

Nowhere outside Australia, for example, can you enjoy a 'Diamantina cocktail', which is truly an Australian drink. When properly made, it consists of a pint of condensed milk, a pint of Bundaberg rum and a well-beaten emu egg.

It goes without saying that the effect of a few of these Diamantina cocktails is truly remarkable.

Left with a genuine Australian hangover, you will find the national pick-me-up a real tonic. This is the 'Murrumbidgee oyster' – a raw egg covered with vinegar and sprinkled with pepper and salt.

Australia has a much less lethal national drink than the Diamantina cocktail. This is post-and-rail tea, brewed in an old blackened billy (which is itself an Australian invention).

You may have a little sugar in the tea, but do not spoil it by adding milk.

Perhaps you have sipped the most expensive Ceylon or China tea from Royal Doulton cups in a fashionable city café or even in more distinguished surroundings, but, believe me, you do not know the taste of real tea until you have sipped post-and-rail tea which has been boiled over an open fire in the Australian bush.

Yes, this is truly an Australian national drink. If you have never tried a mug of post-and-rail tea with a slice of damper liberally spread with 'cocky's joy' you have missed one of life's greatest pleasures. There are, incidentally, few things more Australian than damper with 'cocky's joy', which is the bushman's name for golden syrup.

Kangaroo tail soup is certainly worthy of being classed as an Australian dish. There is no other soup to equal it. Kangaroos are protected in many parts of Australia these days and are becoming too rare to allow kangaroo tail soup to figure regularly on Australian menus. Of course, you can make kangaroo tail soup from a wallaby tail, but don't imagine that you can make it from ox-tail, possibly by adding some hops!

Colonial goose is another truly Australian national dish. It is a boned leg of mutton stuffed with sage, onions and breadcrumbs, and baked.

For full flavour, this dish should be prepared in bush fashion, using a camp-oven instead of an electric or gas oven.

Camp-ovens are rare nowadays, even in the bush, but with one of them the toughest mutton could be baked tender as lamb.

If you would like to sample a national dessert, then I recommend quandong pie. There are still plenty of quandong trees growing in many parts of Australia, from the east coast to the west. A quandong pie is made like any other fruit pie, but the quandongs have a flavour unlike any other fruit.

I find it strange that leading Australian hotels and cafes do not feature quandong pies on their menus, even in towns where quandong trees grow in abundance. But outback settlers still pay reverence to this delicious dish.

Could we have a full-scale menu of Australian dishes? Of course.

We will commence with a plate of genuine kangaroo tail soup, the kangaroos being obtained from those parts of the country where there is an open season and the kangaroos are a pest. Next, a plate of Bateman's Bay oysters, as big as saucers and with a flavour entirely their own; then, fillets of Murray cod or perhaps some Australian graylings, those little native freshwater fish more commonly known as mountain trout; next on the menu is the colonial goose described above, served with boiled stinging nettles, pumpkin and potato; then quandong pie with whipped cream, and, finally, to round off the meal, some Australian bush nuts (*Macadamia ternifolia*), easily the finest table nut that I have ever eaten.

These bush nuts have very hard shells, but, let us say, for the purposes of our banquet, that the shells have been cracked before being brought to the table. There is no reason why we cannot have plenty of these nuts. In recent years they have been cultivated, and they also grow wild in abundance.

Australian wines can, of course, be drunk with our meal. To finish with a real Australian flavour, we shall smoke cigarettes made from cured gumleaves; cigar smokers will be offered a real bush cigar – the porous stem of the flower of the banksia.

Where can we have this meal? I have in mind a little bush pub. So far it is only a dream, of course, but one day I should like to build such a pub somewhere in the great outback, west of sunset.

I have plans to build it on the edge of the biggest mirage in the country, so that patrons will be able to stroll down by the big billabong in the early evenings, after sipping their Diamantina cocktails, to watch the bunyips and swap yarns about the good old days!

Monotonous Cakes

This 1952 sequence of letters to the *Sydney Morning Herald* shows Australia on the way to a gastronomic reawakening. After two world wars, the lean years of the depression and decades of economical eating which was partly justified by public promotion of the virtues of frugality, the nation was entering an era of plenty, prosperity and stability. The 1950s saw the beginning of the end of six o'clock closing and a burgeoning of licensed restaurants and food-and-wine clubs. The correspondence demonstrates the tension between cooks (including pastrycooks) and consumers, each aggrieved and frustrated by the other's lack of adventurousness.

Sydney Morning Herald, October 1952

---

8 October 1952, from Mrs Ruth Baxter, Epping:

Sir,– May I pass comment on the uninteresting variety of cakes presented to metropolitan housewives by the pastrycooks?

Year in and year out it is possible to see the same cakes in the same position in the windows. Yet with so many lovely recipe books about we are still offered sickly mock cream, the good old block cake, and pies in all forms, apple, mince, and meat.

I object to paying fourpence each for unsold cakes wrapped up in coconut and called lamingtons.

Two days later came this response from 'Patissier':

Sir,– May I reply to Mrs Ruth Baxter on 'Monotonous Cakes'?

I am an English pastrycook with Continental experience.

I had great hopes before arriving here of making some beautiful confections.

But I soon found that the average Australian would have none of savarin au rhum chantilly or biscuits a la cuillere; but demanded apple tart and ice cream or jelly and ice cream for sweets in the hotel.

Even the crepes suzette served here is not a patch on the dish served in London's West End hotels.

Similarly, the average shop customer will not try anything that he is not familiar with since childhood.

Mrs Baxter was moved to reply at some length:

Sir,– I do not wish to enter a controversy, but feel that I must offer 'Patissier' some remarks in defence of my fellow countryman's choice of food.

I do not believe that Australians are creatures of habit, because reports show that any new trends in fashions, architectural designs for our houses, gadgets for the home, are welcomed, and absorbing interest always prevails. Attendances are splendid at city and local cooking demonstrations, which indicates that the average housewife is eager to offer her family a new and more interesting menu.

We have been in cafes which supposedly employ a Continental chef, and anxious to try a new dish have, for example, chosen 'meringue glace' – only to be presented with a heavy glass dish which supports a sticky substance called meringue, swamped with ice cream and coloured cornflour flavouring, and in no way representing the delicate and crisp flavour of a glace – so next time, to co-operate with our digestive organs, we choose the more reliable jelly and cream.

While my husband and I were staying at a well-known hotel we were surprised to notice that overseas visitors, who had had the opportunity to taste Continental cooking, chose bacon and eggs for breakfast several mornings in succession, without attempting anything else on the menu – yet at the same time offering their reminiscences of the 'Riviera'.

I still feel that a charming Continental café in Sydney offering delightful confections and unusual meals would be welcomed by Australians.

Meanwhile, Dorothea Sharland weighed into the argument with her comments on monotonous salads:

Sir,– However monotonous the cakes sold in Sydney may be, as your correspondents assert, they could not be more so than (with a few exceptions) our fruit and vegetable salads.

Most restaurants nowadays are sufficiently daring to add grated carrot to the usual salad of lettuce, tomato and cooked beetroot, but other vegetables are equally gratable.

And with our splendid variety of fruit, why are we so often offered the salad of orange, apple, and banana, sometimes tinned?

The Biscuit Factory

Emma Ciccotosto and Michal Bosworth

Emma: A Recipe for Life by Emma Ciccotosto and Michal Bosworth
recounts the ordinary life of an extraordinary woman, supplemented by
'Conversations across a Kitchen Table' and Emma's recipes for simple
Italian staples. Emma was born in the Abruzzo region of central Italy in
1926 and migrated to Australia in 1939. Married at seventeen, she had four
children by the age of twenty-eight when she started work in a biscuit
factory in Fremantle. As she explains, in the 1950s biscuits were generally
packed loose in tins rather than in individual packets.

Emma: A Recipe for Life, 1995

One day I met a woman I knew while I was out shopping, and she told
me I should ask for a job at the Mills and Ware biscuit factory. The
very next day I cycled down and saw the manager. He took one look at
me and told me that I was too small to do the work. I protested that
I was used to hard work and I went back to see him again and again.
The third time I saw him he decided to give me a trial. I went home
so happy and excited, and told the family that I was starting work the
next day. Peter was pleased, because he knew I could not stay all day
in the same house with his mother. That night I went to bed thinking
about work the next morning and I got butterflies in my stomach, but
I knew I had done the right thing for myself.

For my first day at work I wore a black dress with flowers on it. It
was long, as that was the fashion, and when I walked into the factory I
felt everyone looking at me. I felt they were sizing me up and deciding
I was from the country. I will never forget that first day. The fore-
woman put me onto a line of women who were packing biscuits into
tins. No one explained what I was supposed to do, so I just watched the
other women and did the same. Each of them was responsible for two
lines of biscuits on the conveyor belt. They swept off the same number
each time and put them into the tins. I followed them. I didn't know
I was expected to have had some experience before I was able to do
this. The others were surprised when I told them I had never worked
in a biscuit factory before. I was tired after that first day, but pleased

with myself, for I knew I could do the work. I got seven pounds in my first pay packet for my first week's work. Fremantle had begun to improve . . .

I made many friends at Mills and Ware, and it was this I looked forward to when I began. Working conditions were not too good then. It got hot in the factory in summer. There was no air-conditioning, only a few fans that moved the air around but did nothing to reduce the heat. I cycled to work each morning on my old bicycle which I had brought with me from Waroona. It had no brakes and so I used to stop by putting my foot through the spokes of the front wheel. People told me this was dangerous, but luckily nothing ever happened to me. I worked from 7.45 in the morning to 4.45 in the afternoon. We had three-quarters of an hour for lunch, and I usually went home for it. We also had a twelve-minute break both morning and afternoon when we ate some of the company's biscuits and had a cup of tea. After a few years we lost the afternoon break in favour of going home at 4.30, which I preferred. We had to wear a uniform and a white net hat with a band. The women working around the ovens wore blue uniforms, but later all of us wore cream. The men wore white shirts and trousers.

I was twenty-eight when I began at Mills and Ware. In those days there were still a lot of people working there, perhaps as many as eight hundred. Some of the ovens they continued to stoke with wood because they produced a line called Saloon Empire biscuits which they claimed were cooked better in wood-fired ovens than electric ones. These biscuits were rather like the Sao is today, but they were softer. Many women and girls started work with Mills and Ware, but they did not all stay. It was all right if you were a good worker, but if you were slow they told you off again and again, and so many just left.

We had to stand on boards when we were working on the conveyor belt, wrapping or packing biscuits. Because I am short I needed four of these boards. They were short, thick planks that were used to adjust the height and reach of all the workers. They must have spoiled the look of the factory for some of the management, because one day we were told not to use them any more. That was when they decided not to employ girls who were short, or girls who had small hands. Applicants for jobs were measured at the interview. This kind of discrimination did not last long, as most of us who were already working there could not manage without the boards. They made the work much more comfortable, even though we had to pick them up and stack them neatly against the factory wall at the end of each day.

I soon discovered that the manager had been right about some things, because there were some jobs I was too small to handle. I could not reach to take down the trays of biscuits from some of the ovens, but I could do almost everything else. The work was not organised as it is today. When we arrived we stood around the lady foreman and she gave us our jobs for the day. Some girls had to carry tins all day long from one side of the factory to the other to have them filled. Others were sent to certain ovens to handle the biscuits as they came through. When we were doing cream biscuits the single loose biscuits were put straight into tins and sent to a cream room where a machine put cream between them. They had to pass through a fridge before we wrapped them. Some girls were sent to put cellophane around packets. This was a job we hated in summer, because we sealed the cellophane on a hot plate that stood on the table in front of us, and in summer its heat was almost unbearable. Others were sent to lift trays out of ovens to put on racks to cool before we wrapped the biscuits. Some had to ice cakes or spread jam on swiss rolls which then had to be rolled and sliced. Everything was done by hand. You needed a good eye and a steady wrist to do most of the work. Mills and Ware also made puddings and Christmas cakes. To do the puddings we sat at tables and scooped the prepared mixture into tins, weighed them and sent them to be steamed, after which they were sealed. I always think that their Christmas cakes are the best you can buy – they have so much rum in them that they keep for years. But the main lines, the biscuits that kept the factory going, were Milk Arrowroot, Granita and Ginger Nuts. They made them then and they still make them today.

Some biscuits, like Coconut Rings, Fruit Mince Rolls and Ginger Nuts, were packed loose into tins and sent to shops that way. The tins were sent back to the factory, where women had to clean them and remove the sticky label that went around the tin. Later they brought in plastic tubs to pack these biscuits. More and more biscuits were wrapped. Some were harder to wrap than others. All the new girls learned how to wrap by doing masses of little packets which were sold at the Perth Royal Show, but you could make a lot of mistakes. We didn't weigh each packet as we wrapped. We weighed the first one and set it in front so it would act as our model. We were permitted to make a certain number of mistakes, and some packets went out of the factory a little lighter or a little heavier than they should have been, but when you consider that we wrapped such light delicate biscuits as a line called Club Cheese, as well as heavier ones like Custard Creams, it is hardly surprising that the wrapping wasn't always perfect. After I had been there a couple of years the company installed a machine that wrapped Milk Arrowroot and Nice biscuits automatically. It took a long time to get it going properly, but once it went a lot fewer girls were needed because these were two of the main biscuits the factory made. The management was happy; they said they hoped to have all the biscuits wrapped and packed by machine. They were always interested in reducing staff numbers.

Clement's Lunches

Gerald Murnane

The ineffaceable smell of school lunches – squashed banana-on-brown-bread mingled with newly tanned leather – remains with most Australians for their entire life. Recalling the Globite school case, Nancy Keesing writes in *Lily on the Dustbin* (1982) that 'it was the smell that dominated all, recalling countless paper-bags of school lunch and "play lunch"' (which in Queensland is known as 'little lunch').

Tamarisk Row, 1974

Every afternoon when Clement reaches the back veranda and pushes open the fly-wire door, his mother calls out – did I give you enough for lunch today? and he answers – yes thanks. Every morning as he leaves for school she makes him put his hand into his school-bag to make sure he has not forgotten his two brown-paper bags – one for lunch and one for play-lunch. The lunch is always six little triangular sandwiches with at least two different kinds of fillings arranged so that as he eats his way through the stack he never finds the same filling in two successive sandwiches, a cake or a pair of sweet biscuits, and a piece of fruit. The play-lunch may be two fairy cakes or a slice of moist fruit-cake or two cheese cakes or a pair of biscuits with jam between them, but never the same as on the previous day. Sometimes his mother asks him – in all the years you've gone to St Boniface's have you ever had to buy your lunch once? He answers no, because even when there is no bread in the house on a Monday morning she sends him to school with just his play-lunch and waits at the school gate at lunch-time with sandwiches made from fresh bread. Sometimes she asks – have you ever had to take your lunch wrapped in newspaper? He answers no, because even his cakes and biscuits are always wrapped in clean lunch-wrap paper inside a brown-paper bag. And sometimes she asks – have you ever had to sit down to a whole pile of jam sandwiches with no butter? He answers no, because he always has such fillings as cheese and vegemite, egg and lettuce, apple and raisins, dates and nutmeg, peanut butter, or ovaltine mixed into a paste with the butter. His mother is always curious to hear about other boys' lunches and listens eagerly as he tells her how half of his grade run down to Keogh's Korner Shop with threepence for a pie or pastie or fourpence for a whole Boston bun which they eat without any butter or filling, and how some of the others have a stack of jam or vegemite sandwiches without any butter and wrapped in nothing but newspaper. He never tells her how only a few days after he first started school a small crowd of the shabby poorer boys in his grade gathered round and stared as he unwrapped his dainty parcels of cakes and took out his piece of fruit, and how a few days later some boys that he knew, even without a trial of strength, were tougher than himself snatched away his bags and tossed pennies to see who would have Clement's fairy cakes or his apple or even the choicest of his sandwiches. In his very early days at school Clement believes that by allowing the rougher boys to plunder his lunch and play-lunch bags he is securing their friendship or at least making sure that he will be safe during the many lunch-hours when they go around looking for victims to bash or torture. But he soon finds that even though he reaches a perfect understanding with boys like Barry Launder or Michael Harman or Fat Cormack, so that they only have to walk up to him before they go to Keogh's and say – what have you got for us today Killer? and he hands over everything but a few sandwiches to them to share among themselves, he is often one of the first to be hauled before Launder to be dealt with – sometimes only half an hour after he has given the gang all the tasty parts of his lunch. Eventually he tries such tricks as eating all his cakes and fruit on the way to school in the morning or hiding in the lavatory as soon as the grade is let out for lunch or eating his lunch as he walks only a few feet from the nun patrolling the shelter shed. None of these tricks works for more than a few days. In the end one of Launder's gang either bashes him or threatens to bash him until he agrees once more to hand over a fair share of each day's lunch. Then one day a big girl in Therese Riordan's grade, whose name he never discovers and whose face is not pretty enough to inspire or even to interest him, happens to see two of Launder's gang dipping into his lunch bag while he stands patiently by. The girl orders them to give the food back to Clement. When they tell her to bag her bloody head she slaps each of them hard across the face, takes the lunch from them, and sends them running away. For two weeks after that she meets Clement at the school gate each morning and takes his lunch into safe-keeping. Then at play-time and lunch-time she meets him and lets him sit beside her while he eats. Two of three times during those weeks Launder and his gang prowl around just out of her reach shaking their firsts at Clement or holding their stomachs and groaning and crying that they are starving. But they never dare to bash him, even after the girl has left him. Then one day the girl tells Clement that he should know by now how to handle the boys if ever they bother him again, and leaves him to eat his lunch alone once more. About a week later she sees him in the yard and says – those little brats haven't been pestering you again have they? He says – no thank you very much, because he doesn't want to put her to any more trouble. But of course they have been ransacking his brown-paper bags since the first day after the girl left him.

The Oslo Lunch

Redmond Phillips

The 'Oslo lunch' was introduced to Australian schoolchildren in the 1940s as the prototype of a healthy school lunch, full of goodness and vitamins. Essentially it consisted of wholemeal bread sandwiches with cheese, plus an apple and an orange, milk to drink and a small serve of 'Weat-Harts', a wheat germ preparation. It did not survive the 1950s.

a lettuce leaf
with a white grub shivvering
in its wet folds
cheese
brown bread
a glass of milk
and an orange
is what they give you at twelve o'clock
with a pat on the head
and a spartan smile
this is
the
oslo
lunch

for myself
i have a milk shake
3 chocolate frogs
an ice cream
perhaps popcorn
up at the corner shop
this is the anti-oslo lunch

oslo is the capital of norway
i met a man once from norway
a mr jorgensen
a friend of uncle todd
big bald and very pink
he told us many stories about
the norse gods
and the fiords
he had never heard of
the
oslo
lunch
i asked him

Bread Should Not Be Crumbled

Anonymous

While they were doubtless directed to a different audience, the rules of table manners decreed by *Principles of Home Cookery* (1936) appear far more rigid and authoritarian than those of *Australian Etiquette* half a century earlier (page 50). Certainly, different social and economic values set the context, but the intransigence of the 'Thou shalt/shalt not' formula is perhaps indicative of deeper changes in society.

Principles of Home Cookery, 1936

---

1. Be punctual for meals and come properly attired.

2. Men and boys should not seat themselves at table until ladies are seated. Children should remain standing until hostess is seated.

3. When sitting at table the body should be about six inches from the table. One should not lean back in one's chair except between the courses. Avoid placing elbows on the table or fidgeting with table appointments. Soup is taken from side of the spoon and the plate should not be tilted. Bread should not be crumbled into soup or any other food.

Fish is eaten with fish knives and forks, two forks or one fork in right hand and a piece of bread in left. The handles of knives and forks should rest lightly in the hand. Only a small portion at a time should be taken on the fork or spoon.

Place butter or jam on one side of plate, cut the bread in pieces, and then spread with butter or jam.

Fruit should also be cut in pieces and not divided with the teeth. If a fork is used in the right hand, the prongs may be turned upwards, but always hold them downwards when used in the left hand.

Made dishes such as rissoles, curry, mince, etc, may be eaten with fork only. Dessert may be eaten with a fork, a spoon or both, as required. When finished place the knife and fork or spoon and fork side by side on plate, and the plate should not be pushed away. The stones from stewed fruit as plums, peaches, apricots, etc., should be separated from the pulp with spoon and fork and not taken into the mouth. The stones of small fruit, as cherries, may be taken into the mouth and then removed on the spoon. The knife should not under any circumstances be raised to the mouth.

Remain seated at table until the hostess rises.

Conversation at table should be general and pleasant.

Avoid unpleasant topics.

Be attentive to the wants of others.

Bread Rules

Frank Moorhouse

The image connected to the word 'bread' in Australia today is almost invariably a plastic bag, sealed with a small plastic tag, containing uniform slices of a homogenously soft and spongy texture, their outer edges almost indistinguishable from the core. It comes in many more varieties than the two Sydney novelist and columnist Frank Moorhouse would have known – white or brown – but its mass acceptance has made his Bread Rules obsolete.

Loose Living, **1995**

In my childhood bread had more rules about it than any other food (for reasons which escape me). Perhaps the Rules of Bread had to do with the metaphorical weight we give to bread, as in the 'staff of life', cast not your bread upon the waters, the loaves and fishes, we live not by bread alone, knowing which side your bread is buttered on, and so on.

Anyhow – in my family the Rules of Bread were as follows:

The bread was bought from a baker who carried the bread to the house from a horse-drawn cart in a bakers' basket and placed it in the bread compartment built into the side of the house.

The bread was taken from this compartment by the kitchen maid.

At meal times the loaf was placed on a bread board on the table and sliced with a bread knife. The slices had to be just so. Picking the hot fresh bread from the centre of the loaf was an irresistible temptation for a child and punishable by death.

For reasons which elude me, this fresh crust, that is the first outer slice of bread, was highly prized but not so the crusts (the other 'crusts' were the crusty frame of the slice of bread).

It was unacceptable to treat the crust as a separate gastronomic entity by spreading butter along the inside of the crust, something which I found particularly delectable (despite it being proscribed) and which is delectable because of the combination of butter and the aforementioned constituents of the crust.

The butter was transferred from the butter dish by the butter knife to the edge of the plate – never directly to the bread and never with the plate knife.

The bread was buttered with the plate knife from the crust evenly inwards to the centre, but there was something called 'having too much' butter on the bread.

I do not know who set the amount of butter which was considered 'correct' for a slice of bread (I suspect that it is the same Authority which sets all limits in life). I only know that it was less than I considered desirable. I liked my butter spread thickly and suffered severe deprivation throughout childhood for which I have more than amply made up.

If something was to be added to the bread and butter such as jam or honey there was also some decreed amount beyond which it was 'too much'.

Looking back over my turbulent and varied life I can see that seeking 'too much' or asking too much was to become a guiding maxim of my life.

Our bread was then cut into two triangles. Working-class people cut their bread into two rectangles. Small children had their bread cut into four rectangles or four triangles.

One did not eat the slice whole. I was to find that Americans ate the slice whole but that was later, around the time I began sitting on the chair back to front, wearing a baseball cap, chewing gum, and saying 'that's rich'.

The loaf had to be eaten whether stale or not and was never wasted. It could be used as toast or failing that, it could end up as an atrocious dish without a name, made of bread-sugar-and-hot milk or bread and butter pudding which was an also an atrocious dish, regardless of being sweetened with Golden Syrup.

Stale bread, thinly spread butter, and these two dishes, were some of the reasons I listed in my declaration to my family when I left home at thirteen never to return.

Mock Chicken

Chris Gregory

There was an era in Australian kitchens when counterfeiting was common.
***Australian Cookery of Today Illustrated* (c. 1937) gives recipes for 'Mock Duck' (made with sheep's heart); 'Mock Pears' (stewed chokos coloured with cochineal); 'Mock Hare Soup' (made with broad beans and lentils); and 'Mock Cream' (made from butter, cornflour, sugar and milk). Chris Gregory's mock chicken has the same relationship to 'real' chicken as sliced bread to the bread of Frank Moorhouse's childhood.**

Hot Sand, 1997

I grew up in a town called Mount Gambier in the south-east corner of South Australia. Mount Gambier's main industries involved the production of cheese and trees and the subsequent processing of these materials into more useful forms, such as chipboard and extruded cheddar cheese sticks sealed in transparent plastic tubes . . .

If we ate at [our neighbours'] house, we would invariably be served mock chicken or mock fish or some other processed protein product, along with frozen peas and frozen chips. Perhaps their family had to budget so that they could afford to maintain the fallout shelter. In my family, we had no similar concerns.

Mock chicken could be bought ready-made from the butcher or prepared at home. The main ingredient was sausage mince, to which a packet of chicken noodle soup was added for flavour. This mixture was then shaped into drumsticks. A thick wooden skewer was inserted along the axis of each drumstick, like a surrogate leg bone, then the drumsticks would be coated in breadcrumbs and deep fried. The mock chicken was eaten with the fingers, held by the protruding end of the wooden skewer.

I liked eating mock chicken. At the time I liked mock chicken more than I liked real chicken. The texture was more consistent, and the skewer was much more convenient and less disturbing than real chicken bones. Eating mock chicken was like eating a cartoon chicken.

People no longer make mock chicken, because real chicken has become inexpensive . . .

These days I eat a lot of chicken. The chicken is an elegant and highly sophisticated piece of modern technology. In adspeak, chicken has become an affordable luxury: it has maintained an up-market image while being available for a low cost. The price of food is very important for people on low incomes, and the easy availability of a good meat, like chicken, contributes greatly to their quality of life. I feel the same way about chicken as I imagine more politically conscious people feel about the democratic system or universal suffrage.

At the same time, I feel a certain nostalgia for mock chicken. Mock chicken was the product of more optimistic times, when people believed that human beings could improve on nature, when the artificial was valued more highly than the real and before the words natural and artificial became synonyms for good and evil respectively.

Paddy's, 1960s

Charmian Clift

This article was one of a series of light-hearted weekly columns Charmian Clift (1923–1969) wrote for the *Sydney Morning Herald*, after she and husband George Johnston returned in 1964 from ten years living on the Greek islands of Kalymnos and Hydra. Charmian Clift was the author of several novels and other books, and with George Johnston wrote three novels, one of which (*High Valley*, 1949) won first prize in the *Sydney Morning Herald*'s literary competition (unpublished works) in 1948.

The World of Charmian Clift, 1970

'Excuse me, lady! Outa da way, please! Outa da way!'

He was young and swarthy, with shoulders and arms built through generations for labour. Over his hairy Esau pelt he wore ragged shorts and a huge leather apron studded intricately with metal and hung about with wicked-looking curved picks. On his head a blue beret, worn jauntily. And as my friend Toni and I leapt for safety (or even survival) from his hurtling cart of tomato crates he grinned at us with that joyful unselfconsciousness of a Mediterranean male whose inalienable right it is to appraise every female he encounters – of whatever age or condition.

(I have a woman friend who has lived overseas for many years and she says that this is what she misses most in Australia, aside from somewhere to go for a holiday. She doesn't want to be pinched, particularly, but she feels deprived of that glint of recognition in a passing eye, the gallant salute from male to female: Madam, we are comrades and conspirators, and you know it, ma'am, as well as I do.)

And: 'Out of the way! Out of the way!' (or its equivalent) they yelled in urgent accents of Italian, Greek, Yugoslav, Chinese, and even Australian, as we dodged around piled trucks pulling in from places where still things grow in spite of the drought, stacks of aromatic crates, or jumped hastily from the onslaught of those lethal handcarts – dangerously stacked with fruit and vegetables or more dangerously empty – that shot out from every market aperture with the obvious intent of crushing us down into the mulched cabbage leaves and the trodden mint and parsley that bore every evidence of a progress passing.

What was exciting was that we were involved in the progress, shouting in triumph as it passed, as though these huge market vaults were really Persepolis. It was terribly early in the morning, and every single leaf, blade, shoot, root or bulb had the dew or the earth on it.

I have always thought an early morning market to be a celebration. Demeter, who is the earth and the fruits of it. Harvest festivals. Corn Kings and Spring Queens. Poetry – 'Season of mists and mellow fruitfulness'. We survive on the peasantry of grass (those of us who are lucky enough) and the green of chlorophyll is nothing less than the colour of life. We all exist by that cool and cleanly and most commendable virtue of green. (My husband tells of a Chinese army that lived by every soldier getting down on his hands and knees and eating grass and roots.)

This early morning market was a proper celebration. As proper as Covent Garden or the Portobello Road or Never-on-Sunday Piraeus or co-operative Omsk or Tomsk or dear old unco-operative Athens or even, I suppose, a Chinese field where ragged soldiers grubbed around on hands and knees for a grass blade in lieu of wages and commissariat. If the incense smelled predominantly of crushed cabbage and sweaty leather there were wafts of herbs and spices too, and under that vast ecclesiastical roof whole pockets of air that were sodden with the scent of roses (pink and yellow and red and white and tangerine, and every shade of every colour in between).

And all this abundance, this prodigality of leaf, shoot, bulb and tuber, piled up in scented mountains under the echoing roof of this shouting, tumultuous market, came out of the Russian Steppes, out of the Caucasus, out of the Ice Ages that had frozen everything living everywhere else on earth. Plants came out of Siberian forests and high Asiatic plateaux. They filled Europe, they invaded all environments, they called to their aid ancient winds and modern insects and even birds to pollinate them. They were as ingenious and indomitable as man was, and wherever he has gone they have been there too in some form or other, ready for the plough and the spade and the harvesting.

'Do you think,' said Toni conspiratorially, 'that the Mafia are abroad?' (One is inclined to say 'abroad' instead of 'around' in these scented circumstances: there is a marvellous expectation of the Borgias, or their modern equivalent, sliding in to buy strange herbs for dubious purposes.)

I said I thought they were, and we tracked them down through crates and crates of pink tomatoes and mounds of celery and spinach and prodigal heaps of cabbages like green roses and the more intensely greenly deliciously tight curls of broccoli and tortuously spiked Chinese cucumbers and fresh bean shoots and weird mandrake roots that a little smiling Chinese man said were ginger and the whitely gleaming stalks of spring onions. The greens predominated but the earth was there too. You felt you were being offered your fill – thorn and leaf and succulent cell and indomitable tuber.

We didn't find the Mafia, but we found a swooping penguin flock of nuns, all black and white and with their sleeves rolled up and sugar sacks over their shoulders, bargaining with intense and concentrated delight over pumpkins and marrows and black-purple aubergines and red peppers and green peppers and lettuces all crisp and morning-curled and little pink radishes done up like Victorian posies.

'Out of the way! Out of the way!' the voices yelled, and two nuns jumped, black and white and beautifully hooded, spilling all around them spikes of scarlet gladioli and frantically red roses and little tender bunches of maidenhair fern. (And I wanted desperately for Elaine Haxton or Cedric Flower to be there to record it.)

Toni and I bought garlic in white bundles with the straw stems plaited. We bought Chinese cucumbers, not knowing quite how we were going to eat them but not caring. We were given a crate of lusciously pink tomatoes by my landlord, who operates joyously around those parts. We bought roses of a wicked Inca red, and virginal white daisies and little yellow pom-pom dahlias, and we looked and smelled and sniffed until we were quite intoxicated and fell about saying: 'Why shouldn't I buy this?' or: 'I think I want that,' and each saying to the other: 'Now, really.'

What we really wanted, I think, was to capture the penguin nuns for ever, and we wanted to buy guinea pigs, and white rats with pink eyes, and a beautiful mottled snake as thick as a motor tyre or a garden hose, and a Boxer pup who was yearning in spite of his pedigree, and a white rabbit who looked at us with such a boulevardier insouciance that we knew he'd been on stage at some time.

What we did was to buy hamburgers and coffee in some crummy market joint that was patronised by the men in leather aprons and served by Toulouse-Lautrec ladies in incredible hairdos, and around us everything was still roaring with green life and smelling of cabbages.

There are festivals going on all over Australia now. Perth, and Melbourne, and Adelaide. Culture is being served up, and Royalty, and Greek drama, and Russian poetry, and negro jazz in white ties and tails.

Toni and I, being low-life prone, will take the festival of an early morning market. Any time.

Sauce Language

Peter Mathers

The Wort Papers followed Peter Mathers' first novel, *Trap* (1966), which won a Miles Franklin Award. Like *Trap* it shows a lively and ingenious use of language. Tomato sauce has been a staple of Australian tables since the late nineteenth century. In the 1920s it was assumed that the average

family would get through a bottle a week. Commercial manufacture of tomato sauce seems to have begun in Victoria in 1868, and by the 1880s there were several manufacturers (who also produced jams) in Victoria, New South Wales and South Australia.

The Wort Papers, 1972

The basic language of sauce labels: Made only from fresh choice tomatoes; Ideal for lamb & veal & hogget & yearling & mutton & beef & fish & eggs & veges (even the glorious fresh tomato itself is enhanced by a few drops of this tomato sauce); Kiddies more and more (no we are not suggesting our tomato sauce for roast kiddies) but kiddies in ever-growing numbers add it to ice-cream and for a party treat what is more intriguing than tomato sauce in your party sherry? Nett contents 26 fl oz. Glory, glory to the tomato, a species of plant of the natural order Solanacae whose fruits when green make a capital pickle and when ripe and rosy are unexcelled raw or cooked; within its firm skin vitamins swim midst essential seeds and pulp par excellence; scientists have proven its tonic effect upon weak eyes and R.G.C. of Vic. uses tomato ointment on his suppurating buttock bites. The tomato, known in olden times, as the love-apple, induces copious flows from Bartholin's glands, blood engorgement of the penis and a fruitful swelling of the testes; so – down this sauce, farewell remorse, our good advice to you; the natural course, without remorse, our good advice to you; take a Bex or Vincents in a teaspoonful of tomato sauce, add it to Eno's effervescent salts and watch the delectable bubbles; buy six cases today for your fallout shelter; and brides-to-be – use it to placate your suspicious betrothed; *pace in terrum tomate* 26 floz 26 floz 26 f loz 26 flo z oz fl 26 ozl f26 ozlf 26 . . . the tomato requires a rich loam but it is inadvisable to manure heavily at the time of planting which should take place when there is no danger of frost; we recommend Rouge de Marmande, Grosse Lisse, Potentate, Bonny Best and innumerable others depending on local conditions, pests, diseases and frosts; beware the wilt and the voracious thrips or they will inherit your realm . . . *Deus ex Tomate.*

The Perfect Australian Meal

Oscar Mendelsohn

Oscar Mendelsohn (1896–1978) was an industrial chemist with a enthusiasm for food, from both a professional and personal perspective, and for books and writing. He contributed articles on food and drink to the *Sydney Morning Herald* and to *Epicurean* magazine in the 1960s and 1970s, many of which were subsequently published in his book *From Cellar and Kitchen* (1968).

Mendelsohn's 'perfect Australian' menu, which includes oysters but eschews the kangaroo favoured by earlier epicures, reflects the tastes and values of the 1960s, as does his optimistic conclusion commending the globalising vision of Australia's pioneering farmers.

Epicurean, August 1968

In 1947 and 1962 Gallup Polls were conducted in Britain to ascertain what a cross-section of the citizenry believed to be 'the perfect meal irrespective of cost'. Bear in mind that 1947 was in the time of grim austerity but fifteen years later was a period of high affluence. One might reasonably have expected the menus to have reflected at least something of the prevailing economic climate. Here, however, are the selected meals:

The Perfect Meal

1947	1962
Sherry	Sherry
Tomato soup	Tomato soup
Sole	Sole
Roast chicken	Roast chicken
Roast potatoes	Roast potatoes
Peas and sprouts	Peas and sprouts
Trifle and cream	Fruit salad & cream
Wine	Wine
Coffee	Coffee
Cheese and biscuits	Cheese and biscuits

So the only change from the poverty years to the rich ones was the substitution of fruit salad for trifle. Who dare deny the gastronomic conservatism of the British? But selecting the perfect meal is not really so simple a matter. Consider. To be eaten at home or in a hotel or restaurant? The season (summer or winter)? The size and nature of the company? The time available (eg, pre-theatre or a long, leisurely evening)? That far from exhausts the variables.

I now stick out my neck to set down the result of long and anxious thinking to discover the perfect Australian meal.

Data: A leisurely dinner for two at a restaurant, time late spring.

Avocado Oysters: Any one of half-a-dozen brands of Australian true fino sherry, bone dry, aromatic, chilled.

Poached Fillets of Flathead, caper sauce: Penfold's Trameah or Seaview Riesling or Hamilton's Moselle.

Roast Turkey, Walnut Stuffing: Tulloch's Hunter River Red. Fig Sauce (in season) or Brown Gravy Sauce: Crisp baked potato, butter-fried baby marrow.

Rum Omelette: All Saints' Old Muscat.

Coffee: Girgarre Blue Cheese.

Notes: I do not know whether what I call avocado oysters has an accepted name. I have only encountered it once, years ago, at one of those little South Yarra places that come and go wistfully, and I cannot remember any title. It consisted merely of half a ripe avocado 'pear' in whose hollow reposed two, three or four plump 'Sydney Rock' oysters, dressed with lemon juice and pepper. It was ferociously expensive (or as it then seemed) but worth the price. For me it remains the appetiser supreme. As to fish, if the common bodily-hideous Australian flathead were rare it would outprice the whiting and would be sent abroad to compete for glory with Mediterranean red mullet or turbot.

Turkey that is skilfully cooked is perhaps the 'safest' of all main dishes. But how one can tire of it! I once undertook an investigation in outback Western Australia. For three months we stayed at the local hotel. The proprietor ran a flock of turkeys. It was roast turkey every Sunday, cold every Monday and curried every Tuesday. It says much for the culinary virtue of *Meleagris mexicana* that I can still enjoy roast turkey despite these memories.

Rum omelette is, to me, the sweet beyond compare. Curiously, I have never seen it served outside Australia and even here it is chancy.

On one occasion it fell to me to specify the menu for The Fellowship of Trenchermen dinner to be held at – no, I shall not revive the sad past. The Italian proprietor (who has long since sold out) assured me that rum omelettes were one of his celebrities. God, that thick, heavy dough, innocent of the faintest blaze of spirit and apparently even of eggs! I think only an especially flavourous dessert wine can stand up manfully to the rum.

I include a cheese course but, for my own part, I think it is redundant. As to liqueurs, I believe any one of them would react to the detriment of a rum omelette that is a good rum omelette.

Epicurean, October 1968

Someone who read the piece on the ideal dinner menu in this column in the last issue has sent me for criticism his own version, which he constructed to make the best of Australian (ie, indigenous) foods. It goes:

> Appetiser: Cod's roe with sliced cabbage.
> Soup: Oyster.
> Entrée: Grilled fillet of snake.
> Main dish: Lamb or beef.
> Sweet: Mango or paw-paw with water ice.
> Savoury: Cheese.

He adds a sound list of accompanying wines.

However, my correspondent has misread my own intention. I did not suggest that my menu was confined to native Australian materials. I merely put it forward as my own concept of an ideal meal, irrespective of cost.

The stark truth, in my belief, is that it would be utterly impossible to construct an artistic and gratifying formal dinner from all-Australian ingredients. As I have already pointed out, almost everything we eat in Australia is exotic (ie, originally imported). This includes all our meats from rabbit to beef to venison, all poultry, vegetables, fruits, cereals, condiments (except salt), beverages and more. What then is left? Sea food (admittedly superb), some (not all) river fish, a few game birds and Queensland or bauple nuts.

'Bill Harney's Cook Book' is a collection of suggested native dishes that, frankly, makes my sides heave.

My correspondent falls into the common error of believing that paw-paw and passionfruit are Australian, but both are natives of tropical south America. He would need to drop from his menu all the wines, also the cabbage, the meat and the cheese. The snake remains, of course, but I remember that I had to leave the room hurriedly on one occasion in Chicago when my host told me that the cold white meat of peculiar and penetrating flavour we had started to eat was canned rattlesnake.

All the foregoing suggests that the settlers in this Australia of ours did a wonderful job in restoring to productivity an ancient and worn-out continent by introducing the best foods from every quarter of the globe.

Sweet and Sour

Carmel Bird

This dutiful depiction of the cooking mother (or the motherly cook) in Carmel Bird's novel *The Bluebird Café* is at the same time tinged with resentment – at the loss of self, during the transition from bride to mother; and the at Sisyphean side to all cooking, completed only to be consumed.

The Bluebird Café, 1990

My mother is very thin and pretty in this picture, and I have looked at the print of the picture that we have at home, and I have wondered about how such a pretty little person could become so fat and ugly. What did life and time do to her? Were all the fat women with shopping bags and tribes of children once graceful brides with shining hair and shining eyes like Margaret? Yes, all the fat women were once lovely little brides who carried bouquets of lilies.

The lilies have withered and died, and the silk gowns have yellowed and moulded and crumbled, while the dainty hands have mixed and moulded and manufactured jellies and puddings and chocolate cakes with fluffy cream and strawberries and hundreds and thousands, and hundreds and hundreds of legs of roast two-tooth. They have laundered the white linen cloth; they have cleaned the heavy silver, polished the perfect brass; they have mixed sauces and glazes, and plucked from the garden bunches of herbs and armsful of perfumed flowers. They have put the flowers into water in elegant vases and they have placed the vases on tables and surrounded the vases with vessels of pepper and salt and mustard and all manner of sweet and sour condiments, sugar and spice. Snips and snails and puppydogs' tails. (I may be writing a poetry book or a recipe book.) They bake yellow sponge cakes called Lemon Snowdrift, and cream the butter and sugar thoroughly, stirring in the dry ingredients and blending smooth; for the Nectarine Soufflé they beat and beat the whites of eggs until a stiff froth is formed and then they fold and fold the frothy froths into the mixture, lightly. They make creamy ice-cream in three flavours and they pluck fresh fruit from the fruit trees, crisp vegetables from the crisp vegetable garden where rows and rows of beans and peas twine and vine and pop with green, bright juice, and cabbages as blue as moths bunch out and frill and offer welcome shade to sweet pink babies who come there to sleep. The dainty fingers chop the crispy crunchy lettuces with chop chop chop and all is little pieces, strands of lettuce known as mermaid's hair and the locks of hair go green and near transparent onto the prongs of forks. Knives spread with butter things that are spread with butter such as bread and scones and also fruitcake and Christmas pudding sliced into cold slices with boiled threepences inside. Then they start pushing and poking and popping, tossing and slipping and jamming these fruits of the earth, these works of human hands, into their open mouths. The jaws begin to work and the good white teeth, the vigorous pink tongues grind and roll and the saliva begins to flow and bubble as the stomachs drip with smart digestive rivulets and the voices cry for more, more, more. More mushrooms; better Angel Food; jollier jellied bananas; many mounds of Mother's Mandarine and Marshmallow Salad before we die, before we die in an ecstasy of eating in a morris dance of marzipan coated in thick chocolate as dark as sin and dark as crime and dark as whispers in the ears of wandering wizards.

Honey Barbara

Peter Carey

Peter Carey's novel *Bliss* won the Miles Franklin Award in 1981 and was subsequently made into a film. Described as a stylish satire on modern living, it contrasts the unprincipled, amoral world relinquished by Harry Joy (but to which Bettina, his ex-wife, David and Lucy, his children, and Lucy's lover Ken are still attached) with the carefree and natural life of hippie Honey Barbara.

Bliss, 1981

'How do you sleep at nights?' Honey Barbara said, in no way cut by Ken's jibes about changing the world with herbal tea.

'We fuck,' Lucy grinned, 'until we can't do it any more.'

And they all laughed and Honey Barbara, in spite of her resolution not to, shared their dope with them.

'Well,' Ken said, 'why are you crazy? Why do you treat food like shit?'

He was not being unkind but he had tapped a serious flaw in Honey Barbara's character: she could not joke about food. She divided the world into people who ate shit and people who ate good food.

'This food is shit,' she said, 'and if I'm going to live here, Harry and I are going to eat good food.'

'What do you think is Good?' Lucy said, leaning over her folded arms.

'If you don't know, how can I tell you?'

'No salt? No sugar? No meat? No white flour? That sort of thing?'

'Fucking right,' Honey Barbara said, standing up and transferring her attention to the refrigerator.

'Sounds boring to me,' Lucy said. (Ken started bundling up his dope.)

Honey Barbara emptied the fridge in five quick throws, saving only the chilled alarm clock from destruction.

'Come back at dinner time, smart arse,' she said to Lucy, 'and we'll see how bored you are.' Lucy grabbed a can of coke from the garbage can. 'I'll be there,' she said.

She made spinach soup with spinach and potatoes and onions and spiced it with a little nutmeg. She baked potatoes in their jackets, pumpkin, onion, and stuffed mushrooms. She braised the cabbage with onion and apple and garlic and (eager not to lose her first engagement) threw in a little red wine she found in the cupboard. When challenged about the presence of wine later, she denied it all.

She steamed the sugar peas and planned to serve them in a big bowl.

I'll give you boring.

She made her famous apple and rhubarb crumble and sweetened it with the Rolls Royce of honeys. She said 'boring' out loud, like an incantation. She cooked with love and venom in almost equal quantities, the sweetness of one managing to offset the bitterness of the other.

She walked twenty-four miles and came home and baked a loaf of heavy dark bread. She cooked it in a flower pot she stole from the garden, muttering to herself while an electric drill penetrated the steel shell of the Cadillac Eldorado in the front garden.

At half-past seven she showered and washed her hair and applied a dab of Sandalwood Oil.

Everyone had assembled in the dining room except for Joel who had gone out on some errand of his own. Ken and Lucy had washed their hands in tribute to her. They had rubbed them raw with industrial soap and had taken out their Swiss Army knives and cleaned under their split nails with the smaller blade. Ken shaved his battered face and attempted to penetrate his tangled hair with a comb. He put on a white shirt and even stole one of Harry's ties, which he then had to be taught how to do up. Lucy wore a clean white boiler suit. David surprised everyone by wearing an exotic shirt and Gucci sandshoes. He poured the wine, but not before he had given his father the cork to formally approve.

Not since the family lunch (which had ended less enjoyably than it had begun – the duck caught fire and David put it out with a fire extinguisher) had they spread a cloth on the table and even Bettina, her shoes kicked off her sweaty feet, a strong Scotch in her hand, seemed relaxed and happy.

The Christmas Event

Thomas Shapcott

In his short story 'The Christmas Event', novelist and poet Thomas Shapcott, originally from Brisbane, subtly depicts generational differences typical of many Australian families, the gradual changes in taste between the 1950s and the 1980s. In particular, he hints at the discordance between image and actuality, the distance between nostalgic representation and reality when the memories of particular foods, unconsciously exalted, inflated and embellished over the years, are discovered to have no relation to the eating experience.

What You Own, 1991

Mick had made great preparations for the first Christmas with Marion in the little flat. Their first Christmas together. He had bought a decorated tree, a whole series of little surprises hidden in various corners – chocolates in shiny wrapping in the tea caddy, an amusing Chinese god in the laundry basket, a disc of Mary O'Hara singing Irish ballads behind the recipe books, and all prepared with a treasure-hunt series of notes and messages. He had brought in most of the things his mother celebrated the Christmas meal with: a ham, pickled pork, a roast chicken. Marion, under his guidance, had prepared the aspic moulds with asparagus, with peas, and with beetroot. There were to be the potato salad and the bean salad. There would even be nuts, though Mick had never really cared for the dusty walnuts and the daunting Brazil nuts, whose flavour after all the effort of cracking them always seemed like flour. Almonds were not his cup of tea either but for the sake of Christmas and the necessary ritual it was unthinkable to have the table without them. Then there was the fruit.

But on Christmas Eve the waters broke and Marion was driven to the hospital and all the preparations, that time, were abandoned.

Old Molly was delighted to have him stay back at his old home. She had prepared her usual large family Christmas meal, though without definite promises from any of her newly enlarged family as to who would come, and when. Though she forgot things now, not one detail of the activities that had absorbed her could be forgotten. Something performed for twenty or twenty-five years is not easily given up. And most of the food would keep, the big hot Christmas dinners were a thing of the past. Molly had eagerly embraced the post-war turn to sensible meals for a sub-tropical climate. The vegetable aspics, straight from the pages of the *Australian Women's Weekly*, were her great triumph: they looked so colourful and inviting, and were always a talking point. They would keep for days after, though it was only in recent years that they tended not to be eaten immediately.

Ten years later his father died, and Mick insisted the big Christmas meal should be with them, with Mick and Marion. There was a secret flattery in the thought that he, now, might provide the link in the ritual of exchange. There were fourteen grandchildren by this time and Mick's house and yard could take them all comfortably.

It was proper that this year should be a faithful replica of all the Christmas meals their father had presided over, while Molly, their mum, had bustled in the kitchen with the girls until everything was laid out on the family table, a table that had seen all of their children grow up. The endless heated debates about schoolwork and then about sport and politics, current news items thrashed and threaded between mouthfuls of steak and mashed potatoes, local debates in the council justified or disparaged as Molly served up second and third helpings of rice pudding or fruit salad. Endless cups of tea served round as the children brought home their challenges on international affairs and rock 'n' roll music. The rounded lifetime of family meal-sharing merged with all the other sharings that had been taken for granted all those years, from examination results to the first insolent cigarette or Stanley's first date, or Annette's crush on the music teacher. The family dining table was of polished red cedar which was always covered with a heavy blanket to protect its delicate surface.

In his restored Victorian dining room Mick polished the mahogany table himself. They did not use a blanket to cover it – 'Why hide that wonderful timber?' Marion had cried, and he agreed. They ate most of their meals down in front of the TV, with the kids, anyway. He rubbed over the eight balloon-backed chairs, too, then found the Irish lace tablecloth. He put out the good cutlery in neat rows, and brought in all the plates. It was to be a help-yourself smorgasbord, not a sit-down meal. There were simply too many of them, even with the children in the breezeway at their own table (though Mick knew half of them would end up around their parents in the big room).

He set forth the crystal wine glasses, a wedding present from Stanley and his Jean. On the big sideboard Mick placed three bottles of a good red wine and uncorked them. Their father had not been a red wine drinker. In his later years he had, on his doctor's instruction, imbibed a glass of white at each meal. His older preference had been beer, but that, too, in moderation. It was the children who were now all experts in varietal subtleties, who extolled Australia's wonderful vintages and presented their father and each other with bottles of special labels bought during wine-tasting excursions to the Hunter, or the Barossa or the Margaret River.

Everything was as it should be. Marion called Mick to start carving the ham and the pickled pork. He admired the aspic moulds. So did the kids. There were nuts – though pride of place was the huge dish of macadamias. Mick had become reconciled to nuts after he had had pointed out to him the fact that the local Queensland nut, the macadamia, was indeed a world gourmet treat. Growing up they had all simply taken it for granted as something you cracked with a hammer when you were a kid and then gobbled.

'Well, here's to the old man,' Stan spoke up. 'He brought us up well. We were a family.'

'We still are,' Mick offered, looking round at the twenty-three people gathered under his roof, or down in the back garden. The twenty-fourth would have been his father. 'He would have liked this day, this Christmas party,' Mick added, though he himself could not avoid a certain feeling of staleness in the routine, for the first time ever sensing that the aspic side dishes had been without taste and that the cold meat had been unimaginative and predictable. It was as if he were merely an inheritor, lacking some truly independent presence in this stale ritual. It seemed disloyal to think of the new flavours and continental dishes now available in the delicatessen.

Wild Duck

Judah Waten

Judah Waten (1911–1985) was born in Odessa, Russia, but grew up in Australia from the age of three. He wrote many novels, often focused on the experiences of migrants, particularly Jewish, in an alien Australian society, together with essays and short stories. *So Far No Further* focuses on two neighbouring migrant families, one Jewish and one Italian, both of which have prospered in Australia, and describes the inevitable conflict between generations and the difficult romance of Paul and Deborah.

So Far No Further, 1971

Outwardly Paul was calm when he arrived home. He had not held up the meal, which was not quite ready. As it was too cold out on the patio, Giuseppe, Dominico and his wife Emilia, Angelina and her husband Salvatore were assembled in the living room, drinking a home-made white wine. The children were playing in another room; the smallest infants were lying in cots in the hall . . .

Dominico kept asking Paul questions about the University, about his studies as well as student activities. He was curious about the University and the sort of people who went there. Students occasionally dropped into the shop and Dominico would question them too. What lucky people students were, he more than once exclaimed to them.

'And have you seen the young Falksteins lately?' he asked. 'Morris, Deborah. She called into the shop not so long ago. Now there's a fine girl. She has a good heart and a good head.'

Paul felt his face growing hot but he said nothing about Deborah.

'I see Morris frequently. At lectures. We're in the same year, as you know.'

He would have liked to talk about Deborah but he was afraid that his family, especially the women, would see straight into his heart. The women had inbuilt romance detectors; they would know at once. His mother would be the first to know. She suspected something already; she was forever suspicious and she would not leave him alone until he had admitted his interest in Deborah. It would begin harmlessly enough and end in a dramatic denouement. He shrank from that . . .

Maria called them to lunch. They filed into the dining room and sat down at the long table, the children at a separate table at the far end.

'There's wild duck,' Giuseppe announced.

He had shot the duck himself. He had gone with a party of friends to a lake teeming with duck.

'I had to fill my heart with hatred for them to shoot them,' he said.

It was the same when he went shooting quail.

'But, after all, birds are predatory,' he went on, justifying himself. 'They live on creatures smaller than themselves. You must come with me next time, Dominico,' he added half-humorously.

He invited Dominico to accompany him every time he went shooting although he knew his son wouldn't go with him or anyone else.

'You know, father, I have nothing against birds, least of all ducks and quail.' Dominico always gave him the same answer.

'I am soft-hearted, too,' said Giuseppe. 'I am filled with remorse.'

He had always managed to stifle his remorse when the duck or quail became a delicious meal cooked by Maria.

They began the meal with spaghetti. Maria placed the large bowl of steaming spaghetti in the middle of the table. Giuseppe's eyes glistened with pleasure. He loved spaghetti, religiously eating it every day. He preferred it with meat sauce and cheese sprinkled on top of the sauce.

With a cheerful expression he sucked up his spaghetti and sprayed sauce on the tablecloth. Several of the children at their table emulated him, noisily sliding the spaghetti into their mouths and spreading sauce over their hands and clothes.

Maria glared silently at the children and Angelina, also without uttering a word, fixed an angry gaze on her father. Instead she tried, once again, to give him an object lesson, demonstratively turning her fork until all the spaghetti was wound around it and then deftly conveying it to her mouth.

Giuseppe paid no attention to her. She had given him the same lesson many times. After all, she had been educated at a convent where, besides being taught English, arithmetic and geography, she was also taught manners, Australian manners, he thought. He kept his eyes on the plate and went on devouring his spaghetti.

When the stewed duck arrived on the table Giuseppe watched apprehensively, wondering to whom she would give the biggest portion.

There was enough for a battalion. Until recently she had left the food on the table and everybody had helped themselves. But she had to change all that: greedily, thoughtlessly Giuseppe had been known to help himself to almost half the meat, quite regardless of the rest of the family. When she had instituted the new procedure of serving each one, when the dishing-up did not begin with him and he saw her passing food from person to person, he had been known to cry out aloud his fears that not sufficient would be left for himself. Only Angelina had roundly chided him for his behaviour.

Now he was not only served first but he also got the largest helping. He glanced at each plate. Paul's helping was far too large. It was ridiculous to heap up Paul's plate, he thought. Paul wouldn't eat half of it. But that was Maria.

As though asserting that he was first in the household Giuseppe was the first to stretch his hand across the table to pull the bowl of sauce towards him. In his haste he poured a good half of it over his duck. Then becoming aware that the family was watching him, he paused, holding his knife and fork in mid-air with a sheepish expression.

'Take some off my plate, please do. Help yourselves. I don't really care much for the sauce. Forgive me, Maria. It is very good sauce.'

No one made a move. To spare his father further embarrassment Paul passed his plate to him and said:

'Put some on my meat.'

'Of course I will,' Giuseppe said, his head bent towards Paul's plate.

Maria had excelled herself – a wonderful cook, thought Paul: the meal was better than ever. The family settled itself in the lounge to drink coffee and liqueurs. It was a bright room with crimson wallpaper. The sun which was shining outside made it bloom with light.

Paul was anxious to leave but this was not immediately possible without evoking a rebuke from his mother. With a kind of feverish restlessness, drumming his fingers on the small coffee table in front of him, he listened to his father's renewed boastings and Salvatore's absurdities and Angelina's complaints.

Suddenly Paul stood up and said:

'I'm afraid I have to go now.'

'I thought you were coming with us to the Cossotos,' his mother said.

'I'm sorry. I just have too much work to do.'

Maria looked at him balefully for a moment without speaking.

Sicilian Sauce

Venero Armanno

Australian-born, Sicilian-speaking writer Venero Armanno often takes Italian–Sicilian migrant communities as settings for novels and short stories. Food traditions are a strong determinant of life in such families and, not surprisingly, food – hearty, earthy, peasant food – is an integral part of Armanno's writings.

Romeo of the Underworld, 1994

The night of the century's final lunar eclipse is an occasion. I wanted to do something special for Mary.

So here is how you make a proper Sicilian sauce.

First you fill your house with music. It has to be music good enough to put you in a mood for cooking. Second, you uncork a bottle of red wine, drink one glass and keep another handy, and then, third, you start cracking a lot of garlic.

Johnny had a CD of that great pop-opera, *Carmen*, and in the fridge Mary had left a bottle of chianti. I got busy cracking garlic and was soon pan-sizzling beef mince in extra virgin oil. Blue kept me company but he whined until I fed him. I knew how he felt for inside me there was a hunger different from any I was used to.

Maybe it was just the aromas of the kitchen.

With more wine, and a soprano singing, I chopped mushrooms, tomatoes, hot peppers. Mary couldn't have read my mind better if she'd tried, almost everything I wanted was there in the kitchen. When I had all the ingredients bubbling in the covered pan I went looking for candles.

The house took on a gossamer glow.

I went onto the verandah to try and see the moon but it was still obscured by clouds. Blue sat by me and let out a fart. I said to the absent starlight, *Mary come home.* Her ugly green Volkswagen pulled up, engine rattling, and I went back to the kitchen. The sauce simmered that special orange-red of meat and ripe tomatoes.

Mary was covering her ears.

'It sounds like a carnival. Can I turn it down a bit?' Which she did without any prompting. Her face was drawn and her black and white clothes were stained. 'Candles. And you're cooking.'

'There's a lunar eclipse. I thought I'd make something special for the occasion.'

'I think it'll rain.'

'It's still an eclipse, even if you can't see it.'

Mary stood in the kitchen with me. 'I've been working today. Cash in the hand. I'm caring for a grandmother who should be in a nursing home. But her family can't bear the thought of letting her go. She's a little senile and very – ' Mary looked down at herself ' – incontinent.' She seemed uncomfortable. 'They wanted me to start right away. Grandma Henderson has a weight problem. My back is killing me. And I need a shower.'

I uncovered the pan. 'This'll be waiting for you. And a glass of chianti. Okay?'

'Okay.'

Mary left the kitchen, shaking her head at my new-found zest for life. I stirred in the pan and washed endives for the salad and salted the boiling water, then walked around the house with another glass of chianti. A few days earlier I'd realised there were no photographs anywhere. Plenty of art, but no photos.

'It's extraordinary,' Mary had told me. 'Johnny doesn't like himself very much. You won't find a photo of him anywhere.' Or of her, it seemed. Well, I wanted her to know I liked her.

The shower was going, I listened, and then the shower stopped. *Carmen* finished. Mary would be drying herself with one of Johnny's thick towels. I went to the corridor and the blistery glass of the bathroom door was misted over. There were dribbles of condensation running down the glass, steam seeped out from the crack under the door, and inside Mary was pink and naked.

I hurried back to the kitchen.

When Mary appeared she was wearing a daggy-baggy tracksuit, as if she had dressed to put me off. I gave her a big glass of wine and saw her cuffs were rolled back many times – Johnny's clothes.

'God I feel better,' she said. 'What a bloody day.'

There were dark smudges under her eyes and her skin wasn't good.

I gave a final stir in the pot. The spirelli pasta was ready. With the serving spoon I picked up a little of the sauce.

'Have a taste.'

Mary's hazel eyes gave me a prolonged look before she leaned toward the spoon, mouth a little open, pink tongue showing. With a hand she kept the hair away from her face, droplets of water beaded in her tresses.

'Mmm, it's good.'

We were standing beside the warm stove, Mary's hand still holding her hair from her face. I put my hand over hers. Hazel eyes looked into mine. I felt lost in the steam of garlic and basil and tomatoes, in the rich black dirt of Johnny's garden.

I kissed Mary.

Sam Orr Visits Tony's Bon Goût

Richard Beckett

Richard Beckett (1936–1987), who under the name of Sam Orr contributed the weekly feature 'Tucker' to *Nation Review* in the 1970s, completely subverted the writing of restaurant reviews. As Marion Halligan wrote, 'Orr's articles always end up being about how revoltingly drunk he got.' At the same time, however, he helped open the way for a new and less kitchen-focused kind of food writing and, in his serious moments, consistently and persuasively argued for regional gastronomic individuality. He would have been delighted by the recent indications of success with truffle growing in cool-climate Tasmania.

Tony's Bon Goût (Elizabeth Street, Sydney) was opened by Gay and Tony Bilson in 1973 and quickly became a success, critic Leo Schofield writing in 1975 that: 'Almost every food buff in town puts it at the top of his list.'

Nation Review, 26 July–1 August 1974

The first indications that the week was going to be a disaster came with the sounds of screaming and scuffling at the front door of our Leichhardt semi-detached palace. I looked up the hall and there was Scarlet beating away ineffectually at two shadowy figures who were edging their way into the house. 'Come and help me,' she screamed. 'The drunken red faced caucasian hordes have invaded from the south!'

Hastily drawing the Sydney line across the middle of the hallway I beat it out the back way to ask the only other Australian resident in this part of little Italy whether he could possibly lend me his three foxies for a short moment in time. He was willing to help but unable to do so as, he explained, they were at this very moment engaged in their favourite sport of running under the trotting gigs which use the Leichhardt byways as paths to Harold Park. And he also regretted that after this encounter they would be further tied up in a long standing engagement known as attack-the-greyhound-trainer-and-make-Son-of-Havoc-cut-his-pads-on-the-roadway. 'Beats taking the bloody bastards out for a walk,' he said. The curses and oaths, plus the sounds of bouncing rocks in the deepening twilight led me to believe that he was not telling a lie.

Wasting no time in idle conversation I rushed to my corner grocer in the hope of borrowing his doberman pinschers. But he also turned me down, stating that while I was more than welcome to take the male dog, the damned fool would attack no one, and the female was so savage that she would eat me before she reached the real enemy. I trudged back home to be greeted by the sight of Scarlet bound and gagged to our designer award stainless steel standing lamp (so much for trendiness!) and the two invaders crashing through the booze cupboard with gleeful cries. I untied Scarlet as best I could and soothed her with a bumper of brandy. But no sooner was the gag out of the bloody woman's mouth than she started to abuse me as a lily-livered failure, made several insulting references to my sexual capacity and said that I wasn't a writer's arsehole. Tenderly I replaced the gag and poured the remainder of the brandy over her curly locks.

After that I spent a happy hour or so with my southern friends playing the usual boring journalistic game of do you remember when . . . and who's died of the booze lately? That part of the greeting over, my friend said he just had to visit a Sydney pub. At this stage I decided to take matters in hand and get some food into his stomach to prevent him from turning into a walking version of brandy aspic. A little couth food and atmosphere was called for. His companion announced that she was buggered anyway and after seeing her to bed with a hot water bottle and an economy can of tomato juice with a gallon of beef tea on the side we sallied out into the gaily lit city of sin to see what we could find.

Now people had been muttering to me about Tony's establishment for just about a year. At one stage it was a very *in* place for the fat cat advisers of our charming federal leader to sup at. Because of this I had decided to let it pass for a while, waiting for things to return to normal, when the restaurant learned to operate without vast subsidies from the honest taxpayers of Australia. Eventually, as in all things Sydney, the fashion changed and the *in* crowd had gone chittering off to other new and titillating taste treats. It was time for a fair assessment.

As Tony's is a bring your own, the three of us paused briefly in a city liquor lavatory near the restaurant to quietly imbibe a brandy and soda and purchase a couple of bottles of steam from its limited selection (the bottle shop has risen above the flagon level, but only just) and we tottered in to be greeted by a subdued interior for a change – white tablecloths, a few scattered prints and, glory of glories, not a single potted Mexican dwarf palm in sight. Thanking my own personal saviour for this smallest of small mercies I managed to get my beefy faced fool of a friend seated without too much fuss on his part and allowed Scarlet to say a few words, after extracting the promise from her that she would make no further shrill references to my sexual powers.

The menu is French with the usual Australian modifications. There is also a written card with, one presumes, daily or weekly specials. And the specials were the things that appeared to hold quite a lot of interest.

Pausing only for a moment, old red face and myself ordered a *terrine* of piglet and Scarlet opted for celery soup. The terrine, which was served with sharp pickles and tiny olives, was good and firm – and had some taste in it, speaking of much more than the usual grab bag of mixed herbs that so called chefs usually hurl in the direction of this much mistreated dish. Scarlet's celery soup, served with a swirl of cream, was sensational. It was a true French *creme* of vegetable soup, none of your nasty English versions. She said it had potatoes through it as well, giving the soup some body without taking away from the celery taste. My God! I thought, it looks as though it's going to be quite a good night. And it was – in the restaurant – wait for the later disaster.

For the main courses Scarlet chose a duck done with apples, or in the fashion of Normandy. Once again it was very good indeed, the bird crisp and yet succulent, the apples providing the necessary contrast to the richness of the dish. Old red face and myself once again went for the same thing, sweetbreads with truffles. The truffles, of course, were of the canned variety and had suffered accordingly – but there's not one hell of a lot one can do about that in Australia. (An aside here; the Australian bush, especially up Canberra–Goulburn way, abounds in quite a variety of edible fungus, it's just that no one has quite found a poison taster to sort the beasts out. Given the culinary audacity of our visitors from Sicily I have no doubt that in years to come in this country we will eventually see many more edible fungi on the market, especially in Italian greengrocers. And death to the cultivated mushroom say I. Perhaps one day some brave person may even find – with the aid of his faithful and imported truffle pig – the Australian version of that great delicious morsel.)

However, that aside, the sweetbreads were delicious in their cream sauce. They had been properly blanched and cooked. And, whoopee, the vegetables, potatoes and zucchini, were served separately and the zucchini had been cooked properly, still retaining crispness and not taking on the boiled pulp aspect of good old Australian squash.

With the going being so good how could one pass up dessert? We didn't. Scarlet opted for a vanilla souffle, which was high, tall and handsome and tasted as good. The old red faced grumbler from the south went for pears in red wine, which, he said, was almost as good as his own version of the dish. I had a very delicious slice of cake that was described as *à la Chantilly*, but to English-accustomed-food-minds it is probably easier to describe it as a form of charlotte. The whole had been soaked in *kirsch*. Bliss!

Having done this passing imitation of the three little pigs, without the disadvantage of being taken to market afterwards, red face and I, despite Scarlet's warnings, decided that a little cognac would be more than welcome. Unfortunately the corner lavatory did not deal in cognac and so we settled for a bottle of port. Ah, shit and Oh, dear, that is where we fell from grace (that and the fact that we couldn't get a taxi). Inflamed by the bus ride we were forced to endure on the way home, red face and my goodself started to drink the port on the bus. Cries of shame! Shame! No one was amused and Scarlet started to weep. Once off the bus Scarlet fled up the road to our humble home fairly blubbering all the way. Red face and I pursued her in the time honoured Sydney fashion with cries of wassa matterluv, and COME BACK HERE GIRLIE!

Alas she didn't. And so the two of us sat down in the gutter and drank the whole damn bottle didn't we. Oh, why can't I behave? Why can't I grow up? The curse of the schooner hangs over me like the dread shadow of Mordor itself. Woe and damnation to the House of Orr!

Hawkesbury Lunch

Peter Corris

With his Cliff Hardy series, novelist Peter Corris repopularised the crime fiction novel in Australia and, at the same time, became its most successful modern exponent. *The Empty Beach* **shows the seedy side of Sydney but ends with a meal at a restaurant on the Hawkesbury – a barely disguised Berowra Waters Inn, which opened in 1977 and, under the direction of Gay Bilson, became Sydney's top restaurant throughout the 1980s.**

The Empty Beach, 1983

'I'll send a car.'

What could I say? A Fairlane with a taciturn Scot at the wheel arrived at eleven am and we set off north.

He didn't talk well, but he was a terrific driver. We moved smartly against the sluggish flow of traffic down into the narrow streets of Sydney. We got to the river about midday, parked, and I waited for the restaurant boat to pick me up.

'What'll you do?' I asked the driver.

'I'll wait,' he said. 'I have a packed lunch.'

It was a bright, warm day. Spring comes to the Hawkesbury. There were patches of green and yellow on the rocky river banks where grass and wildflowers had gained a hold. The trees were aggressively native, gums that exhibited all the shades from khaki to grey. But we loved them. The other revellers numbered about half a dozen and included a state cabinet minister. Parliament was sitting that day as far as I knew, but the minister had a very pretty young Asian woman with him, so I suppose he could have been on a goodwill mission. I had on my best drill slacks and a denim shirt that I'd ironed. I also had my new walking stick and the bandage was off my ear.

The boat was a wide, flat-bottomed craft with a fringed awning over the seating section and a convincing Johnson outboard motor. A thin, elegant boatman handed us in and whipped the boat out into the current.

Half the people in the boat didn't need lunch and the rest looked like professional dieters. The minister kept his hand on the Asian woman's knee and looked into her almond eyes. I was glad I wasn't driving. The restaurant had a reputation for drinkable wine.

The restaurant is a plain brick and stone affair set right on the river. It has a couple of hundred square feet of unfashionable louvre windows that should look terrible but don't.

Mrs Singer was waiting for us at a corner table commanding the best view of the river. She was dressed to kill in a white linen suit. Her silvery hair had that expensive disarray and her makeup was somewhere between bold and restrained. Up close, there were signs of strain around her eyes and mouth, but she put together a pretty good smile.

'Mr Hardy,' she said. 'That stick and limp are maddeningly attractive.'

'They look better than they feel, Mrs Singer.'

'Marion,' she said. 'What will you drink?'

'Gin and tonic, thanks, like before.'

'Being bashed hasn't affected your memory. I'm sorry you had such a hard time.'

She looked concerned, but not sorry.

The drinks came. She seemed determined to stay off business for a while, and I let her. She was laying on the charm and affluence with a trowel and there had to be a reason. The menu arrived and we chatted about that. She had a medallion of venison and a lettuce leaf. I had a steak. She ordered a bottle of German wine, most of which I drank while she sipped Perrier. She pointed out a few local characters as boats puttered by on the river. I noticed that she'd upped her tar content – she was smoking Rothmans and plenty of them.

No sweets by consensus; on to coffee and down to business. Marion hauled out her cheque book and wrote out a big one for days worked, expenses incurred and some for luck. Lots for luck.

'Thanks,' I said. 'Lovely lunch, too. Now, tell me how I earned it!'

Fried Sausages, Tinned Beetroot

Roger McDonald

In a brief mid-life career as a shearers' cook in the 1980s, which provided the inspiration for his book *Shearers' Motel*, novelist Roger McDonald continued the improvising tradition of bush cooks – to the extent of turning out a batch of biscuits made with flour, sugar, custard powder, vanilla essence and rendered mutton fat: mutton fat shortbread.

Shearers' Motel, 1992

It was five in the afternoon. A ten-ton truck pulling a long, lurching, mud-spattered and dented caravan emerged from the heat-haze behind the shearing shed and surged towards a clump of trees opposite the kitchen. Its roaring progress was slow, probing. He watched through window glass while doing a wash-up of dusty enamel plates and grit-covered crockery. The truck was a bulky twin cab, a six- or eight-seater of the kind used to carry electricity workers out to high-tension power-lines. Two figures were visible up front, a man and a woman. The truck ground slowly past, but he didn't go to the door. He got on with what he was doing.

On the stove behind him potatoes were on the boil. On a tin plate in the fridge were two kilos of sausages pricked and ready. He had carried these and some mince all the way from the Braidwood Butchery, keeping the packages chilled in an Esky. He'd been told to expect station meat ready killed, but forgot to ask Maurice Holgate about it. An oiled frying pan stood ready at the side of the stove. Tonight's menu: fried sausages, potatoes to be served either hot or cold, tinned beetroot and sliced tomatoes on the side. Should he open the five-kilo tin of Gee-Vee pickled cucumbers he'd brought? These were the big questions now. He was no longer a small-time primary producer or a writer selecting phrases with care and frustration. He was Cookie peeling onions with even knife strokes.

There had been another time in his life when he had stood in a kitchen deciding what to do. It had been almost twenty years ago. He had never cooked until then, except for throwing steak in a pan or peeling a hunk of salami and munching it with bread and cheese while tossing back a beer, a novel or a book of poems propped on the table while he ate. Sharon had done the cooking until then. But then they had their first daughter and he began experimenting with recipe books in the long evening intervals before the baby slept. Close to midnight, the table would be spread with Indonesian or Italian food from *Cheap Dishes of the World* and *Continental Leftovers*. Over the years, he had continued this way, doing much of the household cooking. That way he escaped the washing-up. That way he ate when he was hungry. He prided himself on his abilities as an improviser and considered writing a book, *A Man's Book of Scraps*. But he had never been tested till now. He had never cooked the sort of food he had been brought up on: Australian food, it was called – meaty, barley-thick, soapscud-grey soups; stringy roast legs of mutton and coarsely baked potatoes; thick yellow custards and heavy steamed puddings.

By ten that night he had learned almost as much as he was ever going to know about shearers' cooking – short of what he would discover through his own practical experience. Davo and Barbara had given him their pointers. Breakfast: plenty of chops. Morning smoko: heaps of sandwiches, some of them toasted. Lunch: a choice of two dishes, one of them hot. Tea: the roast. They made it sound simple. Davo did. It was basically what Davo liked – what everyone liked, he said.

'Those are your basics, work up from there,' Davo said, ashing his cigarette at arm's length across the table, twirling the tip carefully into an ashtray he'd made by buckling the edge of an empty pineapple tin. 'Never ask people what they want, just give it to them. If they don't like it they'll let you know. Sort of, surprise me, but give me what I'm used to – or else. At one level a cook is never going to get it right. There is no such person as a good cook. Not that that should worry you, Cookie.'

He had served Davo and Barbara their tea three and a half hours before, at six-thirty, exactly on time. They would have been happy to wait. But he wanted to rule the beginning line cleanly off. His first meal: Braidwood sausages done crisply, a mixed fry of onions, zucchini, tomato and capsicum, with potato salad, lettuce, beet-root, pickles, bread and butter on the side. He couldn't eat anything himself – he was too hot, too wrought up, too exhilarated by strange-ness. He drank strong black tea instead. Barbara picked at her plate.

Davo ate everything, and went back for more, washing it down with extra VB.

At ten there were still only the three of them. Nobody else had turned up except for Maurie Holgate arriving with a sheep's carcase, which he hung in the meat house while his cook shone a torch . . .

It was peaceful in the quarters with the shearers over at the shed. Work time snared him again. He leaned back on the kitchen sink, and kept falling asleep for instants of buzzy time. Every sound was clear and identifiable. Movement of wind, thump of heat-expanding tin, scrape of bird claws on the roof: you could dream the day through with those companionable, familiar, lulling noises, as long as you didn't have an inner clock pressing the back of your brain.

Today someone had left their radio going. Odd, he hadn't heard it earlier. He heard a time call. Then Slim Dusty. Anne Murray. Archie Roach. Willie Nelson.

Mentally he ran through the list for lunch: a roast shoulder, which he'd tear and hack into rib-portions, and serve with fresh rolls; plates of salad items – thawed lettuce, squashy red tomatoes, tinned beetroot, sweaty cheese, Fritz, sliced cucumber, pineapple rings . . .

He walked back to the kitchen. He didn't have a clue. It was the last half-hour to dinner (as lunch was called). Simplicity of the table – shiny green surface awaiting placement of bread board, lifting tongs, enamel dishes, tins of food with their tops removed, spoons at the ready. Something Alastair had told him that he was thrashing himself to achieve: 'You've got to have boiling water in your sink, and everything you do, you wash up as you go. You dirty a pot, you wash a pot. As the people are bringing in and emptying their plates, you're not sitting down talking to them, you're washing the plates up. It's just one of those things, you've just got to plan your day, and you've got to plan your next day, what you're going to cook. And really you can see cooks chasing their tail, purely because they're not organised. But if they organise themselves it's absolutely magnificent what they sometimes can do.'

Alastair had told him that a cook could control a team if he was a smart cook and a good cook. 'His existence is lonely, but he's one bloke who's not a member of the team in general, and people will talk to him in confidence.'

He felt about as effective as an ant. But as a touch of pride, had established a habit of laying the serving plates on sheets of newspaper. Today's tablecloth was made up of the executive employment pages of the *Sydney Morning Herald*. The meat was cooling under a flyproof cover. He couldn't put the salad out till just before noon because of the heat. The food was only just tepid in the fridges anyway (even fridge number three, crammed with lettuce and cauliflower, where everything had frozen at first, was running hot as candleflame). Heatwave conditions like this and there wouldn't be much eating done. He could tell that now.

He congratulated himself on judging quantities to the minimum. He didn't just want to be known as a good cook, he wanted to be a cheap cook. The heat was on his side. It was cooking for appearances.

Jugs of cordial crammed with ice were plonked on the mess table. A lot of thought had gone into selecting the colour combination – lemon at one end, lime at the other. The ammoniated odour of Spray'n'Wipe over everything was like a nudge in the ribs – this cook was clean. He started to think about the next shed. He saw his truck moving south, into a cooler landscape, coming under the shadow of a raincloud on a sealed road. He saw steam rising from bitumen, and he lay back with his mouth open, his eyes closed.

Minutes away from twelve and the table arrangement was a symmetry of tinplate. Only one last thing needed – a chilled tin of beetroot. So out to the fridge to get it.

Christmas Traditions

Julie Capaldo

Julie Capaldo's novel *Love Takes You Home* is in part a joyous celebration of Italian foods and traditions (complete with recipes), in part the story of Italian migrants making good in Australia, in part the story of a girl's coming-of-age. The exuberant joie de vivre, conviviality and sensuality typically associated with Italians find full expression in Pino, contrasting with the cheerlessness, apprehensiveness and remoteness of Judy, the narrator's mother.

'Truth and oil always come to the surface – it is an old saying from back home,' Pino said. 'You cannot hide the beginnings, if you don't use good oil the taste will never be just so. I only use extra-virgin olive oil – the olives are gathered by hand one by one and the pickers spread white linen sheets under the trees to catch any that might fall and be bruised. The olives must never touch the ground and they must be pressed immediately.' Pino sprinkled salt over the raddichio. 'Here, take this to the table.'

It was Christmas. I hang onto the memory of it greedily. I was fifteen and after years of refusing the Portellis' invitation for us to spend the day with them, this time Judy accepted. Every year we did something different. One year we went to the beach, took a picnic hamper with cold chicken, coleslaw and potato salad and the three of us sat on the sand and ate and then packed up and went home. Anthony spent the afternoon in his workshop, Judy lay down with a headache and I watched television eating potato chips. Another year we went to the Botanic Gardens – that was as good as the beach – but the worst Christmas was when I stayed in my room.

I was given my own television that year and Judy thought I'd like to watch it so she let me eat in my bedroom. I spent the day watching the religious services, the Queen's Christmas message, 'The Walton Family's Christmas'. Ruby told me her family always ate roast turkey and steamed pudding for Christmas. Her mother started making the pudding from the first of December and poured a spoonful of brandy over it each day. She even hid coins in it until the currency changed and the new money made the pudding go off. After that she kept a box full of sixpences and each year she reused them for the pudding. I told Judy about it but she said it was old-fashioned and nobody ate roasts and puddings for Christmas any more.

The year we went to the Portellis' was when Pino gave me my shoes. Pino and Valda were so pleased we would be with them for the day. 'You know you are family to us, Antonio,' Valda said. 'You must come to midnight mass and celebrate exactly as we do.' So at midnight we all trudged off to the monastery gardens which was where the service was held. Chairs were set up on the grass and an altar had been erected alongside a replica stable with porcelain figures of Mary, Joseph, shepherds and the three kings. As Father Tolmino told the story of Christmas, Michael – Vincenzo and Carinella's grandson – carried out a figure of the baby Jesus and gently placed it in the empty crib. We walked back to Pino's in the crisp night air still singing 'Silent Night'. Valda put coffee on and Pino poured cognacs for everyone. Judy even let me have one. The Doogans from next door were there and we all gave presents to each other. I gave Valda a saint light. It was a statue of Saint Anthony that flashed on and off and it came with a ten-year guarantee. Valda loved it. She cried as she hugged and kissed me. 'Is beautiful. I will keep it in the kitchen. *Grazie, bella, mille grazie.*' That was when Pino gave me a box wrapped in purple tissue with silver ribbon. It looked so beautiful I didn't want to open it. Inside were my shoes. Leopard-skin stilettos that felt and smelt divine. Judy gasped when she saw them. 'They are a bit, well . . . a bit . . . risqué,' she said.

'What is this word? I do not know it,' Pino asked. 'You don't like the shoes? As soon as I saw them I knew Grazia would love them. They are so beautifully made. Look.' He took one and showed it to Judy. 'Handmade, from Firenze. Maybe they are a little too old for her to wear now but later, when she is older, perhaps, that is why I buy them a bit big.'

There was wrapping paper and ribbon all over the lounge room floor. Valda had made up a bed for me in Angelina's room and Judy and Anthony slept in the spare room. When we woke late the next morning, I could smell coffee and cake. The Portellis did not eat breakfast on Christmas morning but had coffee and milk, saving their appetite for dinner. Pino could not understand how people could sit down to a hot roast in the middle of summer. He had his own traditional meal.

We all sat at the dining room table – which had been extended for the occasion and had the kitchen table added on to the end of it. Valda covered both tables in her best white linen sheets. Red and green candles were on the table and Pino had Puccini's *Turandot* on in the background. He served home-made pasta – ravioli filled with minced chicken and parsley – and covered with a Neapolitan sauce. Crayfish, prawns, calamari and baby clams dressed with lemon juice, vinegar, oil and sprinkled with finely chopped parsley. Tossed green salads, plump Jerusalem artichokes, red peppers and home-grown tomatoes dotted with oregano. He raised his glass of wine. 'Back home we say, *Tutte le feste finiscono a tavola* – all the holidays end at the table. *Buon Natale a Tutti.*'

After each course Valda and Angelina whisked the plates away and picked crumbs from the cloth. Fresh plates were set and out came crushed sweet ices flavoured with fresh fruits and a fruit platter of pineapple, strawberries, raspberries, blueberries, cherries, sweet melon and mangoes. With the coffee came almond biscuits and *fritelle*. The women cleared the table and went to the kitchen to wash, wipe and put away, the men slumped in the lounge chairs and crossed their ankles and drifted into sleep. When the last dish had been put away we all went outside and played *bocce*. Pino turned the music up so we could still hear it but Valda yelled that all the noise was making the glasses in her cabinet shake. I watched Anthony that day. He looked more at ease when he was a part of the crowd around the Portellis' table than anywhere else. He straightened his shoulders and smiled. That night we had a light broth for tea, with the leftovers. Pino sang along with the tenors on the record and when we left he hugged us all with tears in his eyes. Anthony called out '*Ciao*' as we drove away and I thought this is what Christmas should be. In the car Anthony whistled '*Nessun Dorma*' and the crease between his eyebrows smoothed.

And then Judy spoke. 'For God's sake Anthony stop that whistling, I've got a splitting headache, all that racket, I hate going there.' And Anthony stopped whistling as Judy went on, 'You have no idea what it's like . . . for me,' and the tears started.

The crease cut back into Anthony's forehead as he asked his wife what was wrong. 'You have no idea what it's like for me,' Judy repeated, 'Pino is such a wonderful cook and Valda's the perfect hostess, how am I expected to compete with that? I can't ask them over for dinner, I can't cook anything as good as Pino can, or if I try he gives me advice on how I should have done it and why it has turned out wrong. So I have to sit there, knowing I can never return the hospitality, knowing they will think I am rude for not returning the hospitality . . .'

'Oh don't fret so, Jude, I'm sure they don't think anything of the sort . . .'

'How would you know?' Judy snapped back. 'You're too busy drinking and carrying on to notice. I don't want to eat there again.'

Wok Cookery

Sharon O'Keefe

Sharon O'Keefe's novel _The Best-Looking Women in Bondi Junction_ is a light-hearted account of the lives of a group of active, lively, young-elderly single women living in Sydney's eastern suburbs.

The Best-Looking Women in Bondi Junction, 1989

Tuesday, 1st October

Julia and I went along for our first cookery lesson tonight. We were quite early so we managed to get the front bench. The instructor, who is male, gave us a short talk about how current attitudes to healthy eating make Wok cookery very appropriate. We all sat up straight and looked terribly responsible about our health. Our first dish was Stir-fried Vegetables. He went on at length about the proper way to cut up vegetables, which raised my hackles a bit. When one has been chopping vegetables every night for sixty years there's not much you don't know. Still, I'm a tolerant woman so I didn't interrupt. Finally we were told we could commence chopping, ourselves – and the race was on. Really, people are so childish, racing to be the first finished. Julia won. When the cooking actually began, the instructor came around to each bench and tried to make a petty criticism of everyone. He said I was cooking our vegetables too slowly and turned up the flame. I responded that he had the flame dangerously high and turned it back down again. He was taken aback that someone should stand up to his nasty little dictatorial ways, and said, rather waspishly, 'Your vegetables won't cook quickly or successfully like that.'

'How many years have you been cooking young man?' I retorted.

At this he pulled a silly face, but I ignored that and gave him the spiel about cooking for more than sixty years.

'Don't try to tell me I'm cooking too slowly.'

Stir-fried vegetables aren't very nice if you ask me. Other people pretended to enjoy their meal and kept saying, 'I love crisp vegetables.'

Tuesday, 22nd October

Really I'm in the wars at the moment. My first big venture back into society – Wok Cookery with Julia – and I was kicked out of the class. Well, not exactly kicked out, but the instructor said I was not happy there. You see, I'd missed a few classes, so I skipped all the way from Stir-fried vegies to Pork with Abalone. I admit that I was not familiar with cooking abalone, but it was not necessary for the instructor to look pointedly at me when he said that those who hadn't cooked abalone before were to follow his instructions carefully and not go off thinking they knew more than God about cooking. I guess I was on the defensive.

Julia was trying to calm me down, saying, 'Don't be ridiculous, that had nothing to do with you.'

I ignored his instructions as much as possible.

'Now Madam,' he said, 'you will please not cook that any longer than I say.'

Well, it was like a red rag to a bull. I doubled his cooking time. Everyone was hoeing into theirs by the time I dished ours up. Julia was looking very embarrassed. We tried to chew the abalone, but it was like rubber. Boy, has he chosen his recipes badly. All this time he was staring at me from across the room, saying nothing. Still without a word, he walked over, took some abalone from my dish and bounced it on the floor. I should have got in quickly and told him what a dreadful choice he had made yet again, but he got in first, telling the class at large that my generation had made Australian food the most boring in the world and here we were resisting improvements because we insisted on overcooking everything. It was a vicious attack and I really had nothing to counter with. All I could do was go on at length about the longevity of people who ate the 'stodge' we cooked once, while everyone now was dying of cancer. I even suggested he looked far from well himself. A bit black under the eyes. This rattled him a bit. I was able to tell the class that my great-aunts and uncles all lived to eighty plus, whereas modern cooking habits had left only my sister Lily and myself in our generation. I neglected to mention that we were the only two of our generation ever. We have no cousins.

So I made a sad exit from Wok Cookery. Julia said we could try something else, perhaps Japanese Cookery, as it's very healthy. I said I'd think about it.

The Cooking Class

Amanda Lohrey

In *Camille's Bread*, Tasmanian-born novelist Amanda Lohrey describes a different kind of cooking class. Marita, the novel's narrator, decides to enrol in a cooking class as part of her resolve to be a better mother to her young daughter Camille, whose staple diet is sliced 'Sunshine Wonderbread'.

Camille's Bread, 1995

Outside in the wide circular foyer there are ten of us sitting on the circular window seats, rifling through *Good Living* magazines or staring at our socks (shoes left at the door), waiting to be summoned. But in this house no-one seems ever to announce the beginning of anything and after a while we just wander down the grand hallway and into the large room at the back where an enormous scrubbed pine table is laid with ten sets of implements; large knife, small knife and chopping board. We stand politely around the table, looking one another over, until a woman with frizzy red hair and a baby on her hip beckons us through into the kitchen proper. Obediently we shuffle in, and cluster around the marble-topped bench.

And there is Johanna Beech, presiding at the bench, waiting, arms outstretched on the white marble. Here then is our sibyl, our witch for the day, and I am willing to be entranced by her: she has a blazing physical charm, a lustrous muscularity that cooks rarely possess, a hint of playful arrogance. Her hair is almost a white blonde, cut very short and covered by a green and white silk Tibetan hat. Ornate silver and green earrings, the size of florins, hang from her small ears. She wears a red silk singlet and her arms are brown and strong, each one graced with a wide gold bracelet. Below the waist she wears black and yellow striped pants, white socks and chunky black Doc Martens. I notice the way she stands with her feet apart; solid, relaxed. She has a wide, sharp, mischievous smile that seems to go with the hat. Here is something clownish but commanding, European yet Asiatic, mystical but grounded; here is something unorthodox but sure of itself.

I observe her square, practical hands. Like all good cooks, she is unhurried. On the large industrial gas range next to her, three saucepans of water simmer in readiness. I know I could never be this calm, this in control.

As she talks, I look down at my menu, *Use Your Noodle*, and make notes in the margins. The large white bowl in front of her is half-filled with green noodles tossed with baby squash, rosemary, olive oil, garlic and something called umeboshi vinegar; a delicate red vinegar made from pickled Japanese plums. I like the way she runs her fingers through the dressed noodles, with relish, with authority, her nails glistening with oil and tiny black droplets of tamari. She smiles. 'Use your hands. Let your fingers flow through the noodles. Enjoy the sensuous feel of it. Let your energy harmonise with that of the food.' Now she is leaning over the pot on the stove which seems to boil with a complacent boil, neither frantic and surging nor lame and flat. I never seem able to get my pots of salted water to boil in exactly this way. My energy in the kitchen is too rushed and indifferent. That's why I'm here, to improve my attitude. And for Camille.

Jo tells us that the quality of the energy we put into our cooking is everything, that in Buddhist monasteries only those considered the most spiritually advanced are allowed to cook. And that is why, in families, mothers do the cooking. Mothers, she says, are more spiritually advanced than fathers. 'Some of them.' It's a male voice. And I am aware, for the first time, of the only man in the room.

'Most of them.' Her eyes twinkle, but she is adamant. 'Women are responsible for nurturing, that is their fate. However they may choose to organise it, or delegate it, is their business, but if they refuse that responsibility entirely they destroy a part of their spiritual self. Of course,' she goes on, 'a part of this is that they must nurture themselves. That's where women traditionally have gone wrong, made martyrs of themselves, nurturing others at their own expense. And then their daughters have reacted in the other direction, and worked on nurturing themselves at the expense of others. Women have to find a way of doing both, looking after themselves and looking after their families.'

From in among the throng comes a faint female groan.

'Alright, alright, it's difficult,' she says, 'but to find that balance is the art of women's genius.'

At this point I feel that some of us are confused as to how we should respond: should we take issue now, as if in a seminar, or shut up and concentrate on our noodles?

Jo is standing over the pot, lifting a long strand of noodle from the water with chopsticks. She is very deft. 'For the Chinese, noodles are a symbol of longevity so they never break them,' she says, 'but I do.' And she breaks off the long noodle suspended above the pot, as if to say: we do it our way; we learn from them, but we are not in their thrall; we have our own smartness. Cooks are wilful.

'Marita,' she says, glancing at my name-tag, 'would you say this was cooked?'

I take the sticky noodle in my fingers, hold it high above my mouth, and nibble on the end. I feel self-conscious. I am aware that he is watching me, nibbling on my noodle. Him, the one at the back, tall, lean and very brown, with black hair pulled back in a ponytail. Before, when challenging Jo, he'd been very serious but now, staring at me, he seems faintly amused.

Already he seems to know a lot about this food: the pickled limes, the bonito flakes, the opaque blocks of agar agar, the buckwheat soba; kuzu noodles, fruit kanten, bunya nuts, bean-thread noodles, kombu strips, nori, shitake and hijiki are clearly not mysteries to him.

Jo has completed her preparations for a kanten of strawberry jelly and is demonstrating the blending of a cream substitute made from cooked oats pureed in a blender with soy milk and maple syrup. 'Being a vegan doesn't mean you have to give up on all creamy foods,' she says. 'We have to have some creaminess in our diet, we have to acknowledge our need for food as consolation for the loss of mother's milk.' She laughs, but *he* is frowning, I notice, although he seems later to approve of her lecture on creative eclecticism. Tradition is a signpost not a straitjacket, she says; we can take Aboriginal bush food, like bunya nuts, and mix them with Ligurian olives. Japanese this, Chinese that – we make our own cuisine, our own synthesis.

'Exactly!' he says, softly but emphatically. I stare at him. His black eyes stare back.

Meanwhile as the jelly – sorry, kanten – sets, she instructs us in the daily ritual of sharpening the knife, and her words ring like an incantation. A poem.

immerse the sharpening stone in water
whet the knife
with small rhythmic movements
pushing the blade away from you
never looking at it.
And then
to test
run along the thumbnail
it ought to catch not slip
– see
perfect

I stand next to him while we cut the carrot shapes for the salad: stars, flowers, wheels and straws. And I notice how expert he is with the knife, how quietly practised but unhurried. I pause and stare into the huge white bowl with red carrot shapes sprinkled with black strands of hijiki seaweed. I feel clumsy.

'Looks good, doesn't it?' he says. I smile, and while he bends his head to resume his chopping I study his broken nose – sort of splayed – which is the thing about him that I like best, a broken nose on a lean head and a lean brown body, and strong hands with square fingers.

'I don't like these shapes,' he says. 'They're kitsch. It's an unnatural look. Ornamental.'

His way of speaking is quiet but precise. A pedant, I think. While we, the women, are ever so polite, he has already challenged her twice. When she tosses the spiral pasta in Ligurian olive oil with torn basil leaves and tofu marinated in mustard and tamari, he gives his disapproving little frown.

'That's a lot of olive oil.'

'It's the best oil in the world,' she says, giving her sharp, mischievous smile. 'Low in cholesterol.'

'It's still a lot.'

Her eyes glint. 'Use to taste,' she says. 'I give no quantities on your menu sheet. You must learn to trust your own palates. Each time you make a dish, you re-invent it. Nothing is ever the same twice.'

Shop Luck

Marion Halligan

Food and eating have assumed a significant role in all of Canberra writer Marion Halligan's many novels. They are not incidental; she maintains that the novels would suffer if the food references were omitted. The scene of Martine's dinner for St Hubert in *The Golden Dress* not only consolidates the character of Martine and advances the story but also provides a link to the reason for her boyfriend Ray's disappearance.

The Golden Dress, 1998

She said, Would you like to come and have dinner with me tonight? And on the way home she buys some simple food. Asparagus. Salmon steaks. Salad leaves. A small fresh goat's cheese. Raspberries. Just pot luck, she told him it would be. Of course it isn't. It's shop luck. The luck of the season. Of a prosperous woman with a job who knows where to find delicious good things.

She wraps the salmon steaks in silver foil, with some thin slices of onion and sprigs of tarragon, with pepper and a tablespoon of vermouth each. Makes dressing in a salad bowl and lays the leaves on top. Ties the asparagus with string ready for steaming. Shaves parmesan to strew over it. Sets the table, no cloth, a plate each, a glass, a big pale yellow linen napkin. Chills white wine that tastes of grass and passionfruit, with a hint of citrus finishing up with ripe peaches, if you believe the label. Showers and puts on her white linen dress and flat sandals. It's all so simple, so plain, so elegant. Taste and money is all it needs.

When St Hubert comes it doesn't take long for him to admire the space and shapes of the flat and the way the light falls in it and the Pellerins on the walls. They stand on the balcony for a while and watch sailing boats crisp and lively on the breezy blue waters of the harbour. The image of the sybaritic life, he says, sailing on a long blue evening. They sit at the dining table that belonged to her grandmother as a bride in another country, that nobody else in the family wants but all are grateful she does. The asparagus is tender and crisp, the parmesan, the right best one from Reggio Emilia, crumbly, nutty, sweet. The salmon *en papillotte* perfectly cooked, just to the point of creaminess. The bread dense and full-flavoured. The salad dressed in olive oil from a certain slope in Tuscany, of antique provenance. The label doesn't claim that Dante actually used it, but gives the impression he might have. A fine pinot noir with the goat cheese, which is still delicate and fresh, no age yet, and the raspberries melt on the tongue.

All this, and a superb cook, says St Hubert.

She thinks, All what? and then remembers what a flirt he is.

She smiles, knowing that this meal has little to do with her being a superb cook, or not.

It's all very simple, she says. A working woman's middle-of-the-week meal.

It occurs to her that St Hubert will know little of working women.

He raises his glass. *Salut*, my dear. He doesn't actually ask what it's all about, but his eyes are curious.

Ray's lost, she says. It looks as though I'm going to have to choose between going to find him and keeping my job.

Ray's lost, he repeated. Lost to himself, lost to the world, lost to you . . . Does he know he's lost, or is it just you who has lost him?

I suppose he knows where he is. I don't know. I mean I don't know whether he knows.

Can't you trust him to know?

Martine considered this. Maybe not, she said. Ray knows about painting, mainly, and that's it. The thing is, nobody seems to be paying any attention. What if he's injured? There's been an accident? . . . Who's looking after him?

Ah, said St Hubert.

But then, I'm a woman with a job, and I have a responsibility to that, too.

Indeed, said St Hubert.

It's a good job. It pays well. But that's not the point. It's my career; you shouldn't give up something like that. Once, maybe, in the past, but it's not the way women live now.

Yes, I do see. The world well lost for love . . . even in its heyday the phrase was an irony.

La Haute Cuisine Australienne

Peter Goldsworthy

Peter Goldsworthy is a wry, witty and sharply observant Adelaide novelist, poet, essayist and short story writer. His story 'La Haute Cuisine Australienne' was published in 1982 when debate on the concept of 'an Australian cuisine' (does it exist? and if so, what?) was beginning to gather momentum.

Archipelagoes, 1982

Kate had been working on the Great Australian Dish for years, but wasn't any closer to realising her ambition at the age of 31 than she had been at 13 when she dunked her first sponge-cube in melted chocolate and coconut.

'Meals were so much simpler then,' she liked to declaim. 'In our mothers' generation. The whole world was so much simpler – more content. A trestle at the church fête groaning with buttered scones and buttered pikelets, a leg of lamb roasting in the oven every Sunday morning was all you *needed . . .*'

She came from one of those small country towns we all seemed to come from. A town in the heart of the Yorke Peninsula, the heart of the wheat belt . . .

'The heart of the *flour* belt. Four pubs, five churches, a six-pack of grain silos – and a thousand ovens full of pudding and cake!'

I knew what she meant – I'd grown up going to the same church fêtes, coming home to the same Sunday roasts . . .

'The food was like everything else in the place. So puritanical. So Anglo-Saxon!'

I seldom had much to say in return – my mouth was usually too full. I was living on a student-pittance in the flat upstairs; every evening found me knocking hungrily at her door. Nail my feet to the floor, I might have said if my mouth had been free. Stuff me with more steak-risotto or rabbit-laksa or chops-and-polenta – or whatever her latest cross-fertilisation had thrown up.

'There has to be a compromise,' she muttered. 'An Australian compromise.'

As I finished one meal she'd already be planning the next, thumbing through lush cookery books while I drank my coffee. Researching, she called it – but to me it looked more like perving. Drooling over the glossy culinary centrefolds, reciting the lists of ingredients to herself like so much sensuous poetry . . .

Gastro-porn. I've heard such books called. Promising everything, delivering nothing . . .

I'd known her for about a year when she got around to opening her dream-restaurant: a year spent eating my way through a new creation every night. Three-hundred-and-sixty-five main courses, from which we selected a final repertoire of seven – one for each night of the week.

It was only a small place – a shopfront on the Norwood Parade with a Sidney Nolan print on one wall, a potted palm against the other, and a few tables squeezed in between. Those few tables were more than enough on opening night – besides mine, only one other was occupied, and that by relatives. Cousins over from the Peninsula on holiday . . .

She served us a kind of steak and kidney pudding – only with yabbies instead of kidneys. It tasted reasonable, I guess – but mine wasn't the most discerning palate. I could eat – and enjoy – almost anything that fitted the dimensions of my mouth.

Perhaps the rest of Norwood felt the same – or perhaps there was too much competition up and down the road. Or perhaps she was too far ahead of her time. Kate barely managed to break even during those first few weeks of business.

'I *know* I can do it,' she told me as I helped wash up her final closing night. 'An authentic Australian cuisine! All I have to do is stumble on it, and the patrons will flock in . . .'

'The only authentic Australian cuisine,' I said, 'is the witchetty grub!'

I didn't see her for a month or so after that – I spent Christmas home on the Peninsula among the puddings and roasts.

When I returned, late January, I received a shock.

She'd redecorated completely – ochre-red paint on the walls, bark paintings in place of the Ned Kelly print, a pile of didgeridoos where the potted palm had stood.

'*Nyina-kati walypala*,' she said. 'That's Pitjantjatjara for take a pew, whitefeller – literally, bring a sit!'

I sat down at a table and she handed me the menu. *Traditional Tribal Tucker*.

'It's all the rage in the States,' she said.

I was incredulous: 'What – Aboriginal food?'

'Well, not exactly. Black food. You know – *soul* food . . . brother.'

I looked through the menu and it all seemed a long way from *my* soul. Unpronounceable fish, fillets of snake and goanna, kangaroo cutlets, galah pie . . . and yes, at the bottom of the list, *witjuti* grubs.

'*Au naturel?*'

'They come in cans,' she replied. 'From Melbourne.'

'And the snake?'

'Snake's off tonight,' she said without trace of a smile, and I guessed that snake was off every night. 'Try the fish instead – or some of the poultry. I'd recommend *kilykilykari* – they're a small native bird.'

'What sort of native bird?'

'Budgies.'

I settled for the fish – barramundi flown south from Darwin the same day, according to the chef. She fetched out two vast platefuls of fish and sat down with me. No other patrons were in sight, and she obviously didn't expect that any would be.

'I'd only have thrown it out,' she said glumly, between mouthfuls.

I was struck by how much weight she'd put on. As though she were eating her way through a whole night's menu – every night.

I thought a little joke might break the ice, and cheer her up.

'What about a drink?' I said. 'Where's the metho list?'

It didn't break the ice – but it certainly broke something.

'What an insensitive thing to say!' she exploded. 'It's not even funny – it's . . . it's *evil!*'

She stood, whisked my half-eaten fish from under my nose, and showed me the door.

'We don't serve racists in this establishment! *Nyuntu ma kumpurawa* – that's Pitjantjatjara for piss off, whitefeller!'

My calls the next day went unanswered; I ate in. Vegemite on toast. And again the next night. I'd put on a bit of weight over the year; perhaps that layer of stored blubber would last me through however many weeks it took to gain forgiveness. Hunger drove me back to her door after four, cap in hand, *mea culpas* at tip of tongue.

I didn't recognise the restaurant at first – she'd knocked archways through the dividing walls and extended along the entire block of shops. The queue outside was fifty metres long – people in white collars and blue singlets, twinsets and caftans, school uniforms and faded denim jeans.

Inside, the crowd was even thicker – standing room only, barely space enough to breathe. Joyful customers jostled for tables as they became vacant, eagerly clutching their plates of food: their slices of sponge and date-loaf, their jam rolls and scones, their buttered pikelets and buttered jubilee cake . . .

Suddenly it was my turn, wedged against the counter while a shop assistant flicked her eyes impatiently from face to face.

'Next?'

In the backroom behind her, I could see Kate sitting at a table piled high with cubes of sponge. I watched as she methodically dipped them in a bowl of melted chocolate, rolled them in a bowl of grated coconut.

She was obviously far too busy to talk.

'I'll have one of those lamingtons,' I said, pointing. 'And a nice cup of tea . . .'

Food is a Statement

Frank Moorhouse

Almost like a modern-day Candide, Frank Moorhouse's 'I' of *Late Shows* is a naïve and bemused observer of contemporary life. Here he wittily applies simple logic to arrive at totally irrational and absurd conclusions.

Lateshows, 1990

One of the sub-committees of the world on which I sit is the dining room/catering sub-committee of the club.

For reasons which I have not yet had explained to me, we have an ex-anti-Vietnam-war poet on the subcommittee. He is now very green. I have heard it said that he is also part of the muesli left. Not being a breakfast eater I am not sure that I understand this expression. He seems to miss the Vietnam war badly.

The poet is forever wanting opinions about his poetry and he campaigns nationally for more poetry readings. But he also worries a great deal about what other people eat.

He wants life-affirming food served at the club. 'Let's get away from roast dinners, and those game birds.'

Game birds are something of which I am very fond.

'It would make a positive statement on behalf of the club and it would demonstrate its awareness of contemporary issues.'

I like clubs because they are oblivious to contemporary issues.

I realised that at some dinner parties in private homes I had been exposed to politically sensitive cuisine chosen to show the household's affiliation with some country's politics – I've found myself eating quite a lot of PLO bread. And houmus and pitta bread. As well as being asked to sign petitions against all monorails world-wide.

'Food is a statement,' the ex-anti-Vietnam-war poet said with troubled seriousness. 'And it goes on making that statement inside you. We vote the way we eat.' I know some very charming people who eat very unhealthy food. I have never seen a connection between personality and diet satisfactorily established.

So this was a novel idea to me. 'Does it go on arguing inside you? The discourse of the digestive juices?' I queried.

'We need food which is good for us – in which yin and yang are balanced. That is biogenic. That is good for the environment.'

I said that when I was young my mother had classes of food which were good for me and not good for me. I seem to recall that eating greens was considered good for me. I do not understand why the food that was good for me was also the food I didn't care for as a child. 'But it would not, I think, be thought good for us now. By some.' And looking at the way things have turned out for me, not so good for me after all.

'I think we know much more about food than our mothers did,' the poet said.

My mother and the race had survived quite some time. Too long perhaps. I realised that there were now many more things for food to do in the world. It could be good for you politically, good for you spiritually, good for you physically, good for the world, good for the environment. I remembered a time when there was simply disdained food and proper food. There was food which became ridiculed for its social style: the prawn cocktail, the Hawaiian steak, the sweet sparkling wines – even rosé – fried rice, Pimms. But I notice that mashed potato and sausages are, happily, appearing on menus. Now we were faced with ideologically sound and unsound food. I have been eating with people where I have sensed that bloody red steaks are considered dreadfully wrong. White Meat Families. It was all very hard. In one White Meat Family the six-year-old daughter had tried to eat me.

'We don't want food which screams out in pain – which says violence of one species against another. All those dead birds on plates. It is cruel food,' said the poet.

The poet said he also opposed elitist food. 'How can we sit here eating caviar while Ethiopians die?'

We were not, as it happens, sitting there eating caviar. It was some time since I had eaten caviar. I said that it was difficult to see the chain of responsibility or the chain of benefit which would flow to Ethiopia by the club not eating caviar. 'We could cause suffering among Iranian fisherfolk if we stopped eating caviar,' I said.

Delly, the table attendant also a member of the sub-committee (and all the sub-committees of the world) de facto, said that she was a part-time vegetarian.

She said that club members were responding well to the word 'wild' on the menus, as in wild rice, wild berries, and wild mushrooms.

I said I believed in the doctrine of *ferae naturae*: 'Every moving thing that liveth shall be meat for you'. I didn't often quote the bible. But it summed up my attitude.

'The alimentary canal is a long passage back to our forbears and their feasts,' I continued. 'To severely change one's diet was to risk disrupting atavistic circuits. Could make us orphans in time.'

'Red meat just has to go,' said the poet, 'and the mucoid-formers.' He suggested that I was falling behind politically. 'It is proven that it generates aggressive behaviour,' he said angrily.

I yearned to fall behind politically, the way I used to fall behind on school excursions and find myself doing not necessarily what I wanted to do but doing what no one wanted me to do, wandering off alone, away from the noise and skylarking, and the teacher's instruction. On my own I would linger over details of inconsequential exhibits of no particular educational interest for no good reason.

I said that to eat wild birds was to make a connection with the living universe and to remind us that we too became food when we die.

I noticed that even Delly looked at me questioningly after this statement.

The Chinese, I told them, had one vegetarian day a year when they remembered and honoured the animals they had eaten that year and that I rather liked that idea.

I went on to say that vegetarianism had been justified by many religions and other theories but the justifications kept changing. 'Vegetarianism is, after all, just a ritual of difference, of self-purity, a way of saying you are superior, for want of any other significant feature to set you apart from the rest of your culture.'

Before the poet and I could come to blows about this Delly said, without conviction, 'Is the strike still on in California? Maybe we shouldn't be eating Californian grapes. Or South African food.'

I said we probably needed someone working at the club to ensure that the food eaten was politically and in all ways, sound.

I reminded them that elephants sometimes went on salt binges.

I had noticed that some of my friends used food to recondition themselves: crash diets and health farms. Another search for purity of self. Fasting. The exorcising of demons. A search for holiness. Attempts to use diet to remake themselves and remake the world.

I suppose if because of the world environmental crisis we have to live one day on synthetic food we would then be sundered from the natural world but at the same time we would be 'protecting' the natural world. We the human species would then truly be orphans of nature.

I left the meeting with Delly to go to a good long dinner where we might play the fool, and where we could contemplate the richness and abundance of food which the good world still offers us, thinking to myself that all meals are always a bigger feast than we sometimes realise.

Real Men Eat Chillies

Hsu-Ming Teo

Love and Vertigo, by Hsu-Ming Teo, won the 1999 Australian/Vogel Literary Award. Born in Malaysia, Hsu-Ming Teo emigrated to Australia with her family in 1977. Her novel, which moves between Singapore, Malaysia and Australia, tells the story of the Tay family through several generations, down to Jonah Tay ('the Patriarch') who decides to give his family a new life in Australia in 1978.

The Patriarch was determined to make us fall in love with Sydney. He was going to take us up to the Blue Mountains on the weekend, drive us to Mrs Macquarie's Chair, make us walk around the Botanical Gardens to Bennelong Point, book us on a Captain Cook Cruise, show us the tourist face of the city. We'll have a *great* time, he told us. He took us to Pancakes at the Rocks and promised me a birthday party at McDonald's so that I could have an ice-cream cake and maybe meet the clown with the big red boots and the sinisterly smiling face. For those few weeks he was so happy to have his family with him once again. He wanted to do everything for us and everything with as. We hadn't disappointed him yet.

True to his promise, one weekend he decided that we should see Katoomba in the Blue Mountains and have a picnic in the park. When I think of family picnics, I hear the hiss of sizzling oil and the clang of the metal wok in the kitchen as Mum cooked rice vermicelli with pork, egg and vegetables. The Patriarch directed operations, packing green plastic plates and cups into a basket and searching for paper napkins. Sonny washed chillies, cut them into tiny pieces and wrapped them in plastic. The seeds stung his fingers and he dreaded the moment when he would have to confess that he could not bear the taste of chillies. The Patriarch did not know this because we never ate together in Malaysia. In the early evening the servants would cook dinner for Sonny and me to eat in the kitchen. Mum and the Patriarch had their meal in the dining room much later. Immigration brought with it the novelty of shared family meals.

'Wait till you see Katoomba,' the Patriarch told us as he selected cassettes to play in the car on the way up to the mountains. He was nothing if not an organised man. 'You'll love it. You've never seen anything like it before. We've all got to get up very early tomorrow so that we can reach there before all the traffic gets on the road.'

All our lives we would arrive at the Royal Easter Show, the premiers of *Star Wars* and *ET*, Christmas parties and school speech nights a good hour before anyone else arrived, just so that we could avoid traffic and queues. The Patriarch was not a man who enjoyed the company of the general public. And although he made Mum take driving lessons and eventually bought her a car, he was the one who always drove when we went out together.

That night Sonny could not sleep. He tossed in bed and thought of the chillies. The following morning he worried about it all along the Great Western Highway up to the Blue Mountains, dreading the moment when his masculinity would be shamed before his father.

The Patriarch was oblivious to Sonny's pain. He drove us to Katoomba first so that we could gape at the petrified claw of the Three Sisters. We hollered across the valley – the first and only time in the presence of the Patriarch – and he smiled in benevolent approval. We listened to the hissing recording of the story of how the Three Sisters came into being and peered into the binoculars – I couldn't focus them properly and all I saw was a smudge of green at the bottom of the valley. We went into the souvenir shop and the Patriarch bought us a Three Sisters paperweight, a Sydney Harbour Bridge pencil sharpener and a plastic ruler with tiny photographs of the Blue Mountains glued along its length. This was our introduction to Australia before it became our home. Vast geographical and artificial structures were shrunk to fit a child's hand, commodified into the implements of education.

From the Three Sisters he drove us back to the town centre so that we could have a picnic lunch. From the car I looked at other families picnicking in the park. The smell of barbecuing meat and the hiss of fat sizzling on hot coals provoked stomach rumblings and mouth-watering cravings for meals as yet unknown and untasted. People were lying in the sun, munching on sandwiches, drinking Coke or beer or cups of wine from Coolabah casks.

Then out we got, the Tay family, with a huge Esky and a brightly coloured groundsheet because it had rained the previous night and the Patriarch believed in preventing rheumatism and arthritis decades clown the track. We found a shady spot because Mum didn't like the sun and we unrolled the groundsheet. The Esky was opened, the icecream containers full of noodles removed. Paper plates were unpacked and dealt out like cards. Schweppes lemonade was poured into cups – what a novelty fizzy lemonade was to us back then – chopsticks paired up and handed round, and Mum started heaping noodles onto the plates. There we sat, cross-legged, solemnly shovelling noodles into our mouths with our chopsticks, sucking and slurping up the longer strands. They dripped from our lips like a tangle of worms. We were an incongruous sight in the park; we didn't fit into the picture.

'Where are the chillies?' the Patriarch demanded. Mum unwrapped the plastic film and laid out the chillies. The Patriarch helped himself and offered them to Sonny. 'Sonny? Want some?'

Sonny was filled with shame. Slowly, hesitantly, he picked up a few pieces with his chopsticks and put them on his noodles. He took a deep breath and thrust a skein of chillied noodles into his mouth. Once again, his eyes watered, his mouth burned and the tips of his ears turned red. He reached for his cup of lemonade and guzzled noisily. He just could not do this. He tried to push the pieces of chilli to the edge of his plate but their hotness infested everything. He couldn't eat that contaminated plate of noodles but he couldn't go for a second helping until he'd finished the first plate. Waste not, want not, the Patriarch always admonished. Sonny's stomach growled hungrily and he hung his head.

'Sonny? Why aren't you eating?' The Patriarch had noticed his untouched plate.

'Can't eat it,' Sonny mumbled.

'What?'

'I said I can't eat it. The chillies are too hot for me. I can't eat chillies.' There. He'd confessed and his shame hung like a bright blade in the air, poised to strike him down before his father's eyes.

'*Hi-yah!* Then why did you want to take chillies?' the Patriarch said.

'I was trying to be a man. You're not a man unless you can eat chillies.'

'Who told you that?'

'Uncle Winston.'

'Talk nonsense! Chillies have nothing to do with being a man. I tell you what, Sonny, you've got no choice, you know. Sex comes from biology, not from chillies. When you study science at school and dissect rats, then you'll see. Give me your plate.' The Patriarch took a spoon and scooped Sonny's noodles and chillies onto his own plate. '*Nah.* Go and get some more *mai fun.* You have to eat or you won't have any energy left to hike down to Wentworth Falls.'

Later that afternoon, after a long bushwalk and the exotic experience of our first Devonshire tea, we drove back to Sydney, back down the Great Western Highway. The setting sun seared the backs of our necks and baked the vinyl car seats. We had to stop by the side of the road once, while I was sick, but I didn't get told off. The Patriarch was in a buoyant mood. His kindness was stunning in its breadth and duration. I loved my father so much. He pushed his favourite Carpenters cassette into the machine and turned up the volume. Music swelled in the car. The Patriarch warbled in joyful song, wondering, along with Karen Carpenter, why birds had suddenly appeared. Mum, Sonny and I joined in the chorus. Absurdly, happily, we flapped our arms like wings and assured the Patriarch that we too longed to be close to him.

Indigenous Deli

Alan Benjamin and Cyril Pearl

Limericks Down Under is an all-Australian collection of limericks based on Australian place names, some familiar and some quite arcane.

Limericks Down Under, 1984

A shearer's cook opened, at Shelley,
An oddly indigenous deli
With the wombat ragout,
The broiled jabiru,
And, for pudding, the sugar-ant jelly.

Sources and Acknowledgements

Armanno, Venero. *Romeo of the Underworld*. Sydney: Picador, 1994

Australian Etiquette, or *The Rules and Usages of the Best Society in the Australasian Colonies*. 'Kangarooing', Successful Dinners. Melbourne: People's Publishing Co., 1885

Banks, Joseph *The Endeavour Journal of Joseph Banks 1768–1771*. Edited by J.C. Beaglehole. Sydney: The Trustees of the Public Library of New South Wales in association with Angus & Robertson, 1962

Barnard, Marjorie. 'The Dressmaker', from *The Persimmon Tree and Other Stories*. Sydney: Clarendon Publishing Co., 1943

Baume, F.E. *Burnt Sugar*. New Century Press, 1934

Benjamin, Alan and Pearl, Cyril. *Limericks Down Under*. Melbourne: Hutchinson, 1984

Bird, Carmel. *The Bluebird Café*. Sydney: Random House Australia, 1996

Boldrewood, Rolf. *The Portable Rolf Boldrewood*. Edited by Alan Brissenden. Brisbane: UQP, 1979

Campbell, Ross. *An Urge to Laugh*. Sydney: Wildcat Press, 1981

Capaldo, Julie. *Love Takes You Home*. Sydney: Reed, 1995. Permission granted by Random House Australia.

Carey, Peter. *Bliss*. Brisbane: UQP, 1981

Ciccotosto, Emma and Bosworth, Michal. *Emma: A Recipe for Life*. Fremantle: Fremantle Arts Centre Press, 1995

Clarke Marcus. 'Chinatown'. Originally published *The Argus*, 8 March 1868; from *A Colonial City: Selected Journalism of Marcus Clarke*. Edited by L.T. Hergenhan. Brisbane: UQP, 1972

Clarke, Marcus. 'Curry'. *Something to Eat*. Melbourne *Herald*, 3 February 1874

Clarke, Marcus. 'Marcus Clarke's Christmas'. Originally published *Australasian*, 17 July 1869; from *A Colonial City: Selected Journalism of Marcus Clarke*. Edited by L.T. Hergenhan. Brisbane: UQP, 1972

Clarke, Marcus. 'On Chops'. *Something to Eat*. Melbourne *Herald*, 23 February 1874

Clarke, Marcus. 'Melbourne Restaurants'. *Age*, July 1879

Clift, Charmian. *The World of Charmian Clift*. Sydney: Ure Smith, 1970. Permission granted by HarperCollins Publishers.

Comettant, Oscar. *In the Land of Kangaroos and Gold Mines*. First published 1890. Trans. Judith Armstrong. Adelaide: Rigby, 1980

Corris, Peter. *The Empty Beach*. Sydney: Unwin, 1983

Dawson, Robert. *The Present State of Australia: A Description of the Country*. London: Smith, Elder & Co., 1830

Edmund, Mabel. *No Regrets*. Brisbane: UQP, 1992

Esson, Louis. *Ballads of Old Bohemia: An anthology of Louis Esson*. Edited by Hugh Anderson. Ascot Vale: Red Rooster Press, 1980

Faulding's Medical Journal. 'Sixpenny Restaurants'. 20 December 1902

Franklin, Miles. *Childhood at Brindabella*. Sydney: Angus & Robertson, 1963. Permission granted by HarperCollins Publishers.

Gilmore, Dame Mary. *Old Days, Old Ways*. Sydney: Angus & Robertson, 1934. ETT Imprint, Sydney 2001.

Goldsworthy, Peter. *Archipelagoes*. Sydney: Angus & Robertson, 1982

Gould, Nat. *Town and Bush: Stray Notes on Australia*. London: George Routledge, 1896. Facsimile edition Melbourne: Penguin, 1974

Gregory, Chris. 'Mock Chicken'. *Hot Sand: An Anthology*. Edited by Susan Kurosawa. Melbourne: Viking/Penguin, 1997. Permission granted by Penguin Books Australia.

Halligan, Marion. *The Golden Dress*. Melbourne: Viking, 1998. Permission granted by Penguin Books Australia.

Halls, Geraldine. *The Last Summer of the Men Shortage*. London, 1976. This edition Adelaide: Wakefield Press, 1995

Howitt, William. *Letters from Victoria, 1852–1855*. First published London: Longmans, 1855. This edition Kilmore, Australia: Lowden Publishing Co., 1972. Letter VII

Illustrated Melbourne Post. 'Christmas in Australia'. December 1864

Inglis, James. *Our Australian Cousins*. London: Macmillan, 1880

James, John Stanley ('Vagabond'). *The Vagabond Papers*. First published 1877–1878. This edition edited by Michael Cannon. Melbourne: MUP, 1969

Johnston, George. *My Brother Jack*. Sydney: Collins, 1964. Permission granted by HarperCollins Publishers.

Kelly, William. *Life in Victoria in 1853; and 1858*. First published London: Chapman and Hall, 1859; this edition Kilmore, Vic: Lowden Publishing Co., 1977

Lawrence, D.H. *Kangaroo*. London, UK: Martin Secker, 1923. ETT Imprint, Sydney 1995.

Lawson, Henry. *The Stories of Henry Lawson*. Second series, edited by Cecil Mann. Sydney: Angus & Robertson, 1964

Lindsay, Norman, *The Magic Pudding*. Sydney: Angus & Robertson, 1918. Permission granted by HarperCollins Publishers.

Lindsay, Norman. *Age of Consent*. First published New York: Farrar & Rinehart Inc., 1938. This edition Sydney: Ure Smith, 1968. Permission granted by Helen, Catherine and Andrew Glad.

Lindsay, Norman. *Pan in the Parlour*. London: T. Werner Laurie Ltd, 1934. Permission granted by Helen, Catherine and Andrew Glad.

Lohrey, Amanda. *Camille's Bread*. Sydney: Angus & Robertson, 1995. Permission granted by HarperCollins Publishers.

Lower, Lennie. 'Etiquette without Tears'. *The Illustrated Treasury of Australian Humour, chosen by Michael Sharkey*. Melbourne: OUP, 1988

Lower, Lennie. *Here's Luck*. Sydney: Angus & Robertson, 1930

Malouf, David. *Harland's Half Acre*. First published London: Chatto & Windus, 1984. This edition Melbourne: Penguin, 1985

Marshall, Jock and Drysdale, Russell. *Journey Among Men*. First published Hodder & Stoughton, 1962. This edition Melbourne: Sun Books, 1966

Martin, A.E. *Sinners Never Die*. First published New York 1944. This edition Adelaide: Wakefield Press, 1992

Martin, Catherine. *An Australian Girl*. First edition 1890. This edition London: Pandora, 1988

Mathers, Peter. *The Wort Papers*. North Melbourne: Cassell Australia, 1972

McDonald, Roger. *Shearers' Motel*. Sydney: Picador, 1992

Melbourne Punch. 'An All-Australian Christmas Dinner'. 10 December 1925

Mendelsohn, Oscar. 'The Perfect Australian Meal'. *Epicurean*, No. 14, August 1968; *Epicurean*, No. 15, October 1968

The Kat. 'Hotel Australia Menu', Vol. II, No. 2, April 1902

Meredith, Louisa Ann. *Notes and Sketches in New South Wales, during a residence in the colony from 1839 to 1844*. London: J. Murray, 1844

Meredith, Louisa Ann. *My Home in Tasmania, during a residence of nine years*. London: James Murray, 1852

Mitchell, Blanche. *Blanche: An Australian Diary: the diary of Blanche Mitchell, with notes by Edna Hickson*. Sydney: John Ferguson, 1980

Moorhouse, Frank. *Lateshows*. Sydney: Picador, 1990. Permission granted by Pan Macmillan Australia.

Moorhouse, Frank. *Loose Living*. Sydney: Picador, 1995. Permission granted by Pan Macmillan Australia.

Mossman, Samuel and Banister, Thomas. *Australia Visited and Re-visited: A narrative of recent travels and old experiences in Victoria and New South Wales*. First published 1853. This edition Dee Why: Ure Smith, 1974

Mundy, G.C. *Our Antipodes: or, Residence and Rambles in the Australasian Colonies*. First edition 1852. This edition London: Bentley, 1862

Murnane, Gerald. *Tamarisk Row*. London: Heinemann, 1974

Murray, Robert Dundas. *A Summer at Port Phillip*. London: Simpkin, Marshall & Co., 1843

Muskett, Philip. *The Book of Diet*. Sydney, 1898

O'Keefe, Sharon. *The Best-Looking Women in Bondi Junction*. Melbourne: Penguin, 1989

Orr, Sam (Richard Beckett). 'Tony's Bon Goût'. *Nation Review*, 26 July–1 August, 1974

Park, Ruth. *Swords and Crowns and Rings*. Melbourne: Thomas Nelson, 1977. Permission granted by Penguin Books Australia.

Pearson, M.J. *Cookery Recipes for the People*. Melbourne: H. Hearne & Co., 1894

Phillips, Redmond. 'The Oslo Lunch'. *Comic Australian Verse*. Edited by Geoffrey Lehman. Sydney: Angus & Robertson, 1972

Porter, Hal. *The Watcher on the Cast-Iron Balcony*. London: Faber & Faber, 1963

Praed, Rosa. *My Australian Girlhood: Sketches and Impressions of Bush Life*. London: T. Fisher Unwin, 1902

Principles of Home Cookery. 'Table Manners'. Sydney: New South Wales Public School Cookery Teachers' Association, Sydney, 1936

Richardson, Henry Handel. *The Fortunes of Richard Mahony*. First published 1917–29. This edition three volumes in one, London: Heinemann, 1930.

Schleman, Joseph. *The Working Man's Haven*. London: R. Simpson & Co., 1882

Shapcott, Thomas. *What You Own: Stories by Thomas Shapcott*. Sydney: Angus & Robertson, 1991

Slessor, Kenneth. *Bread and Wine: Selected Prose*. Sydney: Angus & Robertson, 1970

Sorenson, E.S. *Life in the Australian Backblocks*. First published 1911. Illustrated edition Melbourne: John Currey O'Neil, 1984

Stone, Louis. *Betty Wayside*. London: Hodder & Stoughton, 1915

Stone, Louis. *Jonah*. First published 1911. Third edition Sydney: Angus & Robertson, 1933

Sydney Morning Herald. 'The gentle art of eating'. 2 September 1903

Sydney Morning Herald. Letters to the editor. August 1910

Terry, Michael. 'Dining in Australia'. *The Trident*, Vol. 1, No. 3, July 1939

Teo, Hsu-Ming. *Love and Vertigo*. Sydney: Allen and Unwin, 2000

Thiele, Colin. *Labourers in the Vineyard*. Adelaide: Rigby, 1970. Permission granted by New Holland Publishers.

Thiele, Colin. *The Sun on the Stubble*. Adelaide: Rigby, 1961. Permission granted by New Holland Publishers.

Thirkell, Angela. *Trooper to the Southern Cross*. First published London, 1934. This edition Melbourne: Sun Books, 1966

Thornton. W.P. 'Our Own National Dishes'. *Sydney Morning Herald*. 20 June 1953

Turner, Ethel. *The Family at Misrule*. London/ Melbourne: War, Lock and Bowden, 1895

Vaile, Rita. *Cottage Cookery*. Melbourne: Geo. Robertson and Co., 1892

Vellacott, Helen, ed. *A Girl at Government House: an English girl's reminiscences: 'below stairs' in colonial Australia*. Melbourne: John Currey O'Neil, 1982. First published as *The Autobiography of a Cook* by Agnes Stokes, 1932

Waten, Judah. *So Far No Further*. Mount Eliza, Victoria: Wren, 1971

Watts, Jane Isabella. *Memories of Early Days in South Australia*. Adelaide, 1882. Republished as *Family Life in South Australia fifty-three years ago*. Adelaide: Libraries Board of South Australia, 1978

White, Patrick. *The Eye of the Storm*. London: Jonathan Cape, 1973

White, Patrick. *The Tree of Man*. First published 1956. This edition Harmondsworth: Penguin, 1961. Permission granted by Barbara Mobbs.

Wilmot, Furnley. *The Victoria Markets Recollected in all Tranquillity*. First published in *Melbourne Odes*, 1934. This edition *Frank Wilmot: Selected Poetry and Prose*. Edited by Philip Mead. Melbourne: MUP, 1997

Winton, Tim. *Cloudstreet*. Melbourne: McPhee Gribble, 1991. Permission granted by Penguin Books Australia

Wakefield Press is an independent publishing and
distribution company based in Adelaide, South Australia.
We love good stories and publish beautiful books.
To see our full range of books, please visit our website at
wakefieldpress.com.au
where all titles are available for purchase.
To keep up with our latest releases, news and events,
subscribe to our monthly newsletter.

Find us!

Facebook: facebook.com/wakefield.press
Twitter: twitter.com/wakefieldpress
Instagram: instagram.com/wakefieldpress

www.ingramcontent.com/pod-product-compliance
Lightning Source LLC
Chambersburg PA
CBHW020853270326
41928CB00006B/675